Grammatically CORRECT

The WRITER'S ESSENTIAL GUIDE

to punctuation, spelling, style, usage and grammar

ANNE STILMAN

WRITER'S DIGEST BOOKS

CINCINNATI, OHIO

To Greg,

Who helped me get the idea off the ground,
provided suggestions, reality checks and a laser printer,
and convinced me to work a little nonsense into the examples.

Grammatically Correct © 2004 by Anne Stilman. Manufactured in the United States of America. All rights reserved. No part of this book may be reproduced in any form or by any electronic or mechanical means including information storage and retrieval systems without permission in writing from the publisher, except by a reviewer, who may quote brief passages in a review. Published by Writer's Digest Books, an imprint of F+W Publications, Inc., 4700 East Galbraith Road, Cincinnati, Ohio 45236. (800) 289-0963. First edition.

Visit our Web site at www.writersdigest.com for information on more resources for writers.

To receive a free weekly e-mail newsletter delivering tips and updates about writing and about Writer's Digest products, register directly at our Web site at http://newsletters.fwpublications .com.

08 07 06 05 04   5 4 3 2 1

Cataloging-in-Publication data is available from the Library of Congress at http:// catalog.loc.gov.

ISBN 1-58297-331-8

Content edited by Michelle Ruberg
Designed by Patrick G. Souhan
Cover designs by Stanard Design Partners
Production coordinated by Robin Richie

CREDITS

TABLE OF CONTENTS

A question that might reasonably greet the appearance of yet another handbook on English usage is, does the world really need one more? Presumably every author writing on a well-covered topic believes he or she has something different to contribute, and I am no exception. Many of the publications available on this subject are nothing short of excellent, and some of them delve into topics and levels of analysis not addressed here. I felt, though, that there was a niche for a book that might be seen in some ways as more useable— if less scholarly or broad-ranging—than much of what is already on the shelves.

For one thing, I've sought to liven up what can be a somewhat dusty subject by excerpting passages from very quotable literary works, both classic and modern. Academic explanations of how to use a certain punctuation mark or stylistic technique are all very well, but a "real-life" illustration can be a lot more convincing—and entertaining. My thanks here to all those authors whose work I have cited.

Second, in order to make things a bit more challenging, much of the information is presented in the form of test-yourself exercises. That is, rather than just giving examples of rights and wrongs, many sections contain problem words or sentences that the reader can work through before checking the answers or suggested revisions. Such a hands-on approach is often the most effective way of getting knowledge to stick, as it gives readers a chance to recognize and correct their own errors.

Finally, and most importantly, I have tried to steer a middle course between too little and too much, covering the necessary topics in sufficient detail while avoiding an overly earnest tone. Obviously no single book on this subject can meet everyone's needs, but many lie too close to either end of the spectrum to be fully helpful. At the low end are those that are outright superficial, stating flat do's and don'ts without providing a sense of proportion, and leaving readers confused or unsatisfied. Those at the high end, however may cover the subject with such thoroughness as to be overwhelming. Readers may wish to know when to say *I* and when *me,* when to use *which* and when to use *that,* when to apply the semicolon, when the colon and when the dash. But many of them wish to know all this without having it explained through intimidating terminology and scholarly rules.

That is the premise on which I have based this book. To a large extent, one doesn't need a profound understanding of grammar in order to apply it: The world is filled with articulate individuals who have no aspirations to be linguistics scholars but simply want to learn *how* to do something the right way and get on with it. With this type of reader in mind, I have put together a book that steers clear of jargon and theory, focusing instead on practical strategies and intuitive explanations. A few terminology definitions are unavoidable, but in no case is an explanation presented solely in terms of grammatical constructs. The examples and exercises are designed to show what ambiguities or misinterpretations can result if the rules are not followed. In cases where there is more than one acceptable way to do something, my approach is not to prescribe one over another, but simply to describe the options.

This book is not as comprehensive as some of the others out there because I have chosen to concentrate on those areas that I know, from my years as an editor, to be the ones where writers are likeliest to need help. Many aspects of the language are intuitively understood by almost everybody, and it seems a waste of people's time to review what they are almost certain to already know. Those style guides that take the approach of "leave nothing out" are unquestionably the right choice for anyone learning English as a second language or with an interest in acquiring an academic understanding of how the language works. The readership I am envisioning, however, consists of individuals who already know English well and just want some specific answers on tricky topics. As it is, I realize that many readers will already have a firm handle on much of the material presented here, but I have attempted to provide answers to—or at least reassurance on—the most probable questions.

The book is organized as follows: Part One deals with spelling in a broad sense: hard-to-spell words, frequently confused homonyms, spelling variations and hyphenation. Part Two looks at the complexity and irregularity of English vocabulary: words that are frequently confused with others or are used in the wrong way, or that are often mangled in their plural or negative forms. Part Three tackles the bugbear of punctuation, describing the role of each mark in achieving clarity and affecting tone, and showing how misuses can lead to ambiguity or misinterpretation. Part Four looks at grammar issues that systematically present difficulty: agreement of subject and verb, parallel construction, positioning of modifiers and use of pronouns; it also provides a brief review of some conventions that are sometimes taken too seriously. And finally, Part Five moves on to style issues, ranging from relatively mechanical aspects such as the use of capital letters and italics, to determining appropriate sentence length and avoiding a biased tone.

A perspective I have tried to maintain throughout is that knowing the rules of the language does not mean applying them rigidly and unthinkingly. For one thing, these rules are not carved in stone—a glance at any style guide of another era would show how significantly attitudes to language can and do change. More importantly, writing is a combination of science and art. The guidelines outlined in this handbook are concerned with the former: They are the tools you need in order to be able to express your ideas unambiguously and elegantly. To go beyond mere correctness, however, you must know when to accommodate your style to the expectations of your audience; when to bend a convention to capture a certain effect; when to go with common idiom instead of the rule book. Anyone armed with a pen or a keyboard can write. Good writing is achieved by those who understand innovation, creativity and the needs of their readers.

Anne Stilman
Editor
IBM Software Solutions Toronto Laboratory

PART ONE

Spelling

In this age of online dictionaries and other high-tech writing aids, need authors concern themselves with the details of spelling? For some, the advent of the word processor has relegated the typewriter practically to the status of the quill pen, and the most execrable speller can look good simply by running a spell-check on the finished document before hitting "Print."

The problem is, though, this isn't always the case. There is no denying the value of electronic dictionaries, but relying on them exclusively is risky because the English language just has too many twists. Most spell-check programs lack the sophistication to detect misuse of homonyms (would yours amend *Their maybe moor then won weigh two rite sum words?*), and if used unthinkingly can even introduce errors (witness the concert program that promised a performance of Beethoven's *Erotica* symphony). Some will recognize only one form of a word that can be spelled two ways, and will annoyingly "correct" already valid spellings. The dictionaries may themselves contain errors; after all, some human had to input what went into them, and there is no guaranteeing that accidental typos or outright spelling mistakes didn't occur along the way. And, of course—unthinkable as it may be to some—not everyone works on a word processor.

Hence the need for basic spelling skills remains, and is the focus of this chapter. The information that follows won't turn a poor speller into a good one, but can help alert the reasonably competent speller to some nuances and common pitfalls. It covers the topic in a broad sense, including aspects such as acceptable variations and appropriate use of hyphenation. A good writer is hardly expected to know the spelling of every word, but should have an eye for when something doesn't look quite right, and the common sense to reach for the dictionary if there's any doubt.

Misspellings

COMMONLY MISPELLED WORDS

Exercise

The following list presents some words that many writers get wrong. Correct as many as you can without referring to a dictionary. If you caught the commonly misspelled word in the heading above, you're off to a good start.

abcess	diaphram	idiosyncracy	overlayed
accessable	diaresis	infinitesmal	paraphenalia
accomodate	diptheria	indispensible	passtime
aquisition	disasterous	innoculate	permissable
asterix	ecstacy	interruptable	perjorative
auxilary	eminant	jacknifed	perogative
barbituate	epitomy	knowledgable	perseverence
bellweather	explaination	langour	Phillippines
boundry	fallable	liason	playwrite
Brittania	Febuary	loathesome	pronounciation
committment	flourescent	maintainance	quadriped
compatable	forgiveable	manouver	relevent
concensus	fuschia	mischievious	respondant
conjested	geneology	neccesary	seperate
consise	*grand dame*	noticable	silouette
contraversial	gutteral	*object d'art*	sympatico
deductable	hemorrage	occurance	threshhold
desireable	hierarchial	opthamologist	underly

Answers

[s] ab^cess	[g] diaphram^	[s] idiosyncracy	[i] overlayed
[i] accessable^	[e] diaresis^	[i] infinitesmal^	[r] paraphenalia^
[m] accomodate^	[h] diptheria^	[a] indispensible	[p]asstime
[c] aquisition^	disasterous	in[n]oculate	[i] permissable
[sk] asterix	[s] ecstacy	[i] interruptable	perjorative
[i] auxilary^	[e] eminant	[k] jacknifed^	[r] perogative^
[r] barbituate^	[e] epitomy	[e] knowledgable^	[a] perseverence
bellweather	explaination	[uo] langour	Phillippines
[a] boundry	[i] fallable	[i] liason^	[ght] playwrite
[n] Brittania^	[r] Febuary^	loathesome	[u] pronounciation
committment	[uo] flourescent	[e] maintainance	[u] quadriped
[i] compatable	forgiveable	[e (manoeuvre)] maneuver	[a] relevent
[s] conceensus	[chs] fuschia	mischievious	[e] respondant
[g] conjested	[a] geneology	[s] neceesary^	[a] seperate
[c] consise	[e] *grand dame*^	[e] noticable	[h] silouette^
[o] contraversial	[u] gutteral	*objet d'art*	[i] sympatico
[i] deductable	[h (haemorrhage)] hemorrage^	[re] occurance	threshhold
desireable	[c] hierarchial	[h l] opthamologist	[ie] underly

Haemorrhage and *manoeuvre* are the standard spellings in Britain and some other Commonwealth countries. For more, see "American/British Differences" on page 17.

The preceding may possibly have taught you some spellings you didn't know, but obviously no such exercise could be comprehensive. Its larger aim is to demonstrate just how capricious and counterintuitive English spelling can be, and thereby drive home the importance of always checking the dictionary rather than trusting your memory or judgment. The words presented here have been chosen either because they are difficult to spell, or—more dangerously—because they are so frequently misspelled that the wrong version has become almost conventional and many people don't realize it's wrong. There is no shame in having to look up tricky words repeatedly; the best writers do. Don't risk leaving in an error just because you're "almost sure" something is right and it's too much trouble to go to the dictionary.

The good news is that the majority of spelling errors fall into predictable categories. Keep these categories in mind as you write, so as to be particularly alert for "high-risk" words.

COMMON TYPES OF ERRORS

INTERCHANGING *ANT* AND *ENT* ENDINGS, OR *ANCE* AND *ENCE*

eminent, occurrence, perseverance, relevant, respondent

These endings sound virtually the same, and there's no rule that will tell you which is correct for a given word. (Some words in fact may go either way: *dependant* or *dependent, dependance* or *dependence, descendant* or *descendent.*) Memorize what you can, and check any such word you're not sure of each time you use it.

INTERCHANGING *ABLE* AND *IBLE* ENDINGS

accessible, compatible, deductible, fallible, indispensable, interruptible, permissible

Like *ant* and *ent*, these sounds are indistinguishable to the ear, so you must memorize the right spelling for each word. The more common ending is *able*, so writers are more likely to err when the ending should be *ible*. (Note that some words can go either way: For example, *extendable* and *extendible* are both correct.)

INTERCHANGING *SOFT C* AND *S*, AND *SOFT G* AND *J*
congested, consensus, concise, ecstasy, idiosyncrasy

Watch out for these identical-sounding letters. (A few words can go either way: *jibe* or *gibe*; *supercede* or *supersede*; *offence* or *offense; defence* or *defense; practice* or *practise*. Note, though, that the British distinguish between *practise* as a verb [to practise medicine] and *practice* as a noun [a doctor's practice].)

OMITTING A SILENT LETTER
abscess, acquisition, diaphragm, hemorrhage (or haemorrhage), silhouette

Often a letter whose omission wouldn't change a word's pronunciation is mistakenly left out.

CONFUSION OVER DOUBLE CONSONANTS
accommodate, Britannia, commitment, jackknifed, necessary, occurrence, Philippines, threshold

Words with double consonants tend to be troublesome. Errors include doubling the wrong letter, wrongly doubling more than one and doubling just one instead of two. It's also a common mistake to omit the doubling altogether if the word is a compound where the last letter of the first part and the first letter of the second part happen to be the same (*jackknife, misspelling*—although note that some can go either way, such as *granddaddy/grandaddy*). Conversely, writers sometimes mistake a word for a compound, and double a letter that they shouldn't (*threshold* is *not* a combination of *thresh* and *hold*).

SPELLING WORDS THE WAY THEY'RE MISPRONOUNCED
asterisk, auxiliary, barbiturate, boundary, February, hierarchical, infinitesimal, mischievous, ophthalmologist, paraphernalia, pejorative, prerogative, separate

Certain words are commonly mispronounced, ranging from a failure to enunciate subtle vowels to blatant solecisms. People then may spell these words the way they say them, not realizing that both are wrong.

Separate, possibly the most frequently misspelled word of all time, is a subtle case of this type of error. It's fine to pronounce the first *a* like an *e,* but much of the population then thinks that's how it's spelled as well.

MISTAKENLY SPELLING A DERIVATIVE
THE SAME WAY AS ITS ROOT WORD

disastrous, explanation, maintenance, pronunciation

When one word derives from another, it's *often* the case that the spelling of the root word still holds—but not always. Be aware of the exceptions.

MISTAKENLY KEEPING—OR NOT KEEPING—
THE FINAL *E* OF A ROOT WORD

desirable, forgivable, knowledgeable, loathsome, noticeable

For some words the final *e* is kept and for some it isn't—and writers often guess wrong as to which way it should go. (Note in the discussion on "American/British Differences" on page 17 how some words can go either way.)

GIVING AN UNFAMILIAR WORD THE
SPELLING OF A MORE FAMILIAR ONE

bellwether, guttural, pastime, playwright, simpatico

When a relatively uncommon word sounds like a better-known one *(weather, gutter, pass, write, sympathy),* the spelling of the more familiar word is often mistakenly adopted.

NOT RECOGNIZING EXCEPTIONS TO
FAMILIAR LETTER SEQUENCES

controversial, epitome, fuchsia, genealogy, inoculate, overlaid, quadruped, underlie

Words such as *contradictory* and *contraindication* may take an *a, mythology* and *ethnology* an *o,* and *quadriceps* and *quadrilateral* an *i*—but not all words with these suffixes and prefixes follow suit. *School* and *schooner* contain *sch* sequences, while *chs* doesn't come up very often. Most words that end with an *e* or an *i* sound take a *y,* so exceptions such as *epitome* and *underlie* often get overlooked. Familiar words such as *innocuous, innocent* and *innovate* contain a double *n,* so *inoculate* often picks up an extra one. And since the past tense form of most words that end in a *d* sound is spelled *e-d,* exceptions such as *laid* often get missed.

CONFUSION OVER UNUSUAL LETTER SEQUENCES
diaeresis, diphtheria, fluorescent, languor, liaison, maneuver (or manoeuvre), ophthalmologist

Writers are understandably thrown by words that contain *uo* or *ae* sequences instead of the more familiar *ou* and *ea,* and by words that contain three vowels or four consonants (!) in a row.

SPELLING FOREIGN WORDS AS IF THEY WERE ENGLISH
grande dame, objet d'art

It's easy to trip up on words borrowed from a language not one's own. Be particularly alert for those that are spelled *almost*—but not quite—the same way as their English counterparts.

COMMON TYPES OF TYPOS

A particular variety of spelling mistake is the typo, defined as a spelling error that results from an accidental slip of the finger on the keyboard rather than through systematic ignorance of the correct form. Some words are more susceptible to being accidentally misspelled than others, so when proofing your work, be extra alert for the following:

TRANSPOSITION OF LETTERS TO CREATE A SIMILAR WORD
Watch out for scared cows, casual factors, martial harmony, complaint pupils and the like—words that differ from another only by transposed letters. Note that such errors would not be picked up by a computer spell-checker!

OMISSION OF ONE OCCURRENCE OF A REPEATED LETTER
A number of activites have been planned for the day.

With the advent of desktop-publishing software, typsetting is now often being done by nonprofessionals.

8

Did you spot the errors in *activities* and *typesetting*? They are easy to miss on a quick read, because the missing letters (*i* and *e*, respectively) are present in another position in the word. Double-check any such words very carefully.

"WORD STUTTER"

A common type of slip to to make when typing is to repeat short words such as *the, is,* etc.

Even a sharp eye can easily miss the typo in the above sentence. Some computer spell-checkers are programmed to pick up on repeated words, which is a useful feature.

On a final note, when you are proofing your work, check to see if you have left any extra spaces between words or omitted the space between any sentences. Such typos may not be spelling mistakes, but nonetheless need to be rectified.

Frequently Confused Homonyms

A word may be spelled impeccably as far as the computer spell-checker is concerned—but still be wrong. English is replete with **homonyms**, words that are pronounced the same way but are spelled differently and mean different things. The majority present no problem; few people, for example, would write *brake* for *break* or *see* for *sea*. Certain words, however, get confused with their homonyms systematically. Often the cause is that one of the homonyms is less common than the other, and the writer puts down the more familiar spelling without realizing it has a different meaning from the word that he or she intended.

Exercise
Which word in each of the following sentences is incorrect?

Gordon's face occasionally twitched with a nervous tick.

The wording of her ad peaked his interest.

The report was divided into discreet sections.

She could have born the news better if it had come later.

Tall vases of flowers stood on either side of the alter.

Things did not appear to auger well.

Emmeline's diamond weighed a full sixtieth of a caret.

The villagers struggled to throw off the yolk of their invaders.

The stationary supplies consisted of just a box of paper and a few pens.

It was the only sound piece of advise Bert had ever received from his father.

Dora's known for sticking to her principals.

Her office was little more than a cubical.

Verna believes in giving her staff free reign.

The car comes with duel airbags.

The council for the defendant insists that his client is innocent.

The patient complained that his head felt as if it were in a vice.

It was a considerable time before I regained piece of mind.

Pupils in Mr. Wigglesworth's class knew they had better tow the line.

Registration fees may be waved for low-income students.

The new curtains complimented the furnishings very well.

The campers fell quiet for the role call.

When the police arrived at the scene, they made a grizzly find.

Armand felt as if he'd been put through the ringer.

I was loathe to interfere, but I felt I must.

Philbert knew he would have to prove his metal if he won the promotion.

Her lawsuit claimed that there had been a breech of contract.

It took a long time, but Effie finally got her just desserts.

It was hard to say exactly how it happened; one thing just lead to another.

Usually, the last part of a book to be written is the forward.

Answers

Gordon's face occasionally twitched with a nervous **tick**.
Should be *tic*—a periodic spasm of the facial muscles. Nothing to do with small bloodsucking arachnids.

The wording of her ad **peaked** his interest.
Should be *piqued*—aroused or excited. *Peak* means to be at the maximum (interest has peaked, and will probably soon decline).

The report was divided into **discreet** sections.
Should be *discrete*—individually distinct. (Unless the sections were particularly good at keeping a confidence.)

She could have **born** the news better if it had come later.
Should be *borne*—past tense of "to bear"; that is, handled, coped with. Nothing to do with being born. (Note, though, that another usage of this word is related to birth: To "bear children" is to bring them into being, so a sentence could read *She had borne two children.*)

Tall vases of flowers stood on either side of the **alter**.
Should be *altar*—the structure in a place of worship. *Alter* means to change something.

11

Things did not appear to auger well.

Should be *augur*—bode, portend. An *auger* is a tool for boring holes.

Emmeline's diamond weighed a full sixtieth of a caret.

Should be *carat*—a unit of weight for jewels. A *caret* is a small wedge-shaped mark used by editors to indicate where text should be inserted.

The villagers struggled to throw off the yolk of their invaders.

Should be *yoke*—bondage or servitude. (Unless the invaders had taken to throwing eggs at the locals.)

The stationary supplies consisted of just a box of paper and a few pens.

Should be *stationery*—writing materials. Of course, paper and pens *are* characteristically stationary—not moving. (A mnemonic that might help: Station*e*ry includes *e*nvelopes.)

It was the only sound piece of advise Bert had ever received from his father.

Should be *advice*—the noun. *Advise* (pronounced differently) is the verb. When you advise someone, you are giving advice.

Dora's known for sticking to her principals.

Should be *principles*—code of conduct. *Principle* and *principal* are confused frequently. The first, which is always a noun, can also mean a fundamental law *(the principle of relativity)*, an underlying phenomenon that accounts for something *(the principle of the steam engine)* or the essence or fundamentals of a situation *(in principle, this action should be possible)*. The second has several meanings that all relate in some way to being first or primary. As a noun, it can mean the head of a school *(go to the principal's office)*, a main player *(he's suspected of being one of the principals)* or the main sum of money owed on a loan *(the amount includes both interest and principal)*. As an adjective, it describes something that is prominent *(she plays a principal role)* or important or pressing *(our principal concern is safety)*. A mnemonic that might help: The *principal* is your *pal*. (Right.) Once you have this connection in place, think whether the meaning of the word you want has anything to do with "firstness." If it does, the ending will be *pal;* if it doesn't, the ending will be *ple*. Thus: Dora sticks to her principals if she is known to hang out with headmasters.

Her office was little more than a **cubical**.
Should be *cubicle*—a small partitioned space. *Cubical* means shaped like a cube, with six equal square sides.

Verna believes in giving her staff free **reign**.
Should be *free rein*—that is, not hauling on their reins to control them (figuratively speaking). *Reign* means to rule as a sovereign.

The car comes with **duel** airbags.
Should be *dual*—two, one on each side. *Duel* also has to do with two, but in a somewhat more antagonistic sense.

The **council** for the defendant insists that his client is innocent.
Should be *counsel*—lawyer. *Counsel* is also a verb, meaning to advise or consult with, so a *counselor* is one who counsels (a camp counselor, a guidance counselor, a marital counselor). *Council* is an administrative or legislative group that deliberates or governs, so a *councillor* is one who is a member of a council (a town councillor, a school board councillor). In Britain, government-funded housing is referred to as *council flats*.

The patient complained that his head felt as if it were in a **vice**.
Should be *vise*—a tool for gripping something strongly. Vises (or any other tool) are rarely noted for moral depravity.

It was a considerable time before I regained **piece** of mind.
Should be *peace of mind*—having one's mind at ease. This expression presumably gets confused with *giving someone a piece of one's mind*—that is, telling that person off.

Pupils in Mr. Wigglesworth's class knew they had better **tow** the line.
Should be *toe the line*—conform to expected behavior, as in walking along a prescribed line without deviating one's toes from it. (Unless, of course, Mr. Wigglesworth was in charge of a barge.)

Registration fees may be **waved** for low-income students.
Should be *waived*—to refrain from claiming, to voluntarily forgo something to which one is entitled. Flapping the fees up and down in front of the students would be to little purpose.

The new curtains **complimented** the furnishings very well.

Should be *complemented*—went well with, set off to advantage, enhanced. (Unless the curtains were telling the furniture how nice it was looking that day.) The word *complement* derives from *complete,* so a good mnemonic is to remember the connection between these two words. Thus, one can have a full complement (a complete set) of cutlery, or assign some complementary (additional) course readings along with the main text. A *compliment* is a courteous, admiring or flattering comment. Thus, one can offer compliments (best wishes, regards) of the season, write a complimentary (favorable) review, exchange complimentary (mutually esteeming) remarks or offer complimentary (free as a courtesy) drinks.

The campers fell quiet for the **role** call.

Should be *roll call*—checking attendance by calling names off a list (a roll). Unless the campers are waiting to learn who will play what part in a drama.

When the police arrived at the scene, they made a **grizzly** find.

Should be *grisly*—gruesome, ghastly. Assuming the scene didn't contain a large aggressive bear. Note: *Merriam Webster's Collegiate Dictionary* permits *grizzly* as a variant of *grisly;* however, enough readers would consider this incorrect that writers are advised to make the distinction.

Armand felt as if he'd been put through the **ringer**.

Should be *wringer*—a device for wringing something out, squeezing it dry. The phrase means to feel pressured and exhausted by an ordeal. No bell clappers are involved. (Also note that if you ever say you want to *ring* someone's neck, this means you plan to put a circlet around it.)

I was **loathe** to interfere, but I felt I must.

Should be *loath*—reluctant. *Loathe* means to hate, despise. Note that the pronunciation is slightly different: *loath* rhymes with *oath,* while *loathe* ends in a softer sound, like the *th* in *the.* Note: *Merriam Webster's Collegiate Dictionary* allows *loathe* as a variant of *loath,* but writers would be advised to stick with the traditional spelling. For more on this, see the discussion under "Spelling Variations" on page 16.

Philbert knew he would have to prove his **metal** if he won the promotion.
Should be *mettle*—stamina, courage, worth. Quite unrelated to gold,
brass, etc.

Her lawsuit claimed that there had been a **breech** of contract.
Should be *breach*—violation. This word derives from *break*. Thus,
a breach of honor, breaching a standard, a breach in a wall or a
breach in continuity. *Breech* refers to the bottom or back end of
something: the breech (rear) of a gun, a breech birth (feet or rear
end first) or (archaically) a pair of pants.

It took a long time, but Effie finally got her just **desserts**.
Should be *deserts*—getting what one deserves. Once you realize that
this word derives from *deserve*, its spelling is obvious. All the bad
puns that abound notwithstanding, it has no connection with post-
meal sweets.

It was hard to say exactly how it happened; one thing just **lead** to another.
Should be *led*—past tense of "to lead." This common error likely
results from a confusion with the metal *lead*, which is pronounced
"led."

Usually, the last part of a book to be written is the **forward**.
Should be *foreword*—the words that appear at the front (the
"fore"). Nothing to do with the direction of movement or with being
uppity. (Note that if this is the very first word to appear in your
book, it's one you want to get right!)

Spelling Variations

English contains many words that can be correctly spelled more than one way. Two dictionaries may present the same word differently, and the same dictionary may present alternatives. Often the choice of which spelling to use is up to you—but not always. Writers should have a solid awareness of spelling variations for the following reasons:

• If you are being hired to write some sort of commercial publication, such as a technical manual for a software producer, marketing material for a bank or an information brochure for a government office, you are often expected to abide by a particular style guide. Organizations generally want their publications to have a uniform "look and feel," which includes words always being spelled the same way. For example, a U.S.-based multinational corporation with branches in the United Kingdom might specify that all printed materials that go to the public follow the conventions of American spelling, including those produced by British writers.

• If your writing is "your own"—that is, something you are doing not as part of a job but as a personal project that will bear your name—you may still be expected to abide by the style guide of the publishing house that will be producing your work. Not all publishing houses require that writers go with a particular dictionary, but many do. If you disregard their specifications, it may well mean seeing your manuscript come back heavily marked up by the copyeditor.

• Just because a dictionary indicates that a variant spelling is *legitimate* doesn't always mean it's *appropriate*. If the dictionary you are using allows for unconventional spellings, consider what effect these might have on the tone of your writing. Some dictionaries may endorse spellings that would send a majority of copyeditors lunging for their red pencils.

It is worth mentioning here that dictionaries can be roughly categorized as either "prescriptive" or "descriptive." The former act as guardians of the language, strictly upholding conventional rules of spelling and word usage, and are conservative about adding new entries. Descriptive dictionaries, on the other hand, attempt to reflect language as it is used, whether supported by tradition or not. They are thus more flexible in incorporating unconventional spellings (along with slang, jargon and new terms) on the grounds that it is their responsibility not to decree but to record how words are being used in the real world. Both approaches have validity: Clearly, without the maintenance of standards the clarity of the language would degenerate; on the other hand, language is a fluid entity that changes year by year, driven more by common usage than by linguistic pundits. (Consider how quaint many terms that were in standard usage just a few decades ago now seem.) Hence, whether certain spellings are considered errors or acceptable variants may depend on what source is being used.

AMERICAN/BRITISH DIFFERENCES

Many of the variant spellings in the English language are due to the differing styles of the United States and Britain. For staunch upholders of either the American or the Anglo tradition, the "right" way to spell something will be unambiguous; however, in many parts of the world the path is murkier. (Canadians in particular, with geographical proximity to one country and historical ties to the other, have adapted a hybrid style that borrows from both.)

The following describes several categories of differences between American and British spellings. In *general*—there are many exceptions—American style is to remove letters not necessary for pronunciation, while British style is to retain traditional spellings, which are often more complex.

OR/OUR ENDINGS
Some words end in *or* for American style, *our* for British style.

humor/humour   honor/honour   endeavor/endeavour

(Canadians take note: Even with British style, certain derivative words such as *humorous, honorarium* and *laborious* do *not* take the *u.*)

ER/RE ENDINGS
Some words end in *er* for American style, *re* for British style.

center/centre   fiber/fibre   theater/theatre

IZE/ISE ENDINGS
Some words end in *ize* (or *yze*) for American style, *ise* (or *yse*) for British style.

analyze/analyse   organize/organise
paralyze/paralyse   realize/realise

ED/T ENDINGS
Some past tense constructions that take *ed* for American style take *t* for British style.

burned/burnt   dreamed/dreamt   spoiled/spoilt

SINGLE/DOUBLE CONSONANTS
For some words where the root ends in *l, p, s* or *t,* American style leaves the consonant single before an *ed* or *ing* ending, and British style doubles it.

benefited/benefitted   focusing/focussing
canceled/cancelled   grueling/gruelling
kidnaped/kidnapped   worshiping/worshipping

DROPPING/RETAINING *E*
For some words where the root ends in *e,* American style is to drop the *e* before a suffix, British style is to retain it.

acknowledgment/   aging/ageing
   acknowledgement   usable/useable

E/AE, OE

For words originally spelled with ligatures, American style is to drop the silent vowel, British style is to keep it.

anesthetic/anaesthetic   estrogen/oestrogen

encyclopedia/encyclopaedia   fetus/foetus

medieval/mediaeval   maneuver/manoeuvre

MORE PHONETIC/MORE TRADITIONAL

American style is to simplify spelling, whether by dropping silent endings or by using more phonetic constructions; British style is to retain traditional spellings.

catalog/catalogue   omelet/omelette   program/programme

check/cheque   draft/draught   plow/plough

A question that might arise for writers striving for consistency is, must one go exclusively one way or the other? If you have committed yourself to doubling the *l* in *cancelled,* need you also use *re* endings and *oe* ligatures? The answer is, unless you are expected to abide rigidly by a particular style guide, it's usually acceptable to use different styles for different words as long as you spell each individual word consistently. You should, though, treat all words in the same category alike—for example, if you are spelling *valour* with a *u,* do the same for *flavour.*

Note that, regardless of your style choice, you must always use the original spelling for proper nouns. Thus, for example, even if using American spelling, be sure the British political party appears as *Labour,* not *Labor;* if using British spelling, be sure the complex in New York appears as the Rockefeller *Center,* not *Centre.*

OTHER SPELLING VARIATIONS

Exercise

Outside of American/British differences, there are quite a few words that have acceptable variants within North America (and in other parts of the world as well). For example, every word in the following list is spelled correctly—but can be spelled correctly another way as well. Change it to its other acceptable form.

accidentally	dietitian	memento	skeptical
adviser	dissension	moniker	skullduggery
artifact	enroll	mustache	stony
balaclava	espresso	nerve-racking	sulphur
bandanna	fulfill	numbskull	tendonitis
bannister	gelatin	orangutan	tuque
bullrush	hankie	phony	whiz
caliph	license	pygmy	woollen
cantaloupe	liquefy	raccoon	yogurt

Answers

accidentally	^cdietitian	^omemento	^cskeptical
^oadviser	^tdissension	moniker	skullduggery
^eartifact	enroll	^omustache	^estony
^kbalaclava	^xespresso	^wnerve-racking	^fsulphur
bandanna	fulfill	numbskull	ⁱtendonitis
bannister	^egelatin	^oorangutan	^otuque
bullrush	^yhankie	^ephony	^zwhiz
^fcaliph	^clicense	ⁱpygmy	woollen
cantaloupe	ⁱliquefy	raccoon	^hyogurt

As with the review of misspellings on page 3, this exercise is less concerned with the specific words shown here than with raising your awareness of alternate spellings in general. There are a few words with similar variations (double or single *ls* or *ns*; *f* instead of *ph*; *y* or *ey* endings), but for the most part, what distinguishes these alternate spellings is their sheer capriciousness. Note that the section on mis-spellings gives a number of examples of variations as well.

The existence of variant spellings raises the question, how do you decide which way to go? The answer is—it depends. If you are writing to the specifications of a style guide, you don't have to make any decisions: Typically, you are simply informed which dictionary to use as your authority, and that if it gives two or more variants of a word, to use the first. There is a great deal of sense to this approach, as it saves you from having to come up with your own rules.

If you have been given free rein, make sure you spell the same word consistently throughout: Don't switch halfway through or go back and forth. It is also advisable to maintain consistency across similar categories of words; for example, if you are spelling *fulfill* with a double *l*, do the same with *enroll*. This isn't critical, but it can make your writing look more polished to discerning readers.

There is also the matter of tone. As mentioned in the comparison of prescriptive and descriptive dictionaries, there isn't always a clear-cut distinction between "right" and "wrong" in spelling, and some authorities will permit forms that others would dismiss as incorrect. For example, *Merriam Webster's Collegiate Dictionary* presents the following as acceptable variants:

donut *for* doughnut	restauranteur *for* restaurateur
dumfound *for* dumbfound	revery *for* reverie
loadstar *for* lodestar	sherbert *for* sherbet
loadstone *for* lodestone	straightlaced *for* straitlaced
miniscule *for* minuscule	straightjacket *for* straitjacket
nickle *for* nickel	wholistic *for* holistic

In some cases, it could be argued that meaning is lost by going with the variants. For example, *doughnut* derives from *dough*, *dumbfound* from *dumb* (speechless), *lodestar* and *lodestone* from *lode* (course), not *load*, and *straitlaced* and *straitjacket* from *strait* (tight, constricted or strict), not *straight*. In other cases, the actual pronunciation has been changed from the original *(restauranteur, sherbert)*. As a writer, you must decide where your own comfort level lies. But do remember that even if you can justify an unconventional spelling to your publisher by pointing to a source, you run the risk of some of your readers simply assuming an error on your part; they aren't likely to turn to the dictionary to see if it would vindicate you. It is usually better practice to go with the more standard form of the word.

ALTERNATE SPELLINGS OF FOREIGN NAMES

A special category of alternate spellings is names of people, places or other entities that have their origin in languages other than English. This is particularly the case when the language of origin uses an alphabet other than Latin, so the transliteration is not the original spelling in any case. For example, the following may be spelled more than one way:

Chassid (member of Jewish sect), Hassid or Hasid
Hindustani (language in India) or Hindostani
Leiden (Dutch city) or Leyden
Mao Tse-tung (Chinese leader) or Mao Ze-dong
Tchaikovsky (Russian composer) or Tschaikovsky

A good dictionary will include names of well-known people and places and give the most common variations if any exist.

Hyphenation

I worked with [William Shawn, longtime editor of The New Yorker *magazine] from 1939 until 1987, often from the initial proposal of an idea (he grasped ideas with the speed of light) through the cherished phone call of acceptance and through galley and page proofs. These sessions were mostly brief and businesslike: a word here, a nuance there, a fact to be further clarified. But there is one evening in the late forties that is indelibly impressed on my mind. I had written a long report on a visit to the Argentina of Juan Perón. The narrative ended with Señor Perón unexpectedly introducing me, as he opened elegant French doors in the Presidential palace in Buenos Aires, to Evita Perón. I wrote that I took her hand and found it "stone cold." Shawn and I were going over the proof. The time was around 10 P.M. He became agitated.*

" 'Stone cold,' " he said, "requires a hyphen."

I became agitated. "Put a hyphen there and you spoil the ending," I said. "That hyphen would be ruinous."

"Perhaps you had better sit outside my office and cool off," he said. "I'll go on with my other work."

I took a seat outside his office. From time to time, he would stick his head out and say, "Have you changed your mind?"

"No hyphen," I replied. "Absolutely no hyphen." I was quite worked up over the hyphen.

Sometime around two-thirty in the morning, Shawn said, wearily, "All right. No hyphen. But you are wrong."

We remained dear friends, hyphen or no hyphen, to the end.
—PHILIP HAMBURGER, *in "Remembering Mr. Shawn,"* The New Yorker.

Spelling a word correctly sometimes involves more than just getting the right letters in the right order. A word is considered to be misspelled if it ought to contain a hyphen and doesn't, or conversely, if it ought *not* to contain one and *does*. This section looks at the hyphen as a component of spelling. (For a discussion of its role as a mark of punctuation, turn to page 125.) Its functions in spelling are the following:

- Linking words that make up a compound
- Linking a prefix or suffix to the main word
- Linking words that make up a number

HYPHENATION OF COMPOUND WORDS

A **compound** consists of two or more words that express a single concept. A compound word may act as a noun, a verb or an adjective, or even all three.

Some compounds are written as two separate words with a space between them (**open compounds**), some run the words together (**closed compounds**) and some link them by a hyphen (**hyphenated compounds**). There are no strict rules governing this. Adjectives may be either closed or hyphenated (a *standby* ticket, a *stand-up* comedian, *front-page* news); verbs are usually open but are occasionally closed or hyphenated *(stand by* one's principles, *stand up* for one's rights, *break through* a barrier, *show off* one's skills, start to *shadowbox*, learn to *touch-type);* nouns are most commonly either closed or open, but can also be hyphenated (appear on the *front page,* achieve a *breakthrough*, members of a *shadow cabinet,* serve as a *touchstone,* act like a *show-off*).

Exercise
In the following, which of the words shown in bold should be left open, which closed up and which hyphenated?

back check a hockey player/**back slide** from grace	[verbs]
be a **bed wetter**/the problem of **bed wetting**	[nouns]
a **clear cut** decision/a **clear headed** young woman	[adjectives]
cold cock an opponent/**cold shoulder** an acquaintance	[verbs]
cross breed species/**cross fertilize** crops	[verbs]

a **dead on** guess/a **dead pan** manner	[adjectives]
drop in for a visit/**drop kick** a ball	[verbs]
a **half brother**/a **half moon**	[nouns]
hand feed an animal/**hand write** a letter	[verbs]
the bee's **life cycle**/reach for a **life line**	[nouns]
a **long term** plan/a **long time** companion	[adjectives]
an **off color** joke/an **off hand** remark	[adjectives]
attach a **side car** /suffer from **side effects**	[nouns]
act as a **stand in** /be at a **stand still**	[nouns]
stick handle a puck/**stick up** a bank	[verbs]
set a **time frame** /call a **time out**	[nouns]
a **two fold** increase/a **two way** street	[adjectives]
a **water logged** boat/a **water resistant** watch	[adjectives]

Answers

back-check	backslide
bed wetter	bed-wetting
clear-cut	clearheaded
coldcock	cold-shoulder
crossbreed	cross-fertilize
dead-on	deadpan
drop in	drop-kick
half brother	half-moon
hand-feed	handwrite
life cycle	lifeline
long-term	longtime
off-color	offhand
sidecar	side effects
stand-in	standstill
stickhandle	stick up
time frame	time-out
twofold	two-way
waterlogged	water-resistant

The above demonstrates just how unpredictable the formation of compound words can be. If ever you're not certain which way a particular compound should appear, don't try to reason it through: Check the dictionary. (Note: These words are shown as they are presented in *Merriam Webster's Collegiate Dictionary*. Another source might differ on a few.)

Since the language is constantly evolving, not every compound word will appear in the dictionary, and you will sometimes have to make your own decisions. If the combination you want does not have its own dictionary entry, you may usually assume it should be written as two words. However, with compound words that are relatively new to the language, the rules aren't hard-and-fast. There's a general trend for a new compound to start out as open, to acquire a hyphen as it becomes used more frequently and eventually to merge into one word. Before a consensus is reached, all three forms may be considered acceptable. For example, the computer terms *soft copy*, *soft-copy* and *softcopy* all are commonly seen as both noun and adjective.

COMPOUND NOUNS

With some compound nouns, more than one style may be acceptable. For example:

> carry-over *or* carryover
> lay-offs *or* layoffs
> make-up *or* makeup
> send-off *or* sendoff
> short-list *or* shortlist

Compound nouns that comprise more than two words, such as idioms and phrases, usually take hyphens. This isn't invariable, however, so always check—a good dictionary includes multiword phrases and expressions. If a phrase does not have its own listing, assume it does not take hyphens.

> She's such a stick-in-the-mud.
> He's a Johnny-come-lately.
> The place was just a hole-in-the-wall.

But:

> The deal sounded like a pig in a poke.
> She was his partner in crime.
> The beach was just a hop, skip and jump from the hotel.

If one part of a compound noun is a single letter, the compound is hyphenated or open—not closed.

A-frame	B picture
D day	e-mail
F distribution	G-string
H-bomb	I beam
T square	U-turn
V neck	X chromosome
y-coordinate	z-axis

(Note that with something new to the language, such as *e-mail*, there may not yet be a consensus on how it should appear.)

COMPOUND ADJECTIVES

In the case of compound adjectives, there is an extra complexity to the hyphen situation. If a compound adjective has its own entry in the dictionary, it should always be written as it is shown there (either hyphenated or closed), regardless of its position in the sentence. That is, the combination is considered a word in its own right, and the way it appears in the dictionary is its proper and invariable spelling. However, other than these "permanent" compounds, an almost limitless variety of words can be strung together in a given sentence to collectively form an adjective. These more ephemeral compounds typically get linked by a hyphen if they precede the noun they modify, but not if they follow the noun. For a full discussion on this, turn to page 128.

COMMONLY MISHYPHENATED WORDS

There are some compound words or expressions that are systematically given hyphens they shouldn't have. The following lists a few of these common errors; note in particular that Latin phrases do *not* take hyphens.

No	*Yes*
more-or-less	more or less
on-going	ongoing
under-way	under way
a-priori	a priori

ad-hoc	ad hoc
bona-fide	bona fide
post-hoc	post hoc
vice-versa	vice versa

HYPHENATION WITH PREFIXES AND SUFFIXES

There isn't a single rule here that covers all words containing a prefix or a suffix. Some *never* take a hyphen, some *may* take one, some *should* take one and some *must* take one.

The majority of cases fall into the first category; that is, you run the prefix or suffix in with the word it modifies. For example, you would never use a hyphen in words such as *unsaid, illogical, playing, added* or *countable*.

There are some cases where a hyphen may be a matter of choice. For example, both versions of the following words are legitimate:

anti-hero/antihero	non-aggressive/nonaggressive
bi-annual/biannual	pre-mixed/premixed
co-ordinate/coordinate	semi-private/semiprivate
co-operate/cooperate	sub-optimal/suboptimal
infra-red/infrared	ultra-violet/ultraviolet

It should be noted that the modern trend is to view such hyphens as superfluous, and most scientific, technical, medical and government publications will omit them. Putting them in doesn't do any harm, but the words would read just as clearly and unambiguously without them. If you are using a style guide, follow its rules. If you are making your own decisions, be consistent: Don't randomly use hyphens with some prefixes and suffixes and not others.

In a number of situations, a hyphen is strongly recommended. It is a good idea to use one in the following circumstances:

WHEN THE COMBINATION OF ROOT WORD AND PREFIX/SUFFIX IS UNUSUAL

You wouldn't hyphenate standard words such as *premeditation, worldwide* or *clockwise*. However, references to "*prewedding* arrangements," a "*communitywide* effort" or "his place could use some improvement *furniturewise*" would look a bit odd. Such (relatively) unique constructions would read better as *pre-wedding, community-wide* and *furniture-wise*. That is, include a hyphen if the combination of the root word and its prefix or suffix is not standard and might look peculiar as a single word.

WHEN THE WORD WOULD HAVE A DIFFERENT MEANING WITHOUT A HYPHEN
Compare the following two sentences:

> The team announced today that their star pitcher has resigned.
> The team announced today that their star pitcher has re-signed.

Similarly, if referring to the *re-creation* of an event, *re-covering* a sofa or *un-ionized* molecules, include a hyphen so that readers won't puzzle over who's out having a good time, what illness the furniture is getting over or whether the molecules have any work grievances.

WHEN THE WORD MIGHT BE DIFFICULT TO READ IF IT DIDN'T HAVE A HYPHEN
Consider the words *coworker, coinventor, reprepped, tristimulus* and *doable*. On a quick scan, a reader might process these words as *cow orker, coin ventor, rep repped, trist imulus* and *doab le!* Naturally anyone with a competent grasp of the language would quickly see what was meant, but writing these words as *co-worker, co-inventor, re-prepped, tri-stimulus* and *do-able* makes the reading process a little easier.

WHEN THE ADDITION OF THE PREFIX OR SUFFIX WOULD CREATE AN AWKWARD JUXTAPOSITION OF THE SAME LETTERS

No	Yes
antiinflammatory	anti-inflammatory
nonnative	non-native
preengineered	pre-engineered
multiitem	multi-item
multititled	multi-titled
deemphasize	de-emphasize

intraarterial	intra-arterial
shelllike	shell-like

Finally, there are a number of situations where a hyphen is mandatory. *Always* include one in the following cases:

WHEN THE ROOT WORD IS CAPITALIZED

pre-Columbian
sub-Arctic
un-American
post-Reformation
Buddha-like
Canada-wide

WHEN THE ROOT WORD IS A NUMERAL

pre-1900s
under-18s

WITH CERTAIN PREFIXES; E.G., *ALL, EX, SELF*

all-encompassing	ex-employee	self-esteem
all-knowing	ex-husband	self-care
all-embracing	ex-girlfriend	self-doubts

WITH CERTAIN SUFFIXES; E.G., *ELECT, ODD, FREE*

president-elect	twenty-odd students	salt-free
chairman-elect	thirty-odd dollars	jargon-free
bride-elect	forty-odd couples	nuclear-free

HYPHENATION WITH NUMBERS

Include a hyphen when spelling out any two-word number (that is, from twenty-one to ninety-nine) or fraction.

twenty-nine
one hundred sixty-two
one-third
four and three-quarters

With a fraction that includes a two-word number, hyphenate *just* the two-word number: Do not add another hyphen, or it may become unclear just what numbers are linked with what.

No	*Yes*
one-twenty-fifth	one twenty-fifth
sixty-five-hundredths	sixty-five hundredths
five-one-hundredths of a percent	five one-hundredths of a percent

Problem Words

The English language is the sea which receives tributaries from every region under heaven.

—RALPH WALDO EMERSON

Between the various invasions of the British Isles and British colonization, about 80 percent of English has foreign origins. The huge vocabulary of the language naturally leads to occasional errors on the part of its users, and the challenges go further than just coping with the wildly unphonetic orthography. When putting down what they want to say, writers must sort through a plethora of similar-sounding words, words that have almost—but not quite—the same shade of meaning, and words that take unexpected forms in their plural or negative states. This chapter reviews some common errors.

Frequently Misused Words

Homonyms (discussed on page 10) aren't the only words that frequently get mixed up. The following exercise presents words that are all too often wrongly substituted for others or used in the wrong sense—and in some cases don't even exist, except in popular imagination. Note that unlike confused homonyms, where the wrong word at least *sounds* right, most of these errors would be evident in speech as well as in writing.

Exercise
Each of the following sentences contains an inappropriate word. How would you correct it?

The change didn't have a big affect on our plans.

Temperatures this week are expected to be seasonal.

Eustace couldn't precede until the wild applause had died down.

The idea was greeted with strong censor.

The only route was along a narrow torturous road.

We're looking to hire people with exceptionable skills.

Fortuitously, the weather cleared up just in time for the picnic.

I was not at all adverse to getting a raise.

The screaming kids and blaring radio made for a noisome evening.

Exhausted, Minnie went to lay down on the sofa for a while.

There was concern that his legal victory could set a dangerous precedence.

There was no good rational for putting things off any longer.

His writing always had to be heavily edited in order to be comprehensive.

Parents are assured that their children will be provided with healthy meals.

Olga's comment seemed to infer that her resignation was imminent.

If you're going to Antarctica, don't forget to bring your camera.

Women comprise slightly over half the population.

Less than half the employees voted for the plan.

A large amount of dishes were broken when the shelf collapsed.

The exam includes both a verbal and a written part.

Hopefully it won't be necessary for us to go to such extremes.

Errors like spelling mistakes make a résumé look bad.

Her ideas were light-years ahead of her time.

The noise was literally enough to raise the dead.

The team is stronger than ever, and is expected to decimate last year's record.

We applied ourselves to the task with diligency.

They decided to buy the house, irregardless of the cost.

The photographs of the injured birds were heartwrenching.

Fortunately, there was no reoccurrence of the trouble.

If the problem still persists, call your service representative.

If you order now, you will receive a free gift.

We hope to transition from the old schedule to the new one by next month.

The consultant managed to architect a solution to the problem.

Answers

The errors in the above exercise fall into a few categories.

In each of the following sentences, the appropriate word has been replaced by one that sounds similar although not identical. In some cases, writers don't know the correct word and use one that's more familiar; in others, they intentionally use a "fancier-sounding" word, not realizing it doesn't mean the same thing; and in yet others, they are equally likely to confuse two similar-sounding words.

The change didn't have a big affect on our plans.
Should be *effect*—the consequence or result of something. *Affect,* a verb, means to influence or act upon. Thus, when you *affect* something, you have an *effect* on it.

The above definitions are the most common meanings of these words, and are the ones that writers are most likely to mix up. However, just to complicate things further, there are other, less common usages for each word as well. *Effect* may also be used as a verb, meaning to accomplish, bring about, cause to occur (the committee tried to effect a change). *Affect* can mean to fancy something, usually in a pretentious way (affect Eastern dress), to cultivate a style (affect a bored demeanor), to put on deceptively (affect an English accent; speak in an affected manner) or to stir emotionally (such a sight must affect any who see it; she was very affected by his story). As a noun, with the pronunciation on the first syllable, it refers to emotions (the patient exhibited a lack of affect).

Temperatures this week are expected to be seasonal.
Should be *seasonable*—typical of or suitable for the time of year. *Seasonal* means occurring only at a particular time of year (fruit picking is seasonal employment). It's quite striking how many radio weather announcers refer to "seasonal" conditions.

Eustace couldn't precede until the wild applause had died down.
Should be *proceed*—continue. *Precede* means to go before (she asked the clients to precede her into the meeting room).

The idea was greeted with strong censor.
Should be *censure*—criticism, condemnation. *Censor* means to officially prevent or destroy forms of communication—publications, films, Internet exchanges, etc.—that are deemed to be morally objectionable or subversive (her writing was censored in her home country). The words are related, though: A person given to censure is *censorious*.

The only route was along a narrow torturous road.
Should be *tortuous*—winding, twisting. *Torturous* means painful (the visit was torturous, and he was glad to flee).

We're looking to hire people with exceptionable skills.
Should be *exceptional*—extraordinarily good. *Exceptionable* means offensive or objectionable—that is, something that one would take exception to (the drunk's behavior was exceptionable).

Fortuitously, the weather cleared up just in time for the picnic.
Should be *fortunately*—luckily, happily. *Fortuitously* means something unplanned, happening by chance or fortune (it was a fortuitous meeting; we just happened to run into each other at the airport).

I was not at all **adverse** to getting a raise.

Should be *averse*—reluctant. *Adverse* means unfavorable (the flight had to be postponed due to adverse weather).

The screaming kids and blaring radio made for a **noisome** evening.

Should be *noisy*—marked by loud sounds. *Noisome* means malodorous, bad-smelling (noisome fumes were rising from the sewer grate).

Exhausted, Minnie went to **lay** down on the sofa for a while.

Should be *lie*—the word used to describe the action or position of the subject of the sentence (I tried to lie as still as possible; he decided to lie low for a while; the clouds seemed to lie right over the treetops; the money was lying there in plain view). To *lay* means to set something or someone down; that is, it applies to something *acted* upon by the subject (just lay that box on the table; would you lay the baby in her crib; lay your head on my shoulder).

Adding to the confusion, *lay* is also the past tense of *lie* (she was exhausted and lay down; he lay low until the storm blew over). The past participle of *lie* is *lain* (after she had lain there for a while, she got up). Both the past tense and past participle of *lay* are *laid* (I laid the box on the table; he laid his head on the pillow; she had laid the money on the counter). It's a common error to use *lay* instead of *laid*, as in *She lay the money down and left.*

There was concern that his legal victory could set a dangerous **precedence**.

Should be *precedent*—something that will authorize or justify a subsequent event. *Precedence* means to go before or take priority (manners took precedence at her table).

There was no good **rational** for putting things off any longer.

Should be *rationale*—justification or underlying reason. *Rational* means logical, reasonable (his demeanor was calm and rational).

His writing always had to be heavily edited in order to be **comprehensive**.

Should be *comprehensible*—understandable, intelligible. *Comprehensive* means including all necessary details or information (the list is as comprehensive as it need be).

Parents are assured that their children will be provided with **healthy**
meals.

Should be *healthful*—supportive of good health. Another appropriate word would be *wholesome*. Strictly speaking, the word
healthy refers to the health of the noun that follows—and it's not
the health of the meal that's of concern, but that of the person eating
it. (Although one would obviously prefer not to sit down to diseased
food.) Some authorities permit its use as shown above, and it's commonly used this way in speech. In formal writing, however, it is better
to use one of the other words.

In each of the following sentences, the appropriate word has been
replaced by one that is related in meaning or concept, although not
similar in sound.

Olga's comment seemed to **infer** that her resignation was imminent.
Should be *imply*—hint, say indirectly. *Infer* means to guess, surmise
or conclude something without being told it explicitly (I think I can
infer what you're trying to tell me). Thus, the speaker (or writer)
implies; the listener (or reader) infers. Note: *Merriam Webster's
Collegiate Dictionary* permits the use of *infer* as a synonym for
imply; however, enough readers would consider this incorrect that
writers are advised to make the distinction.

If you're going to Antarctica, don't forget to **bring** your camera.
Should be *take*—transport away from where one is currently located. *Bring* means to transport towards where one is currently
located. Thus, it would be correct to say *If you're coming to Antarctica, don't forget to bring your camera*—assuming the speaker is
already there—or *If you're going to Antarctica, don't forget to
bring me back a souvenir*. Similarly, one would *take the dog out
for a walk*, but tell an expected guest to *feel free to bring your
dog*. Usually, no misunderstanding results from using *bring* for *take*,
but the words do indicate different perspectives. For example, *I took
all the old chairs to the new house* implies that it's the packing up
of the chairs that is the focus, whereas *I brought all the old chairs
to the new house* implies that the focus is on the chairs' arrival.

Women **comprise** slightly over half the population.
Should be *constitute*—make up. *Comprise* means to contain or

include (her collection comprises old playbills, movie magazines and stage memorabilia). The parts constitute the whole; the whole comprises the parts. Note: *Merriam Webster's Collegiate Dictionary* permits the use of *comprise* as a synonym for *constitute;* however, writers are advised to make the distinction.

Less than half the employees voted for the plan.
Should be *fewer*—not as many individual entities. *Less* should be used only to refer to a smaller quantity of a single entity (my recipe uses less sugar; the other route takes less time).

A large **amount** of dishes were broken when the shelf collapsed.
Should be *number*—the quantity of individual entities. *Amount* should be used only to refer to how much there is of a single entity (they do a great amount of business on weekends; what amount of flour does this take).

The exam includes both a **verbal** and a written part.
Should be *oral*—spoken, as opposed to written. As used in the above sense, *verbal* simply means involving words, so it would apply equally to both oral and written modes. (One could properly say an exam contained a verbal and a mathematics part, or a verbal and a motor skills part.) Used in another sense, however, the word does mean oral: for example, a verbal agreement as opposed to a written one.

In each of the following sentences, a word is used in an ungrammatical way.

Hopefully it won't be necessary for us to go to such extremes.
Should be *We hope* or *It's to be hoped that.* Strictly speaking, *hopefully* means full of hope (hopefully, she looked through the job ads; he went hopefully through the day's receipts). Certainly, the use shown above is very common in speech, and some modern authorities feel it should be viewed as legitimate since it doesn't present any ambiguity and the alternatives often sound stiff. In formal writing, however, it is advisable to avoid this usage—at least for now. Another few years may see it gain full acceptability.

Errors **like** spelling mistakes make a résumé look bad.
Should be *such as*—meaning that spelling mistakes are among the

things that make a résumé look bad. *Like* means similar to (he got a bike just like his brother's), so the above sentence seems to say that it is errors that *resemble* spelling mistakes that are the problem, not spelling mistakes themselves. In speech, where the context usually makes it unambiguous, the word is commonly and harmlessly misused, but stricter standards should apply in formal writing.

In each of the following sentences, the problem words are ones whose meanings are often just plain misconstrued.

Her ideas were **light-years** ahead of her time.
Should be *many years* or just *years*. A light-year isn't a unit of time; it's the distance that light travels in one year, about 5.8 trillion miles (even the nearest star is light-years from Earth).

The noise was **literally** enough to raise the dead.
Should be *virtually* or *practically*. *Literally* means—literally! This word does not belong with metaphorical expressions, and using it as in the above example, or saying such things as a flustered executive literally lost his head, or children watching a circus were literally bursting with excitement, would raise some rather unpleasant images. A correct use is when you are referring to something normally metaphorical that is happening in reality (the astronauts were literally walking on air; the bumbling farmhand literally put the cart before the horse) or when you want to emphasize that something that might appear to be an exaggeration is in fact accurate (the book contains literally thousands of useful tips; it took literally a split second for the gasoline to catch on fire).

The team is stronger than ever, and is expected to **decimate** last year's record.
Should be *smash, obliterate* or some similar word. *Decimate* should not be used to mean total destruction. Strictly speaking, it means to destroy one-tenth of; more generally, to destroy a significant portion of (the herd was decimated by disease).

The following sentences contain nonwords: words not in the dictionary. *Any* dictionary.

We applied ourselves to the task with **diligency**.

Should be *diligence*. This error possibly arises from an association with similar words—*assiduity, alacrity, industry*.

They decided to buy the house, **irregardless** of the cost.

Should be *regardless*. This error likely arises from a confusion with the similar word *irrespective*.

The photographs of the injured birds were **heartwrenching**.

Should be *heartrending*. This extremely common error—which is made regularly by members of the media, who should know better—presumably arises from a confusion with the similar word *gut-wrenching*. Keep your internal organs straight!

Fortunately, there was no **reoccurrence** of the trouble.

Should be *recurrence*. The word does mean "to occur again," but does not follow the general rule of adding *re* to the root word.

The following sentences contain redundancies. Keep in mind that some words carry inherent meanings that should not be repeated by any modifiers.

If the problem **still** persists, call your service representative.

If you order now, you will receive a **free** gift.

The first should be just *persists*: Anything that is persisting is, by definition, still happening. The second should be just *gift*: A gift, by definition, is free. (Examples such as the latter are typical of marketing hype, whose practitioners can't seem to resist the temptation to use words that they think will grab the consumer.)

The following sentences contain examples of inappropriately using a noun as a verb (or verbing a noun, as this problem is called in the editing trade).

We hope to **transition** from the old schedule to the new one by next month.

The consultant managed to **architect** a solution to the problem.

The first sentence should read *make the transition*, and the second, *design* or *come up with*. Resist the temptation to save a word or two, or to sound fancy, by forcing a noun into an unnatural role. In fairness, some words that were once only nouns have eventually evolved; a section on this topic in Strunk and White's classic 1935 handbook *The Elements of Style* looks suspiciously at the now-re-spectable *hosted*, *chaired* and *debuted*. However, until something has gained dictionary status, or at least general acceptance, do not make your own grammatical rules.

> *'Vienna Station received another signal from Locksmith this morning, fully prioritised.'*
>
> *'Fully whatted?'*
>
> *'Er . . . prioritised, sir.'*
>
> *'Christ.'*
>
> *'. . . Will you be around for initialling appropriation orders later in the afternoon, sir?'*
>
> *'Well, young Reeve, after a brief luncherising and half an hour's memorandorising Cabinet, I'll be at Lord's.'*
>
> *'Right, sir.'*
>
> *'So if you want me to signatorise anything, send Simon Hesketh-Harvey round, he's a member. Now I must go and lavatorise. And while I'm away for God's sake try and learn to speak English.'*
>
> STEPHEN FRY, *The Liar*

Plural Formations

Cat, cats. Tree, trees. House, houses. Life would be simpler if all plurals followed the rule of adding *s* to the singular, but unfortunately the outliers are rampant, and quirky plurals present yet another stumbling block to writers wrestling their way through the exceptions that dot the English language. One reason for the irregularities is that many words have been borrowed from other languages, and for some the plural in the original language has become the correct form in English as well. To complicate matters even further, some nouns have two acceptable plurals, and one form may be considered more appropriate than the other in certain genres of writing. In a number of cases, the different plural forms actually have different meanings.

This section reviews the rules that govern irregular plurals and discusses exceptions and variations. For examples of plural words that are commonly taken for singulars and vice versa, see the discussion of unusual plurals and singulars under "Agreement Between Subject and Verb" on page 219.

WITH COMPOUND WORDS WHERE THE PRINCIPAL NOUN IS FOLLOWED BY A MODIFIER, THE PLURALIZING *S* GOES AFTER THE NOUN

Note that this holds whether the compound is open or hyphenated, and in some cases even when it is closed.

attorney-general	attorneys-general
mother-in-law	mothers-in-law
court-martial	courts-martial
rule of thumb	rules of thumb

right of way	rights of way
passerby	passersby

Compounds ending in *ful* usually take the *s* at the end: *handfuls, mouthfuls*. Some, however, can go either way: *spoonsful* or *spoonfuls, bucketsful* or *bucketfuls*.

If there is no clear principal noun, the plural applies to the entire compound: *hand-me-downs, pick-me-ups, will-o'-the-wisps*.

WORDS ENDING IN A SIBILANT SOUND— S, SH, SOFT CH, X OR Z—ADD ES

lens	lenses	fox	foxes
bass	basses	topaz	topazes
rash	rashes	the Jones family	the Joneses
speech	speeches	the Katz family	the Katzes
match	matches	the March family	the Marches

Note that these plurals do *not* take an apostrophe. For more on this, see the discussion under "Apostrophe" on page 199.

In a few cases, the final *z* or *s* must be or may optionally be doubled before the *es*: for example, *quiz—quizzes, bus—buses* or *busses*.

WORDS ENDING IN IS CHANGE TO ES

basis	bases
crisis	crises
hypothesis	hypotheses
thesis	theses
parenthesis	parentheses

WORDS ENDING IN A CONSONANT FOLLOWED BY Y CHANGE TO IES

twenty	twenties
harpy	harpies
patty	patties
family	families
brandy	brandies

If the *y* is preceded by a vowel, it usually does not change: for example, *galleys, donkeys. Money,* however, may become *monies* or *moneys.* Note that proper names always keep the *y*: the *Kennedys,* the *Applebys,* the *Emmys,* the *Tonys.*

WITH WORDS ENDING IN *F* OR *FE*, SOME CHANGE TO *VES*, OTHERS ADD *S*

A number may go either way.

chief	chiefs
roof	roofs
knife	knives
life	lives
leaf	leaves
hoof	hoofs *or* hooves
scarf	scarfs *or* scarves
dwarf	dwarfs *or* dwarves

Note though that the plural of *still life* is *still lifes,* not *lives;* and the hockey team is the Toronto Maple *Leafs.* While *dwarf* can go either way, the astronomical term is *white dwarfs,* not *dwarves.*

WITH WORDS ENDING IN *O*, SOME ADD *S*, OTHERS ADD *ES*

A number may go either way.

portfolio	portfolios
stereo	stereos
contralto	contraltos
potato	potatoes
tomato	tomatoes
ghetto	ghettos *or* ghettoes
banjo	banjos *or* banjoes
zero	zeros *or* zeroes

The general rule is that the *e* is included if the *o* is preceded by a consonant and not included if the *o* is preceded by a vowel, but there are enough exceptions that it's best to check. (Be aware that dictionaries may differ.)

SOME WORDS OF ITALIAN ORIGIN THAT END IN *O* CHANGE TO *I*, BUT MAY ALTERNATIVELY ADD *S*

concerto	concerti *or* concertos
basso	bassi *or* bassos

LATIN WORDS ENDING IN *US* CHANGE TO *I*

For some—not all—it is acceptable to add *es* instead.

alumnus	alumni
stimulus	stimuli
locus	loci
focus	foci *or* focuses
fungus	fungi *or* funguses
nucleus	nuclei *or* nucleuses
radius	radii *or* radiuses

In cases where both forms are legitimate, the Latin plural is preferred in more formal writing.

LATIN WORDS ENDING IN *UM* CHANGE TO *A*

For some—not all—it is acceptable to add *s* instead.

bacterium	bacteria
medium	media
datum	data
millennium	millennia *or* millenniums
memorandum	memoranda *or* memorandums
symposium	symposia *or* symposiums
honorarium	honoraria *or* honorariums

In cases where both forms are legitimate, the Latin plural is preferred in more formal writing.

Note that for some Latin words the English plural has become the standard. For example, pluralizing *museum* and *auditorium* as *musea* and *auditoria* would look more pretentious than correct.

LATIN WORDS ENDING IN *A* ADD AN *E*

For some—not all—it is acceptable to add *s* instead.

alumna	alumnae
larva	larvae

alga	algae
vertebra	vertebrae *or* vertebras
persona	personae *or* personas
antenna	antennae *or* antennas

Use *antennas* for TV and radio aerials, but *antennae* for insects. Use *personas* for the demeanors put on for others (she assumes different personas for different occasions), but *personae* for fictional characters (as in *dramatis personae*). In cases where both forms are legitimate, the Latin plural is preferred in scientific and academic writing.

LATIN-DERIVED WORDS ENDING IN *X* EITHER CHANGE TO *ICES* OR ADD *ES*

appendix	appendices *or* appendixes
index	indices *or* indexes
matrix	matrices *or* matrixes
cortex	cortices *or* cortexes

It is usual to use *indices* if referring to indicators (several indices are used to measure economic progress). For all these words, always use the Latin plurals in scientific and academic writing.

GREEK WORDS ENDING IN *ON* CHANGE TO *A*

| criterion | criteria |
| phenomenon | phenomena |

If *phenomenon* is being used to mean a remarkable person, rather than an observable event, it is pluralized with an *s* (those young musicians are phenomenons).

MANY FRENCH WORDS THAT END IN *EAU* MAY ADD EITHER *X* OR *S*

beau	beaux *or* beaus
chateau	chateaux *or* chateaus
milieu	milieux *or* milieus

Use the French plurals in more formal writing.

HEBREW WORDS ADD *IM* (FOR MASCULINE WORDS) OR *OTH* (FOR FEMININE WORDS)

In a number of cases, it is acceptable to add *s* instead.

kibbutz	kibbutzim
Ashkenazi	Ashkenazim
Sephardi	Sephardim
cherub	cherubim *or* cherubs
seraph	seraphim *or* seraphs
mitzvah	mitzvoth *or* mitzvahs
matzo	matzoth *or* matzos

Use *cherubs* to refer to appealing children (both their daughters were perfect cherubs), and *cherubim* to refer to actual angels.

SOME ENGLISH WORDS TAKE UNPREDICTABLE PLURAL FORMS

one mouse	two mice
one die	two dice
one foot	two feet
one ox	two oxen
one goose	two geese
one man	two men
one child	two children

SOME WORDS ARE THE SAME IN BOTH SINGULAR AND PLURAL FORM

one moose	two moose
one deer	two deer
one aircraft	two aircraft
one series	two series
one sweepstakes	two sweepstakes

Native speakers easily absorb these plurals along with the more predictable ones. For those learning English as a second language, there is little to do but roll the eyes, tear at the hair and grimly memorize each one.

Negative Formations

Unreliable. Irreversible. Disloyal. Indecisive. Impractical. Atypical. Counterintuitive. Illiterate. Abnormal. Deactivate. Misremember. Antiracism. Nonaddictive. Maladjusted. Childless. Cholesterol-free. Just as not every plural is formed by adding *s* to the singular, not every negative is formed by adding *un.* One of the challenges of the English language is the variety of add-ons that can be united with base words to create their opposites. Sometimes the reason for using a given prefix or suffix has to do with the meaning of the negative word, sometimes with the form or the etymological root of the base word. The result of all this variation is that negative words present yet another pitfall to the unwary writer, and are the source of many common errors.

Varied as they are, negative prefixes and suffixes aren't utterly arbitrary. Their specific meanings are as follows:

A- OR AN-
(an before a vowel or the letter h)

Without, lacking, absent	achromatic, asexual, amoral, anaerobic, anhedonia

ANTI-

Opposite of	antimatter, Antichrist, anticlockwise (alternative to counterclockwise)
Preventing or alleviating	antidepressant, antifreeze
Combating or defending against	antimissile, antiaircraft, antibiotic
Opposed to or hostile to	antimonarchist, antivivisectionist, anti-Semitic

COUNTER-

Opposite of or contrary to	counterpressure, counterculture, counterclockwise
Opposing	countermove, counterespionage

DE-

The reverse of	de-emphasize, de-escalate, deforestation, decompose
Depriving of	dehumanize, demagnetize
Removing from	declassify, decontaminate, dehumidify, deinstitutionalize

DIS-

The reverse of	disrespectful, disagreement, disadvantage, discontented
Excluding or taking away	disbar, disarm, disenfranchise

DYS-

Abnormal or impaired	dyslexic, dysfunctional, dyspeptic

E-

Deprived of, missing	emasculated, edentate (lacking teeth)

MAL-

Bad, wrong	malformed, maladministered, malfunctioning
Poor, inadequate	malnourished, maladroit

MIS-

Bad, wrong	mistranslate, misuse, misshapen, misperceive, misfortune

NON-

The reverse of or absence of (the equivalent of putting *not* before the base word)	nonrepresentative, nonexistent, noncommercial, nonintoxicating

| Of little importance or lacking a normal positive aspect | nonissue, nonevent, noninformation |

UN-, IN-, IL-, IM-, IR-
Largely the same as *non:* the reverse of or absence of

Some words take *un*	undrinkable, unaltered, undressed, uninspiring, unenforced
Some take *in*	inattentive, inability, incapable
Some words starting with *l* take *il*	illegal, illegitimate
Some words starting with *b, m* or *p* take *im*	imbalance, immobile, implausible
Some words starting with *r* take *ir*	irrefutable, irrevocable

Note, however, that many other words that begin with these letters take the prefixes *in, un* or *non.*

-LESS
| Without, devoid of | witless, shoeless, peerless, motionless, classless |
| Unable to do or to be done | helpless, countless, resistless |

-FREE
| Unencumbered with; not containing something undesirable | crime-free, smoke-free, frost-free, caffeine-free |

There is clearly a great deal of overlap, which is why you have to check the dictionary for any word you're not certain of. If no official negative construction for a word is given, it is usually most appropriate to create its negative by prefixing it with either *un* or *non,* sometimes adding a hyphen if the combination looks a bit shaky.

To complicate matters further, in a few cases a negative prefix differs for different forms of a word: *incomplete* but *uncompleted, unrepressed* but *irrepressible, undisputed* but *indisputable.* And while some base words have more than one acceptable negative construction *(uncommunicative* or *noncommunicative, mistreated* or *maltreated),* you must be aware that a dictionary may permit variants that many readers would view as incorrect. For example, you would be advised to go with *infeasible* rather than *unfeasible* and *antihero* rather than *nonhero,* even though these variants are listed in some dictionaries. (See the discussion of prescriptive and descriptive dictionaries on page 17.)

In a few cases, different prefixes added to the same base word create different meanings. Some common misuses are shown below.

Exercise
Correct the following sentences.

She was disinterested in his story, and tried to change the subject.
Children's pajamas should be made of inflammable material.
Statistical analysis found the results to be insignificant.
Many of the inmates came from highly nonfunctional families.
Young children start out immoral, and must be socialized.
If the pegs don't fit in the holes, check to see if they're nonaligned.
The coach stated that he was very unsatisfied with the refereeing.
Her office was wildly unorganized.
The foreign minister was an expert at planting misinformation.

Answers
She was **disinterested** in his story, and tried to change the subject.
Should be *uninterested*—bored by. *Disinterested* means impartial or objective; that is, having no personal stake—interest—in an outcome (they agreed to have their dispute arbitrated by a disinterested third party).

Children's pajamas should be made of **inflammable** material.
Should be *nonflammable*—not easily ignited. *Inflammable* means flammable! (As in *inflame.*)

Statistical analysis found the results to be **insignificant**.
Should be *nonsignificant*—failing to reach a certain criterion that would indicate that an experimental effect was real, not occurring by chance. *Insignificant* means trivial, unimportant, inconsequential (she always managed to make him feel small and insignificant).

51

Many of the inmates came from highly **nonfunctional** families.
Should be *dysfunctional*—working badly or pathologically. *Nonfunctional* means not working at all (be sure to replace any nonfunctional batteries).

Young children start out **immoral,** and must be socialized.
Should be *amoral*—that is, morality is not an issue here. Children initially have no sense of right or wrong. *Immoral* means having bad morals (she felt that to take his money would be immoral).

If the pegs don't fit in the holes, check to see if they're **nonaligned**.
Should be *misaligned*—not in a straight line. *Nonaligned* is a political term—now somewhat dated—referring to countries without political alliances to either the Western or the Communist bloc (the nonaligned nations were supportive of the measure).

The coach stated that he was very **unsatisfied** with the refereeing.
Should be *dissatisfied*—unhappy or displeased with. *Unsatisfied* means not having had enough of something (dinner was meager, and he left the table feeling unsatisfied).

Her office was wildly **unorganized**.
Should be *disorganized*—badly organized. *Unorganized* means not organized, in the sense of either not sorted (two years after she moved, her papers were still unorganized) or not forming a labor union (the workers at the largest plant were unorganized).

The foreign minister was an expert at planting **misinformation**.
Should be *disinformation*—information that is deliberately misleading. *Misinformation* is information that is wrong, but not necessarily intentionally so (teenagers often trade misinformation about birth control).

PART THREE

Punctuation

The word *punctuation* derives from the Latin for "point." That is, the marks within a sentence *point* to the various meanings of its words, making sense of what otherwise might be a string of sounds. They serve two functions: They define how the various elements of a sentence relate to each other, thereby ensuring clear and unambiguous communication, and they help to establish the tone. The first function is more mechanical and hence more easily learned; the second is part of what distinguishes the skilled writer from the novice. Sometimes the reason for selecting one mark over another has more to do with achieving a certain nuance than with major differences in meaning.

In dialogue, punctuation helps to convey intonation and style of speaking, so that the reader "hears" a character's words the way the writer intended. Subtleties such as pauses, emphases, hesitancy and changes in pitch can all be achieved through the appropriate marks.

Punctuation marks defy easy categorization, because all play more than one role and different marks may be used for similar purposes. This chapter follows the convention of grouping them by their main or best-known functions, as follows:

- Marks used to separate elements within a sentence—comma, semicolon and colon.

- Marks used to end a sentence—period, question mark and exclamation point.
- Marks used to link related elements—hyphen and slash.
- Marks used to set off digressions from the main flow—parentheses, dashes and brackets.
- Marks used with quoted material—quotation marks and ellipses.
- A final mark, the apostrophe, is distinct enough not to be grouped with any other. (In fact, some authorities do not consider it a punctuation mark at all, but part of the inherent spelling of a word.)

This ordering has been done with a recognition that the distinctions are not in fact that neat. Take the terminal punctuation marks: Periods have functions other than ending a sentence; question marks and exclamation points occasionally appear in the middle of a sentence; a sentence may end in an ellipsis or a dash rather than in any of the above. Similarly, dashes may be used not only like parentheses but also like colons, to separate elements, and sometimes like hyphens, to link elements. Missing letters and words may, depending on the specifics of what is being done, be indicated by periods, commas, semicolons, apostrophes, hyphens, ellipses or dashes. Thus, along with reviewing its various roles, the section devoted to each mark provides cross-references to any other marks that can perform a similar function, and discusses when it is appropriate to select one mark over another. Most sections end with a discussion of style conventions, including instructions on how to position the mark when it exists alongside another.

Basic Sentence Structure

In order to understand the logic behind some rules of punctuation, particularly those pertaining to the comma and the semicolon, it is necessary to understand the basic components of a sentence. Read this section before turning to the review of the comma, because that section makes multiple references to the terms defined here.

SUBJECT, PREDICATE, CLAUSE

A grammatically complete sentence includes, at a minimum, two things: a subject and a predicate. The **subject** is any sort of entity—a person, a place, an object, an abstract concept, a pronoun that refers to some entity identified elsewhere or an action functioning as a noun. The **predicate** gives some information about the subject, either describing it or identifying an action that it performs or that is performed upon it (its "predicament"). If any object is affected by the subject's actions, that object is part of the predicate as well. Together, a subject and a predicate constitute a **clause**. A sentence may contain more than one clause.

In the examples below, the subject and predicate are separated by a slash.

- Usually, the subject precedes the predicate.

   Fish/swim.

Subject is a concrete noun; predicate identifies an action performed by the subject.

   The silence/was shattered.

Subject is an abstract noun; predicate identifies something done to the subject.

I/rest my case.

Subject is a pronoun; predicate identifies an action performed by the subject plus the target of this action (called the **object**).

Fifi/is no rocket scientist.

Subject is a proper noun; predicate describes the subject.

Skiing/is my favorite winter sport.

Subject is a gerund, an action functioning as a noun; predicate describes the subject.

To drive a Zamboni/was his ambition.

Subject is an infinitive, an action functioning as a noun; predicate describes the subject.

• The predicate may precede the subject.

Off went/the runners.
Out came/the sun.
On the table lay/an illuminated manuscript.
Off in the distance were/the elephants.
Speeding over the crest came/the cyclists.
There's/my missing briefcase!

• A clause may contain more than one subject. This is referred to as a **compound subject** (if linked by *and*) or an **alternative subject** (if linked by *or*).

Ella and her sister/are both contortionists.
Pushing and shoving/will not be tolerated.
Either Saturday or Sunday/should be a good day for starting the
   revolution.

• A predicate may provide its subject with more than one description, or have it performing more than one action, or have it performing that action upon more than one object, or have more than one object affected by that action. This is referred to as a **compound predicate**.

His arms/were tanned and brawny.
[two descriptions]

The storekeeper/looked at the money in the till and sighed.
[two actions]

Joanne/ate an entire box of cookies and six Dove Bars.
[multiple recipients of the action "ate"]

The mayor/gave Mike and me citations for bravery.
[two entities affected by what was given]

INDEPENDENT CLAUSE, DEPENDENT CLAUSE, CONJUNCTION

An **independent clause** (also called a main clause) is a clause that can stand alone. It thus can be either part of a sentence or a complete sentence. All the examples above are sentences consisting of a single independent clause.

Conjunctions are words that link other words or groups of words together and determine how they relate to each other.

The conjunctions *and, but, or, for, nor, yet* and *so* are used to join elements of equal grammatical weight. They may therefore be used to join two (or more) independent clauses.

The first car we considered getting was the better buy, but the second was a prettier color.

The wind suddenly picked up, and the temperature dropped precipitously.

He knew he'd better finish by Tuesday, or he'd be in trouble.

A **dependent clause** (also called a subordinate clause) is a clause that cannot stand alone, because something about it implies that there is more to come. On its own, a dependent clause is left hanging, its meaning incomplete. It must be combined with an independent clause in order to form a complete sentence.

One type of dependent clause is essentially an independent clause with a subordinating word tacked on. Specifically, it opens with a conjunction that indicates a dependent relationship with information elsewhere in the sentence. For example, if you took the independent clause *it was raining heavily* and added the subordinating conjunction *since*, you would no longer have an independent clause but a sentence fragment: *since it was raining heavily*. This fragment could, however, function within a larger sentence: *Since it was raining heavily, we took a taxi.*

Other subordinating conjunctions include *because, now that, although, even though, if, even if, as if, as, as soon as, before, after, when, whenever, despite, rather than, in order that, provided that, so that, whereas, while, unless* and *until.* Unlike the conjunctions used to link independent clauses, which would not normally be used to open a sentence (although see the discussion of this on page 262), these words may appear either at the beginning or in the middle.

In another type of dependent clause, the subordinating word is the subject itself. For example, if you replaced the noun in the independent clause *the fire was burning brightly* with the subordinating pronoun *which*, you would no longer have an independent clause but a sentence fragment: *which was burning brightly.* This fragment could, however, function within a larger sentence: *We huddled around the fire, which was burning brightly.*

PHRASE

A **phrase** consists of a group of related words, but it doesn't qualify as a clause because it does not contain both a subject and a predicate. (It may contain a noun, a verb or both, but these don't constitute a clause unless they are in a specific relation to each other, as described above.)

Like a dependent clause, a phrase is not expected to stand alone. In order for a sentence that contains a phrase to be grammatically complete, the phrase must either precede, follow or lie within an independent clause.

Ever the comedian, he couldn't resist one last parting shot.

She raced off *to tell the news.*

Checking through the receipts, I came across something unexpected.

The twins, *by the way,* insist they had nothing to do with the shark turning up in the bathtub.

SENTENCE FRAGMENT

A **sentence fragment** is a group of words that is punctuated as a sentence—that is, it begins with a capital letter and ends with a terminal punctuation mark—but does not meet the criteria of "grammatically complete" as defined above. A dependent clause or a phrase, standing alone, constitutes a sentence fragment.

Just because a fragment isn't grammatically complete does not mean it can never stand alone. Some fragments can stand independently because they don't need anything added to add meaning.

Big deal.
No way.
Fat chance.
Over and out.
Pity.
If you insist.
To be sure.

More complex sentence fragments may be used intentionally for effect. A fragment stands out more emphatically on its own than if it were merged into a larger sentence.

It was hopeless to try to convince her to lend him the car that night. *Or any night, for that matter.*
We ended up doing the job ourselves. *Which, all things considered, turned out for the best.*
He dumped the contents of the purse onto the table. *A cheap comb, some crumpled tissues, a tattered address book, a few coins.*
I said I would be here on time. *And here I am!*

You should employ this type of construction cautiously, but do use it if it is the best way of capturing the nuance you want.

Comma (,)

The comma is by far the most-used punctuation mark, typically out-numbering all the others put together. Its basic role is to function as an interrupter, separating a sentence into distinct units.

Most of the comma's numerous functions fall into the following categories:

- Separating the main elements of a sentence from each other
- Setting off a parenthetical element from the rest of the sentence
- Separating elements in a series
- Setting off dialogue or quotations
- Indicating omitted words

Note: Before beginning, be sure that you have reviewed "Basic Sentence Structure" on page 55.

AVOIDING COMMAS WITHIN CLAUSES

Using the comma properly means knowing both where to put it—and where not to. Breaking up a string of words that ought to be treated as an indivisible unit will send just as confusing a signal to the reader as letting discrete units run into each other. This section reviews the main scenario of an "indivisible unit"; other scenarios where commas are not appropriate are described farther on.

DON'T SEPARATE ANY OF THE MAIN PARTS OF A CLAUSE

A clause focuses on a single idea or on closely related ideas, and therefore should not be broken up. In general, you should not put commas between the subject and the predicate, between the parts of a compound subject or between the parts of a compound predicate.

The commas in the following examples are *incorrect,* and should be removed.

DON'T SPLIT THE SUBJECT AND PREDICATE

Rodney and his brother, were the worst female impersonators we'd ever seen.

DON'T SPLIT THE SUBJECT AND PREDICATE,
EVEN IF THE PREDICATE COMES FIRST

Discreetly nestled in the tissue paper, was a small plaster bust of Elvis.

DON'T SPLIT THE VERB PART OF THE PREDICATE
FROM THE REST

What he likes best about the condominium is, its no-frogs policy.

DON'T SPLIT A COMPOUND SUBJECT

The desire to succeed, and the ability to do so are not the same thing.

DON'T SPLIT THE TWO ACTIONS IN THE PREDICATE

Lily stomped down to her dungeon, and slammed the door.

DON'T SPLIT THE TWO DESCRIPTIONS IN THE PREDICATE

The meeting was brief, and to the point.

DON'T SPLIT THE TWO ENTITIES AFFECTED BY THE ACTION

Dudley planned to study astrophysics, and numerology.

DON'T SPLIT THE TWO RECIPIENTS OF THE ACTION

She lent her sister, and brother-in-law two thousand dollars.

Exceptions

Do put a comma within a clause if ambiguity would result without it. Consider the following sentences:

The instructor gave out a sheet that described his course and explained how the grading would be done.
She complained that he'd made a mess and stormed out in a snit.

61

It was a shock to everyone when the consultant was arrested and the
whole venture fell apart.
In Part II of the exam, answer questions A and B or C.

In the first example, did the instructor give out a sheet and explain
the grading—or did he give out a sheet that contained a description
of the course and an explanation of the grading? It isn't clear whether
the action of explaining gets attributed to the instructor or to the
sheet. This sentence would be clarified by adding a comma either
between the two actions performed by the instructor or between the
action of the instructor and the details of what the sheet contained.

The instructor gave out a sheet that described his course, and explained
how the grading would be done.
The instructor gave out a sheet, which described his course and explained
how the grading would be done.

In the second example, does the final action connect with *she* or
with *complained that he'd*? If the first scenario is intended *(she
stormed out in a snit)*, a comma should be added, even though it
would break up two actions performed by the subject. If the second
scenario is intended *(she complained that he'd stormed out in a
snit)*, this would be clarified by adding *had* to the last verb.

She complained that he'd made a mess, and stormed out in a snit.
She complained that he'd made a mess and had stormed out in a snit.

In the third example, were people shocked by the arrest, and the
venture subsequently fell apart—or were they shocked by both the
arrest and the loss of the venture? A comma would clarify the first
scenario; changing the form of the verbs would clarify the second.

It was a shock to everyone when the consultant was arrested, and the
whole venture fell apart.
It was a shock to everyone to learn that the consultant had been arrested
and that the whole venture had fallen apart.

In the fourth example, is everyone expected to answer question
A, and then choose between B and C? Or is the choice between
answering *both* A and B, or C alone?

In Part II of the exam, answer questions A, and B or C.

In Part II of the exam, answer questions A and B, or C.

It may also sometimes be beneficial to break up a clause that is long or complex, even if not ambiguous. Skilled writers have a feel for when a comma would be a good idea, even when it isn't required according to the strict rules. Basically, you should consider putting a comma within a clause any time you sense that doing so would make the sentence easier for readers to follow.

Exceptions aside, if commas aren't normally used within clauses, where do they go?

First, the no-comma rule applies only when there are no more than two parts to a compound subject or two subunits of any part of the predicate. Commas *are* needed within a clause whenever there are three or more such parts, or two or more adjectives in front of a noun. This is described in "Separating Elements in a Series" on page 79. Second, commas are needed within a clause if it contains any embedded parenthetical text. This is described in "Setting Off Parenthetical Elements" on page 71. Third, commas are used to separate clauses from each other and to separate clauses from other elements in the sentence. These scenarios are described in the next section.

SEPARATING THE MAIN ELEMENTS OF A SENTENCE

What's the difference between the following two sentences?

They settled only the budget issues, and work schedules and technical matters had to be tabled until the next meeting.

They settled only the budget issues and work schedules, and technical matters had to be tabled until the next meeting.

In case A, only the budget was settled; work schedules and technical matters had to be tabled. In case B, the budget and work schedules were settled, and technical matters had to be tabled.

When sentences contain multiple chunks of information, the boundaries between these chunks must be clear. Commas clarify precisely where one unit ends and the next begins. The syntax—the order in which the words appear—is not always a sufficient cue, because the same words that link elements together may also serve to link subunits within a single element.

WHEN TWO INDEPENDENT CLAUSES ARE JOINED BY A CONJUNCTION, PUT A COMMA BETWEEN THEM

Consider the following sentences:

> Dustcovers had been placed on the tables and the chairs, and all the smaller items had been packed away.
>
> They left early, for the concert was horrific.
>
> They left early for the concert, and arrived there in good time.
>
> Her apartment was tiny but pleasant, and she had decorated it tastefully with old auto parts.
>
> Her apartment was tiny, but the rent was astronomical.
>
> The director reviewed the proposal, and her assistant passed it on to the producer.
>
> The director reviewed the proposal and the financial figures, and her assistant wrote up the report.
>
> He missed her so, and wrote every day.
>
> He missed her, so he went on his own.

In the first example, look at what would happen if no comma preceded the conjunction linking the clauses:

> Dustcovers had been placed on the tables and the chairs and all the smaller items had been packed away.

Without a comma, it isn't clear at what point the sentence shifts direction. Were dustcovers placed on just the tables, and the chairs had been packed away along with the smaller items—or were both tables and chairs covered?

Even in sentences with no ambiguity, the absence of a comma might cause a fleeting confusion or hesitation on the part of the reader *(Are we still on the same topic here, or on a new one? Oh, I see . . .)*. For instance, in the second example, if no comma preceded the conjunction *for,* the reader might momentarily see it as a preposition, as it is in the third example. A comma sends a clear signal that whatever follows it will involve a shift of direction. In sum, without commas, a sentence may become clear only once it is read through; with them, the reader is on top of things all along.

Exception

If both the independent clauses in a sentence are brief and simple, and there is no risk of ambiguity if a comma is not included, it can be acceptable to omit it. It's never wrong to include it, but sometimes you may think it overly formal or cluttering. Let the tone and context of your writing guide your judgment as to whether a comma is really needed.

> This decision is final and there will be no discussion.
> The food was okay but the music was lousy.
> She begged him to stay so he did.

DON'T USE A COMMA TO SEPARATE INDEPENDENT CLAUSES THAT ARE *NOT* LINKED BY A CONJUNCTION
The punctuation in the following sentences is *incorrect:*

> The chairs and coffee tables were worth restoring, the rest was rubbish.
> He stealthily parted the curtains, he looked inside.
> I think we'll be able to work together, you'd better start being more punctual though.
> You can bake them or fry them or steam them, there are various options.
> She could have taken on the task, nonetheless she decided not to.

This type of construction is called a **comma splice** (*splicing* means to unite two things by fastening their ends together), and is an error because it sends a confusing signal. A comma is intended only for "light" separations, and sets up an expectation in the reader that whatever follows it will be closely related to what came before. Accordingly, the reader isn't anticipating the greater shift in direction that occurs, and may have to backtrack to make sense of the sentence. There are three remedies for comma splices: Add a conjunction, break the clauses into two sentences or use a semicolon instead of a comma. For a discussion of the last option, turn to page 93.

Exception

If a sentence is short and the style is casual, you can sometimes get away with a comma splice. It's never technically correct, but you may sometimes decide that a comma "feels" better than the more formal semicolon. It's a matter of context.

The critics hated it, the public loved it.

I doubted she would show up, she was so unreliable.

WHEN AN INDEPENDENT CLAUSE IS PRECEDED BY ANOTHER ELEMENT, PUT A COMMA AFTER THE INTRODUCTORY ELEMENT

An independent clause may be preceded by a dependent clause, a phrase or a single word.

DEPENDENT CLAUSES

In the following examples, the dependent clause appears in italic type.

Whenever you're ready to eat, the dining table will be cleared.

Whenever you're ready to eat the pie, I'll take it out of the freezer.

If you have finished, your wine waiter will be happy to make a suggestion for a digestive.

If you have finished your wine, may I pour you some tea?

Although I'd love to stay to help clean up, I just remembered nine urgent appointments.

After the ceremony was over, the guests all leaped into the hot tub.

Because the weather was so bad, the Polar Bear Club held a special mandatory swim.

Since you insist, I'll let my eyebrows grow back in.

When the phone finally rang, she hurled it out the window in a fit of pique.

Why the need for a comma? Just as with two independent clauses, it may not always be immediately obvious from the syntax (word order) alone when the first clause has ended and the next has begun. For example, compare the first two examples above. In both cases, the comma signals when the end of the dependent clause has been reached—but this happens in different places. In the first case, the action of eating is unconnected to any object; here, the first clause is complete right after the verb *eat*. In the second case, the action of eating applies to an object (pie), and here the first clause is not complete until the recipient of the verb is identified. Suppose you omitted the comma in the first sentence:

Whenever you're ready to eat the dining table will be cleared.

If no comma appeared after *eat*, the reader might momentarily expect that the sentence will go on to identify what was eaten. This expectation, however, will cause the sentence to fall apart, turning its first part into *Whenever you're ready to eat the dining table* (!), and the remainder into a meaningless string. Faced with this non-sense syntax, the reader must go back and reassess the sentence to make sense of it. The comma eliminates any possibility of confusion.

PHRASES

Just as with dependent clauses, when a phrase comes first in a sentence, readers need to be shown precisely where it ends and the main clause begins.

In the following examples, the phrases are shown in italics.

According to his study, people want more say in how the weather is forecast.

To see the fall colors at their best, try taking your Blues Brothers shades off.

Leaning over the balustrade, we could just see the runaway merry-go-round horse plow into a huge display of Kewpie dolls.

At the age of eighty-three, Irma took up snowboarding.

Beginning at dusk, the frog sent out a call of apparently unrequited passion all through the night.

Reading being her obsession, Katie's first act upon starting her sentence was to find the prison library.

Struck by a sudden idea, he feverishly began to learn Ancient Greek.

Next to synchronized swimming, mud wrestling was her favorite sport.

Note that a phrase itself is not subdivided by commas, because, like a clause, it may be considered a unit.

INTRODUCTORY WORDS

A single word can also serve to introduce an independent clause.

Therefore, it just won't be possible to finish building the opera house in time for the first act.

Understandably, she's reluctant to take on the responsibility of escorting a dozen fourteen-year-olds to Las Vegas.

Piqued, he went back to polishing the bedsprings.

Snarling, she ripped up the crossword puzzle.

Sadly, his dog didn't live to see him develop the anti-postman device.

Exception

If an introductory element is short and the sentence would be quite clear without any breaks, you may sometimes make a decision to leave the comma out.

Finally he got up to leave.

At one o'clock the skies opened.

Naturally I tried to avoid the issue.

When an independent clause is *followed* by another element, rather than preceded by it, the punctuation rules are a bit more complex. Here, whether or not you separate the elements with a comma depends on the relationship between them, as described below.

WHEN AN INDEPENDENT CLAUSE IS FOLLOWED BY AN ELEMENT THAT IS ESSENTIAL TO ITS MEANING, DO NOT PUT A COMMA BETWEEN THEM

"Essential to its meaning" means that if the concluding element were removed, the independent clause would no longer be saying the same thing. It would still be grammatically intact (by definition, an independent clause can always stand alone), but the overall message of the sentence would have changed.

The majority of constructions that involve a dependent clause following an independent one fall into this category. Putting a comma between the clauses would be both inappropriate, because you don't want to break the connection between them, and unnecessary, because the opening word of a dependent clause sends an unambiguous signal that a new element has begun. That is, unlike the conjunctions *and* and *or*, which could be joining subunits within a clause, subordinating conjunctions appear only at the beginning of a clause.

The Rutabaga Festival will be held on Saturday *unless it rains.*

She had little income *until the sales of her herring-flavored ice cream took off.*

We won't finish on time *if you persist in sneezing.*

She waited impatiently *while he finished dancing the schottische.*

The presentation went smoothly *because the hecklers were all lulled to sleep by the overheads.*

We went straight to the "Avoiding Stress in the Workplace" seminar *after the power breakfast.*

Sheldon looked at his macaw *as if he suspected it of laughing at him.*

Similarly, when the concluding element is a phrase, do not separate it from the independent clause if the information in the phrase completes the meaning of the clause. In the following examples, if the italicized words were removed, the remainder would still be grammatically intact but something would be lost.

He went to market *to buy a fat pig.*

A new bylaw was passed *to ensure that no boiled cabbage would be served within city limits.*

She did well in the calculus course *by promising to give the instructor her secret recipe for pirogies.*

They were praised *for their efforts in setting up the downtown bungee-jumping site.*

We spotted the intruder *lurking inside the grand piano.*

Meet us at the tractor-pull *at twelve o'clock.*

He ended up in bed *with a bad case of angst.*

WHEN AN INDEPENDENT CLAUSE IS FOLLOWED BY AN ELEMENT THAT IS *NOT* ESSENTIAL TO ITS MEANING, DO PUT A COMMA BETWEEN THEM

A phrase or dependent clause may simply be acting to provide additional information, rather than modifying what's happening in the rest of the sentence. A comma serves as a signal that the sentence is shifting direction.

Compare the following two sentences:

Lynn was all ready to leave when Jeremy showed up.

Lynn was all ready to leave, when Jeremy showed up.

In case A, Lynn is awaiting Jeremy and will take off with him as soon as he appears; that is, her departure is dependent on Jeremy's arrival. In case B, there are two separate items of information: Lynn is about to leave (whether on her own or with someone else), and just then Jeremy happens to show up.

Similarly,

> He didn't like her because she was successful and talented.
> [He liked her for other reasons].
>
> He didn't like her, because she was successful and talented.
> [And presumably he wasn't].

In each of the following sentences, there is a distinct shift in direction between the independent and the dependent clauses: that is, one piece of information is followed by another, rather than the meaning of the first clause being dependent on the second. Therefore, they are separated by a comma.

> He threatened to fire me, *as if I cared.*
> She ran for miles, *until her legs gave out.*
> He's never had a job in his life, *unless you count that two-week stint as a taster at the chocolate factory.*
> She had to hurry to get the house spotless, *since the cleaning lady was expected that morning.*

The rule is the same for phrases: Put a comma before a concluding phrase if the information in it does not directly affect the meaning of what comes before. In the following examples, each phrase does not do more than add additional information or commentary to the clause that precedes it.

> She got up to leave, *having satisfactorily reduced him to a quivering jelly.*
> He leaped up from the exercise machine, *promptly throwing his back out.*
> We found her in the washroom, *angrily scrubbing the ketchup off her tiara.*
> They stood by the window, *oblivious to the meteor shower raining past it.*
> He pole-vaulted off the stage and over the fence, *leaving his fans howling in frustration.*

The issue of how to deal with phrases and dependent clauses that lie *within* independent clauses, rather than before or after them, is addressed next.

SETTING OFF PARENTHETICAL ELEMENTS

What's the difference between the following two sentences?

> Jack thought Melvin should have his head examined.
> Jack, thought Melvin, should have his head examined.

In case A, someone named Jack is thinking about someone named Melvin; in case B, Melvin is thinking about Jack.

What would happen: if we removed the words *thought Melvin*? We would be left with:

> Jack should have his head examined.

In case A, the sentence is completely changed by the removal of these words: It is no longer referring to the right head. Case B, in contrast, may have *lost* something—the fact that Jack's head-examining need is merely a matter of someone's opinion—but at least it still refers to the same head. The words enclosed by commas in case B are an example of a parenthetical element—text that is not critical to the basic structure of the sentence. The defining characteristic of a parenthetical element is that if it were removed, the remainder of the sentence would still be grammatically and semantically intact. Some information would be lost or diminished, but the essential meaning would not be altered.

Parenthetical text may be set off from the rest of the sentence by three types of punctuation marks: parentheses, dashes or commas. Parentheses (discussed on page 144) are best used when the element is a decided digression and its removal would have little or no effect on meaning: that is, they de-emphasize. Dashes (discussed on page 154) serve to draw particular attention to the element, making it stand out; that is, they emphasize. Commas should be used when the element is an integral part of the sentence but does not call for any special attention. Enclosed by commas, a parenthetical element just works its way quietly into the sentence, without fanfare.

The remainder of this section describes various types of sentence constructions involving parenthetical elements. It is important that you clearly distinguish these from nonparenthetical elements, so that you know both where commas *should* go and where they should *not* go.

USE COMMAS TO SET OFF WORDS OR EXPRESSIONS
THAT ARE "INTERRUPTERS"

A sentence may contain some words that interrupt its flow but don't interfere with its meaning.

Some may be asides; that is, text that is included simply for emphasis or effect, or as additional commentary.

> The meeting was, *to say the least,* a total fiasco.
>
> The committee is, *generally speaking,* reluctant to rock the boat.
>
> The rest, *as they say,* is history.
>
> The contract fell through, *by the way.*
>
> Ernie's first book of poetry wasn't a resounding success either, *remember.*
>
> *Needless to say,* my friend Cassandra's predictions always materialized.

Some may serve to tie in a point with a preceding sentence.

> Her resignation, *therefore,* is inevitable.
>
> *In fact,* the profits for the second quarter were up slightly.
>
> *However,* all was not lost.
>
> The more expensive printer, *on the other hand,* would cost less to maintain.

Some may contain information that is necessary to the overall point, but is parenthetical in the sense that you could take it out without changing the meaning of what is left.

> Her lecture on moose calls, *he was happy to report,* went very well.
>
> His story of being abducted by giant lizards, *when I stopped to think about it,* made little sense.
>
> The food she had just eaten as a mid-morning snack, *he pointed out,* had been intended to last the week.

In all the above cases, if the parenthetical element were removed, the sentence would be essentially unchanged: *The meeting was a total fiasco; Her resignation is inevitable; His story of being abducted by giant lizards made little sense.*

Caution: When parenthetical text comes in the middle of a clause, be sure not to neglect the closing comma. It is a common error to write sentences such as *The meeting was, to say the least a total fiasco* or *Her resignation, therefore is inevitable.*

Exception

If a parenthetical word or expression doesn't break the continuity of the sentence, it is sometimes acceptable to omit the commas altogether. If you are uncertain whether or not to include commas, say the sentence aloud, spontaneously, and decide if a pause sounds right.

> She did in fact pay the loan back.
> The course in my opinion is a joke.

IF A SUBJECT IS FOLLOWED BY A NONRESTRICTIVE DESCRIPTOR, USE COMMAS TO SET OFF THE DESCRIPTOR. IF IT IS FOLLOWED BY A RESTRICTIVE DESCRIPTOR, DO *NOT* USE COMMAS

When an element that either follows or lies within an independent clause provides some information about the subject of that clause, this information may be considered either restrictive or nonrestrictive. A **restrictive element** acts to identify precisely which subject, out of various possible ones, is being discussed. A **nonrestrictive element**, while it adds more information about the subject, does not serve to further identify it—in this case, the subject is already fully identified. (Some authorities call these relationships *defining* and *nondefining*, or *limiting* and *nonlimiting*. The meaning is the same.)

A nonrestrictive element is parenthetical in the sense that it is not critical to the meaning of the sentence; if it were removed, the meaning of what remained would still be intact. In contrast, if a restrictive element were removed, meaning would be lost.

Compare the following two sentences:

> By two in the morning, the only people still at Shirley's party were her oldest friend, Susan, and her neighbor George.
> By two in the morning, the only people still at Shirley's party were her friend Susan and her upstairs neighbor, George.

In case A, the name *Susan* is nonrestrictive, since by definition one can have no more than one *oldest* friend. The inclusion of *Susan* is adding more information about this friend—her name— but omitting it wouldn't introduce any ambiguity as to which friend is meant. In contrast, *George* serves to identify which neighbor was

73

there. Saying just *her neighbor* would not be enough, since Shirley can be expected to have more than one neighbor.

In case B, *Susan* loses the comma (unless Shirley has only one friend in the world), while *George* picks it up (unless there is more than one upstairs flat).

The first comma in both sentences is, of course, to separate the introductory phrase *By two in the morning* from the main clause.

Restrictive and nonrestrictive elements can be names, words, phrases or dependent clauses. In the examples below, restrictive descriptors are shown in bold type, and nonrestrictive ones in italics.

> Under cross-examination by the defense counsel **Allan Watt,** the constable acknowledged that he had failed to record the incident in his memo book.

There is more than one defense counsel, so the one being referred to must be identified by name. The constable seems to have been referred to already.

> Under cross-examination by the defense counsel, Allan Watt, *the constable,* acknowledged that he had failed to record the incident in his memo book.

There is only one defense counsel, so this person need not be named in order to be identified. The witness is identified by name, and the mention of his position is simply providing additional information about him.

> My boss, *Pat,* has invited the mystic **Madame Zizi** to speak at our budget-planning session.

Pat is nonrestrictive: Presumably the writer has only one boss. *Madame Zizi* is restrictive: The world contains many mystics.

> My colleague **Pat** has invited the city's best-known mystic, *Madame Zizi,* to speak at our budget-planning session.

Pat is restrictive: More than one colleague is assumed here. *Madame Zizi* is nonrestrictive: The mystic has been narrowed down to only one possible person.

> Zelda showed up at the party with her brother, *Mark,* and her husband, *Hal.*

Zelda apparently has only one brother, and his name happens to be Mark. She also, quite properly, has only one husband, and his name happens to be Hal.

> Zelda showed up at the party with her brother **Mark** and her husband **Hal**.

Zelda apparently has more than one brother and has brought the one named Mark to the party; on the husband front, she has some explaining to do.

> The next-door neighbors, *a pair of curmudgeonly retirees,* would sit on their porch and hurl insults at passing squirrels.
>
> The next caller, *a doctor,* defended the policy.
>
> The old rocking chair, *the one that had sat unused in the basement for years,* fetched eight hundred dollars.
>
> Teachers **using the controversial book** were strong defenders of its usefulness.
>
> Mimi, *the neighbor two doors down,* was organizing a street sale.
>
> Mr. Douglas **the storekeeper** warned Mr. Douglas **the street vendor** to stay off his turf.
>
> The house **with the rock garden** is up for sale.
>
> The downtown core, *once considered doomed,* is making a comeback.
>
> Art **once viewed as valueless** is now commanding high prices.

Clauses too can act as restrictive or nonrestrictive descriptors, as described next.

IF A DEPENDENT CLAUSE IS NONRESTRICTIVE, MARK IT OFF WITH COMMAS. IF IT IS RESTRICTIVE, DO *NOT* USE COMMAS

As described in "Basic Sentence Structure" on page 55, in one type of dependent clause, the subordinating word is a pronoun. This type of dependent clause can function as a restrictive or nonrestrictive descriptor, the same way that a word or a phrase can.

To illustrate: Suppose we have a passage of text that describes two men approaching, one of them dawdling behind the other. The reader is then told:

> The man *who had lingered behind* suddenly quickened his pace.

Saying just *The man suddenly quickened his pace* wouldn't be sufficiently informative: The setting contains two men, so it wouldn't be clear which one is meant. Thus, the clause *who had lingered behind* acts to identify which of the two possible individuals is meant: that is, it is restrictive.

In contrast, say the text describes a woman and a man approaching, and mentions that the woman advances but doesn't say yet what the man does. The reader is then told:

The man, *who had lingered behind,* suddenly quickened his pace.

This otherwise identical clause is now nonrestrictive. It is adding more information about the man—that he had lingered—but it is not serving to further *identify* him: He is already fully identified, since in this case he is the only man. Here, the subject *would* be as fully identified if the sentence read simply *The man suddenly quickened his pace.*

In the following examples, restrictive clauses are shown in bold type, and nonrestrictive ones in italics.

Those prisoners **who had not participated in the riot** had full privileges restored.

The barber, *who had not missed a day of work in fifteen years,* was in his shop as usual.

The boutique **where I bought my wedding dress** went out of business last month.

The boardwalk, *where the wind was strongest,* was no place to be walking that afternoon.

They left the beach **when the shark arrived**.

By next week, *when the test results are in,* I'll be able to give you a better answer.

Customers **whose numbers haven't been called yet** are asked to please wait outside.

The first person to speak up was Mr. Holland, *whose weakness for lost causes was legendary*.

Usually, text will contain enough context so that the intended meaning will come through unambiguously even if commas are not used correctly. It is possible, however, for the comma to be the sole source of information as to whether a clause is restrictive or not.

For example, compare the following two sentences:

Boris pulled into the lot and handed his keys to the attendant, who was standing next to the booth.

Boris pulled into the lot and handed his keys to the attendant who was standing next to the booth.

What differing information do these two sentences give us? Answer: Whether one or more parking attendants were present. If there is no prior mention of any attendants, nor any inherent reason why there should be either one or more than one, the only source of this information is the presence or absence of the comma. In case A, the comma that precedes the clause *who was standing next to the booth* tells us that this information is nonrestrictive; that is, there was only one attendant, and incidentally he or she happened to be standing by the booth. Phrasing this sentence as *Boris pulled into the lot and handed his keys to the attendant* would serve to identify the recipient of the keys just as well. In case B, the absence of a comma tells us that this same clause is serving to identify which of two or more possible attendants is meant. That is, the one by the booth took the keys; perhaps another was at the far end of the lot and a third was busy with another driver.

IN A DEPENDENT CLAUSE, USE *WHICH* IF THE CLAUSE
IS NONRESTRICTIVE, AND *THAT* IF IT IS RESTRICTIVE
In the previous examples of restrictive and nonrestrictive clauses, the only factor that changes is the presence or absence of a comma. The words functioning as the subject—who, whose, where, etc.— are the same for both types of clause. In one case, though, the subject changes as well. Specifically, you use the pronoun *which* for a nonrestrictive clause, and the pronoun *that* for a restrictive one.

Compare the following two sentences:

The newspapers, which are on the coffee table, should be saved.
The newspapers that are on the coffee table should be saved.

These sentences differ in two ways: One has commas and uses *which*; the other has no commas and uses *that.* How does this affect the meaning? In case A, which is nonrestrictive, the implication is that the newspapers—all the newspapers—should be saved, and incidentally, they happen to be on the coffee table. If this sentence read simply as *The newspapers should be saved*, it would be missing some information (the location of the papers), but would still fully identify what needed to be saved. In case B, which is restrictive, the implication is that only certain papers are to be saved. That is, it's okay to get rid of the ones on the floor, the kitchen table, the magazine rack, etc.—but be sure to save those on the coffee table. Here, saying just *The newspapers should be saved* would *not* convey the full information necessary to identify the subject.

Other examples are presented below.

She cut him a slice of cake, which he promptly devoured.
He chose the slice of cake that was the bigger of the two.

They got as far as Fort Simpson, which is west of Yellowknife.
The town that they settled in is Fort Simpson.

I decided to buy the brand that cost less.
I decided to buy the no-name brand, which cost less.

Let's start off by discussing the issues that seem to be the most urgent.
Let's start off by discussing item two, which seems to be the most urgent.

How critical is it to use *which* and *that* correctly? In most cases, an error will probably not confuse your reader.

Keep your writing style simple, and avoid words which are obscure or pretentious.
They went to watch the Stanley Cup parade, that was wending its way downtown.

Although the above sentences are incorrect, it would take a very literal-minded reader to interpret the first to mean that one should eschew all words when writing, and the second to mean that the town was filled with various Stanley Cup parades of which one happened to be heading downtown. In both these cases, the context is sufficiently clear to make the error forgivable. However, consider the next examples:

After assessing the inventory, they decided that the prints which were heavily water-damaged were probably not worth restoring.

> Ensure that the power switch which is on the left side of the panel is
> turned on.

These sentences present a conflict. In the first, the word *which* implies that the clause *which were heavily water-damaged* is nonrestrictive, meaning that all the prints were damaged—but the absence of commas implies that it is restrictive, and that only certain prints were damaged. In the second, the use of *which* implies that there is only one switch and it happens to be on the left side—but the absence of commas implies that of the various switches, the one on the left is the one that should be turned on. The result in both cases is ambiguity, which can be resolved only if the text contains prior information that clarifies which possibility is intended. In the absence of such information, it is not clear if the writer erred in using *which* for *that*, or in omitting the commas. Remember the general rule: *Which* takes a comma, *that* does not.

A final comment on the *which/that* rule: It is a North American convention, not a universal one. British writers will happily use *which* for restrictive clauses, and indeed in most cases the meaning is clear. Disregarding the distinction is not a problem as long as you know to avoid constructions that may be misconstrued.

SEPARATING ELEMENTS IN A SERIES

What's the difference between the following two sentences?

> The only ones to show up were Monica and Bram, Sally, Bruce and
> Penelope, Arthur and Ethel, and Humphrey.
> The only ones to show up were Monica and Bram, Sally, Bruce and
> Penelope, Arthur, and Ethel and Humphrey.

In case A, Arthur and Ethel came as a couple; Humphrey is odd man out. In case B, the couple are Ethel and Humphrey, with Arthur on his own. If there were no commas to show where the breaks between elements occur, the sentence could be interpreted either way.

Whenever you construct a sentence that contains a list of elements of equal grammatical weight, you must use commas to separate them. The elements can range from single words to phrases and clauses.

IN A LIST OF THREE OR MORE ELEMENTS, SEPARATE THE ELEMENTS WITH COMMAS

Each element up to the second-to-last one *must* be followed by a comma, and the second-to-last one *may* be: that is, it's a style decision. A comma in this position is called a **serial** or **series comma**, and some writers put it in and some don't.

In the following examples, no serial comma is used:

Edna's lifelong dream was to open a restaurant specializing in Thai, Ethiopian, Polish and Mediterranean cuisine.

She thought the green, pink, cream and lilac of the curtains went perfectly with the navy, maroon and burnt-orange of the carpet.

Arnold crafted his reply slowly, thoughtfully and meticulously.

Thelma's educated, conservative middle-class parents found it hard to accept her career choice, her lifestyle or her values.

His documentary employs home movies, photographs, archival footage and interviews to paint the portrait of its subject.

If elements are particularly long or complex, you sometimes might want to separate them with semicolons instead. For a discussion of this role of the semicolon, see page 91.

USE A SERIAL COMMA IF IT MAKES TEXT CLEARER OR MORE READABLE

As stated above, use of the serial comma is a style decision, and its omission does no harm in sentences where the elements are short and their relationships are obvious. In some cases, however, its absence could result in awkwardness or ambiguity. Thus, even if you are not using it as a rule, you should make an exception any time it seems necessary. For example:

Breakfast consisted of orange juice, toast and marmalade and coffee.

Here, *toast and marmalade* is a unit that constitutes the second-to-last element in the series. The absence of a comma, while technically acceptable, makes for a clumsy cadence: orange juice—toast—and marmalade—and coffee. This part of the sentence would read better as *orange juice, toast and marmalade, and coffee.*

The next example presents a more serious problem:

The panel consisted of three professors, two historians and an economist.

How many people were on the panel: three or six? Being a professor is not mutually exclusive with being a historian or an economist. If the intention is to describe six distinct individuals, a serial comma would clarify this: *three professors, two historians, and an economist.* If the latter two occupations are the professors' specialties, this part of the sentence should appear as *three professors: two historians and an economist.* (For a discussion of this role of the colon, turn to page 97.)

Similarly,

> Before beginning assembly, ensure that you have all the following parts and that you have paired those that go together: C-460, M-100 and R-560, G-100, R-100 and T-340 and T-640.

Which is the pair here: R-100 and T-340, or T-340 and T-640? The absence of a serial comma makes it unclear which parts constitute a unit. Inclusion of the comma would clarify whether the writer means *R-100 and T-340, and T-640* or *R-100, and T-340 and T-640.*

Finally, sometimes the length or complexity of the elements in a series calls for the use of the serial comma. For example:

> Teachers need hours outside of class time to plan new curricula, grade tests and papers, meet with parents, consult with specialists about students with academic or behavioral problems, and work one-on-one with children who have special needs.

> The consultants independently ranked each survey item on its relevancy and clarity using a 10-point scale, completed open-ended questions pertaining to the appropriateness of the items, and offered suggestions for the elimination or addition of items.

If the serial comma were omitted in these sentences, readers might have to strain to see where one element ends and the next begins.

In summary: If it is your choice not to use the serial comma, that's fine, but let clarity override consistency if an exception seems necessary.

PUT A COMMA BETWEEN TWO ADJECTIVES THAT PRECEDE A NOUN, PROVIDED THOSE ADJECTIVES ARE OF EQUAL WEIGHT

In most cases, commas are needed only when you have at least three items in a series: You wouldn't use them for just two. For example, you wouldn't put a comma in *Arnold crafted his reply slowly and meticulously* or *Teachers need hours outside of class time to plan new curricula and meet with parents*. You do, however, need to separate two items when those items are adjectives modifying a noun.

Her bold, innovative rhythms had the audience swaying to the beat.

The relaxed, laid-back atmosphere was a pleasant change.

The door opened with a grating, creaking sound.

A grumpy, tired-looking waiter took our order.

This rule holds only if the adjectives are of equal weight, meaning that they both modify the noun equally. To determine whether they do, use this test: Would the sentence still "sound right" if you reversed the adjectives, or if you put the word *and* between them? For example, you could say *innovative, bold rhythms* or *bold and innovative rhythms*; *a tired-looking, grumpy waiter* or *a grumpy and tired-looking waiter*.

In contrast, consider the adjectives in the following sentences:

He went in for a routine physical checkup.

A purple-clad French skater was next on the ice.

In my opinion, he's a long-winded, pretentious, pompous old bore.

You wouldn't say *a physical routine checkup* or *a routine and physical checkup*; *a French purple-clad skater* or *a purple-clad and French skater*; *an old pompous bore* or *a pompous and old bore*. In all these cases, the second adjective effectively forms a unit with the noun: *a physical checkup, a French skater, an old bore*. Accordingly, the adjective that precedes this unit is treated as if it were the only one: that is, no comma. (In the last example, the first two adjectives, of course, take commas because of the three-or-more rule.)

Also, do not include a comma between two adjectives if the first adjective is modifying not the noun but the other adjective. For example:

She wore a pale green dress.
[*pale* modifies *green*, not *dress*]

Early spring days are often very cool.
[*early* modifies *spring*, not *days*]

In some cases, such adjectives should be linked by a hyphen. For a discussion of this role of the hyphen, turn to page 128.

SETTING OFF DIALOGUE AND QUOTATIONS

When a sentence consists entirely of dialogue, you punctuate it exactly as you would any other (with the addition of quotation marks, of course). If it contains both dialogue and nondialogue components, you need to set off the dialogue with commas.

IF DIALOGUE IS PRECEDED BY ANY TEXT, PUT
A COMMA AFTER THE INTRODUCTORY TEXT

The nurse warned, "Patients are going to be hurt by these cutbacks."
She answered, "Don't be ridiculous."
He exclaimed, "Of course I didn't!"

It is also acceptable, though less common, to use a colon instead of a comma. See "Other Uses of the Colon" on page 103.

IF DIALOGUE IS FOLLOWED BY ANY TEXT, PUT A COMMA
BEFORE THE CLOSING QUOTATION MARKS
This applies whether the concluding text comes at the end of the dialogue, breaks it in the middle or surrounds it.

"The policy is discriminating and elitist," wrote one of the irate parents.
[on its own, dialogue would end in a period]

"In the three years I've lived here, I've never had any trouble," she
assured him.
[on its own, dialogue would end in a period]

He shrugged and said, "Please yourself," and walked away.
[on its own, dialogue would end in a period]

"I wouldn't try it," he cautioned, "unless you're quite certain you know
   what you're doing."
[on its own, dialogue would not contain any internal punctuation]

"If you finish early," she suggested, "how about if we go out for coffee."
[on its own, dialogue would contain a comma in the same place]

"But I never . . .," he faltered.
[dialogue ends in an ellipsis]

Exceptions

If the dialogue ends in a question mark or exclamation point, or is
broken off by a dash, do *not* add a comma.

"Bah!" he said.
"Are you sure?" she asked.
"The only thing is—" he began.

For a discussion on the distinction between ellipses and dashes,
turn to page 186.

SET OFF NONDIALOGUE QUOTATIONS WITH COMMAS
ONLY IF OTHER RULES CALL FOR IT

Other than direct speech, words may be enclosed by quotation
marks because they are a quote from some other source or a title,
or are intended to be brought to the reader's attention in a particular
way. In these cases, set the quoted element off with commas only if
you would do so if these same words were *not* within quotes.

For example, use commas if the quoted text is preceded by an
introductory element, if it is parenthetical or if it is part of a series:

According to the mediator, "a breakthrough is expected tonight."
As Dickens said, "The law is a ass."
The scene reminded me of the line by Robert Frost, "The woods are
   lovely, dark and deep."
The afternoon seminar, "Planning for a Comfortable Retirement," was
   already sold out.
More and more workers these days are fearful of layoffs, "rightsizing" and
   pay cuts.

Do not set a quoted element off with commas if it would not take them otherwise.

> A lawyer representing the patients said that the agency "has increasing concerns for the quality of care in psychiatric institutions."
>
> Critics claimed that the program "would lead to even greater divisiveness."
>
> The "new, improved" stain remover proved to be not quite that.

For a discussion of the use of quotation marks, turn to page 172.

INDICATING OMITTED WORDS

An **elliptical construction** is a phrasing where one or more words have been deliberately dropped because they can be readily inferred.

Sometimes words can be dropped without any ado:

> We were sure that we would win.
> We were sure we would win.
>
> I looked distrustfully at him, and he looked distrustfully at me.
> I looked distrustfully at him, and he at me.
>
> She isn't quite as tall as I am.
> She isn't quite as tall as I.

In other cases, however, you need to indicate that something is missing. The way to do this is to put a comma in the place of the absent words.

USE A COMMA TO INDICATE OMITTED TEXT IF THE SENTENCE WOULD READ UNGRAMMATICALLY WITHOUT IT

> To err is human; to forgive, divine.
> In spring her garden was ablaze with daffodils; in summer, pansies; and in fall, asters.
> His first novel sold six copies and his second, six thousand (although admittedly all were bought by his mother).

Including the omitted words would be perfectly acceptable grammatically; stylistically, however, it may sound a bit ponderous. Saying the same thing in fewer words often makes writing appear less awkward and more polished.

OTHER USES OF THE COMMA

Aside from its main functions, the comma has a few minor mechanical applications.

SEPARATING NUMBERS
In dates, it is used to separate the day from the year:

> June 12, 1996
> January 1, 2000

In numbers greater than three digits, it is used as a thousands separator:

> $3,459
> 139,897
> 694,775,107,326,960

Note, though, that in some countries a space is used instead:

> 139 897

In text, it is used to separate two numbers that lie next to each other:

> In 1994, 3 candidates ran for the position of school trustee.
> Although the final tally was 983, 247 submissions had to be discarded.

SEPARATING REPEATED WORDS
> Whatever it is in here that smells, smells awful.
> She finally came in, in a huff.
> Whatever he does, he does well.

SEPARATING PLACE NAMES
> Miami, Florida
> Moose Jaw, Saskatchewan

Semicolon (;)

It was her prose that gained [Mrs Albert Forrester] that body of devoted admirers, fit though few, as with her rare gift of phrase she herself put it that proclaimed her the greatest master of the English language that this century has seen. She admitted herself that it was her style, sonorous yet racy, polished yet eloquent, that was her strong point; and it was only in her prose that she had occasion to exhibit the delicious, but restrained, humour that her readers found so irresistible. It was not a humour of ideas, nor even a humour of words; it was much more subtle than that, it was a humour of punctuation: in a flash of inspiration she had discovered the comic possibilities of the semi-colon, and of this she had made abundant and exquisite use. She was able to place it in such a way that if you were a person of culture with a keen sense of humour, you did not exactly laugh through a horse-collar, but you giggled delightedly, and the greater your culture the more delightedly you giggled. Her friends said that it made every other form of humour coarse and exaggerated. Several writers had tried to imitate her; but in vain: whatever else you might say about Mrs Albert Forrester you were bound to admit that she was able to get every ounce of humour out of the semi-colon and no one else could get within a mile of her.

—W. Somerset Maugham, *The Creative Impulse*

The functions of the semicolon fall into two main categories:

- Separating elements, when a comma would be insufficient or unclear

- Linking elements, as an alternative to joining them with a conjunction or breaking them into two sentences

In the first case, the semicolon is required for clarity. In the second case, it is chosen over other equally clear constructions in order to achieve a certain tone or emphasize a relationship.

SEPARATING ELEMENTS

The most straightforward role of the semicolon is to act as a substitute for the comma, to mark a pause or shift in direction in a sentence. While there is some room for judgment as to when to use it, this should *not* be taken to mean that it is merely a fancy-looking comma, interchangeable with the latter at your whim. For the most part, its role is subject to predictable and objective guidelines.

Note: Before beginning, be sure that you have reviewed "Basic Sentence Structure" on page 55.

USE SEMICOLONS TO SEPARATE ELEMENTS THAT ARE THEMSELVES SUBDIVIDED BY COMMAS

Normally, elements in a series are separated by commas (see page 79). If, however, the elements are divided into subelements, commas wouldn't clearly indicate where one group of subelements ends and the next begins, because they would be indistinguishable from the commas within the groups. In such a case, use semicolons instead. For example:

> The sources of information about each patient included reviews of videotapes, nursing notes and the researcher's log; inspection of registers, indices and medical records; and an interview with the doctor.

Here, the semicolons make it clearer where the items categorized under "reviews" and "inspection" each end.

Similarly,

> To assemble the structure, you will need a hammer and a drill; size A, B and D nails; quarter-inch, half-inch and three-eighths-inch drill bits; and a level.

Here, the semicolons serve to distinguish the various tools and supplies.

Put semicolons between all main elements in a series even if only one of them contains internal commas. That is, be consistent: Don't use a semicolon just in the one place where it seems to be needed, and commas elsewhere.

> The competition drew contestants from Georgia and Alabama in the south; New York, New Hampshire and Connecticut in the northeast; and Oregon in the northwest.

USE A SEMICOLON TO SEPARATE INDEPENDENT CLAUSES THAT ARE LINKED BY CONJUNCTION-LIKE WORDS

Certain words and phrases act like conjunctions in that they establish a relationship between clauses, but they are not conjunctions. (Actually, they are categorized as adverbs, because they modify the words they are associated with.) Their defining characteristic is that they indicate a particular relationship between the information they belong with and information elsewhere. A scan of the list below (which is by no means complete) should make this trait clear.

accordingly	for example	instead	otherwise
afterwards	furthermore	later	preferably
also	hence	likewise	rather
anyway	however	meantime	similarly
as a result	ideally	meanwhile	specifically
besides	in brief	moreover	still
certainly	in conclusion	namely	subsequently
consequently	in contrast	nevertheless	that is to say
conversely	in fact	next	then
currently	in short	nonetheless	therefore
earlier	in particular	notwithstanding	thus
eventually	indeed	on the other hand	to wit
finally	initially	ordinarily	understandably

Any of these words or phrases can act as an introductory element to a clause, and many of them can also appear either embedded in the middle as a parenthetical element or at the end as a concluding element. In all these positions, they usually would be set off by commas.

Subsequently, the negotiations broke down.

In short, the trip was a resounding success.

His feelings were hurt, understandably.

It was my best performance ever, in fact.

The presentation, however, was an embarrassing calamity.

The meeting, therefore, was canceled.

As introductory elements, these words can appear either at the beginning of a sentence, to link it with an earlier one, or at the beginning of a second clause, to link it with the first. In the latter case, separating the clauses with a comma would create the error known as a comma splice (see page 65), and the reader might have a fleeting uncertainty as to whether the conjunctive word is a concluding element to the first clause or the opener to the next. Accordingly, the stronger separation of the semicolon is needed.

I'd rather have the report by tomorrow; however, Monday will do.

He didn't think he'd have anything to contribute to the meeting; besides, he wasn't interested in the topic.

Max finally showed up two hours late; understandably, he met with a frosty reception.

She thought she was early; in fact, she was the last to arrive.

We waited and waited; eventually, we gave up.

No progress was evident; nevertheless, they persevered.

A final comment on the use of these conjunction-like words: Some are very similar to actual conjunctions. For example:

The argument was going nowhere, so we decided to drop it.

The argument was going nowhere; hence, we decided to drop it.

The apartment was small and dark, but the price was right.

The apartment was small and dark; however, the price was right.

These is essentially no difference in meaning between these pairs of sentences. The ones with commas tend to look a bit more casual; the ones with semicolons, a bit more formal. When either way would do, your choice should depend on the tone of your writing. No single style is the most appropriate for every situation.

USE SEMICOLONS IF COMMAS MIGHT CAUSE A SENTENCE
TO BE MISREAD OR OTHERWISE DIFFICULT TO FOLLOW

Even when elements are not subdivided, commas sometimes would not suffice to mark the divisions between them. For example, what if you came across a description like the following in some assembly instructions:

Part A attaches to B, C and D attach to E, and F attaches to G.

It would be very easy to mistake *B, C and D* for a series; that is, to start reading the sentence as *Part A attaches to B, C and D*. The rest of the sentence then falls apart: . . . *attach to E, and F attaches to G* (??). A second pass would probably set you straight, but no sentence should have to be read twice to be clear. Semicolons would prevent any confusion, ensuring that each clause is kept distinct from the others.

Part A attaches to B; C and D attach to E; and F attaches to G.

RECOMMENDATION: IF YOU FEEL A COMMA WOULD NOT
BE STRONG ENOUGH, USE A SEMICOLON INSTEAD
EVEN IF IT IS NOT TECHNICALLY REQUIRED

Normally, independent clauses linked by a conjunction are separated with a comma. However, if an independent clause contains any internal commas, you may sometimes choose to use a semicolon as the separator instead. As with a series that contains subelements, the purpose is to make it immediately clear to the reader where one main element ends and the next begins. For example:

It is often useful to discuss your research ideas with others before you begin to write, as the questions that arise from the discussion may help clarify things in your own mind. Your consultants may be experts in your field, or they may know nothing of its methods and assumptions; they may be familiar with your particular research project, or they may be completely unacquainted with it; and they may be seasoned investigators or just starting out their own careers.

Similarly, at times you may decide to use a semicolon simply because the elements in a series are long. Given that commas perform so many functions, it may not always be immediately apparent what purpose a given comma is serving—is it separating one main element from the next, separating subunits within a main element or separating grammatical units within an element, such as a clause from a concluding phrase? Divisions that are obvious when sentences are short may become fuzzy with longer constructions, and the reader may sometimes have to pause or backtrack to stay on top. Using the stronger separator of the semicolon makes the divisions stand out better. For example:

> Recruiting participants for the study included screening all subjects to ensure that they had no contraindicating medical conditions; distributing an information sheet describing the protocol to those subjects meeting our inclusion criteria; arranging for eligible subjects to participate in post-treatment discussion groups with the goal of providing feedback to the researchers; and designating a group leader to attend these sessions and coordinate the discussions.

All this sentence is ultimately doing is listing four activities, and if its elements were shorter, commas as separators would work just fine *(Recruiting participants included screening subjects, handing out information, setting up discussion groups, and designating a group leader)*. However, because there is so much going on, the divisions between elements are easier to see if semicolons are used instead. Just what constitutes "long" elements will be a matter of judgment; there isn't some magic number that decrees when semicolons become necessary. The only guideline that can be given is to use them if you have reason to think they would make a sentence easier to read.

Finally, even if adjoining elements do not contain any internal commas and are not that long, you may sometimes decide to separate them with semicolons if each one deals with a distinct subject, in order to make this distinctiveness stand out more clearly. (See page 55 for the grammatical definition of "subject.")

> Not so long ago, authors turned in manuscripts composed on typewriters, and their entire text would have to be rekeyed by a typesetter. These days, they usually provide the publisher with their work on a computer disk; any editorial changes are made directly on

> this disk; and the revised work is then printed out on a desktop laser printer to produce the final camera-ready copy.

> My criteria are that the building must be no higher than three stories; the main rooms must have lots of light; the parking and guest parking must be adequate; and the neighbors must not be nosy.

Apply this last use of the semicolon with discretion, however. Just as with long elements, it's a judgment call. Do *not* use semicolons in any situation where commas would be adequate.

LINKING ELEMENTS

The previous section looked at the uses of the semicolon in promoting clarity. In that role, it is simply put in places where commas would otherwise go, and no other change to the sentence is involved.

This section describes a different role of the semicolon: that of forming elegant alternatives to other sentence constructions. Knowledgeable application of this punctuation mark can serve to tighten up loose wordings, elucidate or emphasize subtle relationships and add polish to your writing style.

RECOMMENDATION: CONSIDER USING THE SEMICOLON
IN PLACE OF A CONJUNCTION
Consider the following sentences:

> His offer sounded too good to be true, so I didn't believe it.
> [two independent clauses linked by *so*]

> Doreen was starting to worry, for Leo was now two hours late.
> [two independent clauses linked by *for*]

> We didn't have the heart to continue, as it all seemed so futile.
> [independent clause followed by a dependent clause starting with *as*]

> Sol is the practical one in the family, whereas his brother is the dreamer.
> [independent clause followed by a dependent clause starting with
> *whereas*]

There is nothing wrong with any of these constructions, and they certainly contain no ambiguity. In each case, however, it would be possible to omit the conjunction, since it could easily be inferred. If this is done, the comma is no longer the right separator, since putting it between two independent clauses would create a comma splice. The semicolon is the proper mark instead. In this role, it acts as a sort of stand-in for the missing conjunction, sending a signal to readers that there is some implicit and self-evident relationship between the clauses it separates.

> His offer sounded too good to be true; I didn't believe it.
> Doreen was starting to worry; Leo was now two hours late.
> We didn't have the heart to continue; it all seemed so futile.
> Sol is the practical one in the family; his brother is the dreamer.

Aside from shaving off a word, an advantage to omitting conjunctions is that an over-exactitude in spelling everything out can render your style a bit ponderous. Writing often comes through as subtler, more sophisticated, if you leave a few blanks for your readers to fill in for themselves. (For other strategies, see the discussions of elliptical constructions on page 85 and the suspension hyphen on page 135.)

Of course, omitting conjunctions isn't appropriate in all cases. Sometimes a conjunction couldn't easily be inferred, and a sentence might look puzzling without it.

> She longed to stay till the end of the talk; she had to leave.

The connection between these clauses isn't immediately obvious, so the sentence comes through as mildly confusing. It may be a bit of a strain for a reader to deduce that the missing conjunction must be *yet* or *but*.

In other cases, different conjunctions might be possible, so omitting the intended one might cause a reader to put the wrong interpretation on the sentence.

> The task clearly would be difficult; I would have a day to do it.

Is the missing word here *and? but? since? so?* Is one day plenty of time or not enough time? In the absence of a conjunction, the intention of the second clause could be misconstrued. Other parts of the text might provide enough context to clarify the writer's intentions, but on its own this sentence is not communicating them.

RECOMMENDATION: CONSIDER USING THE SEMICOLON TO UNITE TWO SEPARATE SENTENCES

Two independent clauses that are closely related in meaning don't have to be either linked with a conjunction or separated by a semicolon: A third alternative is to have each stand alone as a separate sentence. Often this will be appropriate and effective. However, if the clauses are essentially two halves of a whole—that is, they are not merely on the same topic, but the second one completes the first—then separating them to this degree may obscure or downplay their relationship. If your goal is to help the reader pick up on their connection, you may better achieve this by running them together in one sentence, either by adding an appropriate conjunction or by using a semicolon. The semicolon may be the more appropriate choice in cases where the relationship can't be neatly captured in just one word, and where the reader should be able to infer it in any case.

In some cases, sentences can be run together with no change:

The early bird gets the worm. The early worm gets eaten.
The early bird gets the worm; the early worm gets eaten.

Only Cora showed up to help with the move. The others all found excuses to stay away.
Only Cora showed up to help with the move; the others all found excuses to stay away.

His old apartment had been dark, cramped and dirty. His new one was worse.
His old apartment had been dark, cramped and dirty; his new one was worse.

Aside from helping to elucidate relationships, combining sentences this way often makes writing smoother, turning a series of short, choppy sentences into text that flows.

A caution about using the semicolon as an alternative to conjunctions or periods: Don't overdo it. It's a strong punctuation mark, and sprinkling it too liberally throughout a document will cause it to lose its impact. Even if you can justify each individual use, having semicolons show up in sentence after sentence becomes tedious. Don't make the mistake of trying to make your content look more important by peppering it with fancy punctuation.

STYLE CONVENTIONS

- You may leave either one or two spaces after a semicolon. Just be consistent.
- When a semicolon follows quoted text, place it *after* the closing quotation mark. (See page 182.)
- When a semicolon immediately follows italicized text, italicize it as well.

Colon (:)

The colon acts as a signal of anticipation, drawing the reader's attention to what comes after it. (In the classic reference book *Modern English Usage*, the grammarian H.W. Fowler describes it as "delivering the goods that have been invoiced in the preceding words.") Like the semicolon, in some cases it is required, and in others it is used for effect. Its functions fall into the following main categories:

- Introducing the text that follows
- Strengthening connections or adding emphasis

Writers are often unsure about the distinction between this mark and the semicolon. A discussion of their differences and similarities is presented at the end of this section.

INTRODUCING WHAT FOLLOWS

Use a colon when the first part of a sentence is an introduction, a lead-in, or a buildup to what follows.

USE A COLON WHEN A SENTENCE
CONTAINS A "QUESTION/ANSWER"
A colon serves to cue readers that a sentence consists, in a sense, of a question and an answer. That is, it conveys the signal that the text preceding it has just raised an implicit question, to which the remainder of the sentence is about to provide a response.

> The situation was becoming desperate: Supplies were running low, and winter would soon be setting in.

Implied question: What was desperate about the situation? Answer: low supplies and imminent winter.

One aspect struck him as particularly odd: It was midafternoon on a clear, mild day, yet the streets were totally deserted.

Implied question: What was odd? Answer: unaccountably deserted streets.

There's an issue that we absolutely must address: Will our current level of funding be enough?

Implied question: What's this issue? Answer: whether funding is sufficient.

The text preceding a colon should be a complete independent clause. Do not put a colon after a sentence fragment—a phrase or a dependent clause—that would dangle awkwardly on its own. The colons in the following examples are *incorrect*, and should be removed:

In a word, the plan was: ridiculous.
When they looked at the design more closely: the flaws became evident.
From the top of the hill: the entire scene could be surveyed.

You can sometimes get away with putting a colon after a sentence fragment, provided it's one that wouldn't sound unreasonable standing on its own. (Experienced writers have a sense of when sentence fragments would be acceptable, and will occasionally use them for effect. See page 59.)

A word of caution: Testing has not yet been completed, so any results must be considered preliminary.

Implied question: What's there to be cautious about? Answer: preliminary results.

So far so good: As we had hoped, the results supported our hypothesis.

Implied question: What was good? Answer: affirming results.

The text following the colon does not have to be an independent clause.

Only one thing would satisfy her craving: a large chocolate mousse.

He guessed what would come next: a torrent of tears and recriminations.

USE A COLON TO INTRODUCE A LIST

This function is really just a subset of the one described above. The lead-in part of the sentence states the nature of the list, and the remainder provides the details.

Any scientific measure must meet two vital criteria: reliability and validity.

There are a number of core courses that every student must take: English, history, math and science.

Only two questions remain: How did he do it, and why?

These are the most urgent staples we're out of: milk, eggs, lettuce, oatmeal and catnip.

There must always be a colon when the lead-in part of the sentence contains the words *the following* or *as follows*.

The system is based upon the following principles: It should be acceptable to both patients and staff, it should be applicable to a wide range of diagnoses and it should possess a high degree of face validity.

The following tools are needed: a hammer, a Phillips screwdriver, a hacksaw and a wrench.

The compromise was as follows: We'd each attend one workshop, and then cover for the other person.

Put a colon after the lead-in sentence when the list items that follow are laid out vertically.

Every camper must bring the following items:
a knapsack
a flashlight
a sleeping bag
a canteen
a book of ghost stories

Again, do *not* use a colon to introduce a list if the lead-in text could not stand alone. The colons in the following examples are *incorrect* and should be removed:

99

> This program enables you to: move text around, change its appearance, add graphics and run a spell-check.
>
> She's particularly good at sports such as: tennis, squash and racquetball.
>
> The next section presents: an overview of our last study, a review of the background literature and a detailed rationale for our current work.

STRENGTHENING CONNECTIONS OR ADDING EMPHASIS

This section describes a subtler role of the colon: that of clarifying relationships or underlining a point.

RECOMMENDATION: USE A COLON
TO MAKE CONNECTIONS CLEARER

When one unit of information expands on or derives from another, you can make their relationship more obvious by linking them with a colon. The colon alerts the reader to the fact that whatever was just said has some special significance, so particular attention should be paid to what follows.

Compare the following two passages:

> Glancing at the calendar, Morton made a mental note to buy a card that afternoon. He had not forgotten Great-Aunt Alma's birthday in eight years. The one time he had, she had temporarily cut him out of her will.

> Glancing at the calendar, Morton made a mental note to buy a card that afternoon. He had not forgotten Great-Aunt Alma's birthday in eight years: The one time he had, she had temporarily cut him out of her will.

In version A, the reader has no way of anticipating that the information in the second sentence—Morton's keeping track of the birthday—has any particular significance. He's apparently a thoughtful guy who remembers old ladies' birthdays, that's all. But then the next sentence comes along and forces a reinterpretation of this impression. In version B, while the reader still won't know Morton's motive until the end, the colon makes it clear that there *is* a motive; that is, there's more to Morton's card-giving than just being a good nephew. Unlike version A, the reader will not have to stop and reconcile the last sentence with its predecessor: The relationship will have been anticipated.

Consider the next example:

> Profiles are text commands that contain commands. You can edit them, but always keep a backup. If you change them incorrectly, the behavior of the editor may be affected.

> Profiles are text commands that contain commands. You can edit them, but always keep a backup: If you change them incorrectly, the behavior of the editor may be affected.

In version A, the reader might see the three sentences as three independent items of information, and fail to pick up on the critical connection between the last two. In version B, the colon alerts the reader to the fact that there is a particular reason for keeping a backup copy, and that this reason is about to be explained.

Similarly,

> Voters approved the controversial amendment by an extremely narrow margin. The count was 18,278 in favor and 17,916 against.

> Voters approved the controversial amendment by an extremely narrow margin: 18,278 in favor and 17,916 against.

In version A, the reader must expend a bit of extra energy figuring out that the purpose of the figures given in the second sentence is to illustrate the narrowness of the margin. In version B, the structure makes this connection instantly obvious.

RECOMMENDATION: USE A COLON TO ADD EMPHASIS

Judicious use of the colon can serve to make a point more emphatic. If your intention is to draw a contrast between two elements, this contrast may come through more forcefully if the elements are in immediate juxtaposition, rather than being placed in different sentences or separated by intervening text.

Compare the two passages below:

> The next witness testified that she had been fired from her job as a line supervisor. Her offense was that she had tried to organize the factory's 200 workers, who earned an average of $90 a week.

> The next witness testified that she had been fired from her job as a line supervisor. Her offense: trying to organize the factory's 200 workers, who earned an average of $90 a week.

The text in both cases is basically the same, but the message is subtly different. A contrast exists between the reference to an "offense," which implies some inappropriate behavior, and the actual actions of the subject, which seem to be laudable. Assuming the writer is trying to portray the subject's actions in a sympathetic or supportive light, version B achieves this better. In version A, a reader who wasn't paying close attention might get the impression that the writer as well as the factory owners viewed these actions as a genuine offense. In version B, the colon heightens the contrast, thereby making it clear that the word *offense* is being used ironically.

Consider the two versions of the next example:

> Wife assault cannot be dismissed as merely a symptom of marital problems. It is a criminal activity that is a manifestation of the abuser's inability to deal with frustration and anger.

> Wife assault cannot be dismissed as merely a symptom of marital problems: It is a criminal activity that is a manifestation of the abuser's inability to deal with frustration and anger.

Here, version A has less impact than version B, since the contrast between the key words—the relatively benign "marital problems" versus "criminal activity"—is diminished by putting them in separate sentences.

If the goal is to run these two sentences together, would not a semicolon or a dash do as well? The answer is no, for somewhat subtle reasons. The first part of this sentence is acting as a "buildup" to the second, in that it tells the reader what wife assault is *not*. The colon then conveys the message that the remainder of the sentence will set you straight as to what it *is*. (Put in the terms given earlier, the implied question is, Well, if wife assault isn't a marital problem, what is it?, and the answer is, A criminal activity.) Neither the semicolon nor the dash quite performs this function. The semicolon does not act to draw the reader's attention to what follows it, and while the dash does, it does so for purposes other than answering a "question" raised in the first part.

Aside from the impact on meaning that the colon can confer, note how it offers some stylistic advantages by allowing you to run choppy sentences together, thereby achieving a better flow, and sometimes allowing you to drop a few words, thereby making your writing more concise.

OTHER USES OF THE COLON

The colon has a few mechanical applications, as described below.

SEPARATING THE NUMBERS IN A RATIO

4:1   3:2

Note that if you were writing these numbers out as words rather than numerals, you would use the word *to* instead of a colon: *four to one; three to two.*

SEPARATING THE HOUR FROM THE MINUTES

1:30   5:45

Note that the British style is to use a period instead (1.30; 5.45).

SEPARATING A MAIN TITLE FROM THE SUBTITLE

The Fatal Shore: The Epic of Australia's Founding

"Universality and variation in moral judgment: A longitudinal and cross-sectional study"

SEPARATING LEAD-IN TEXT FROM SPOKEN WORDS IN DIALOGUE

The uproar subsided, and I tried again: "Ladies and gentlemen!"

He suddenly turned to her and said: "Why me?"

Similarly, it may be used instead of a comma to introduce a quotation.

SEPARATING LOW-LEVEL SUBHEADINGS AND FIGURE OR TABLE IDENTIFIERS FROM THE TEXT THAT FOLLOWS THEM

The Colon: The colon has the following functions . . .

Figure 12: Diagram of developmental diversity.

Alternatively, a period or a closing parenthesis may be used.

SEPARATING A CHARACTER'S NAME FROM HIS
OR HER LINES IN SCRIPTS AND SCREENPLAYS
Alternatively, a period may be used, or the character's name may
appear on a separate line.

COLON OR SEMICOLON?

Some writers are confused by the distinction between the colon and
the semicolon, and in fairness, there are a few cases where either
mark might do. How do you decide which one to use, then? It depends on context and tone. The colon is a "stronger" mark, one that
increases the emphasis of what is being said. Consider the difference
in nuance between the following two sentences:

> Time was ticking away; he had to make a decision soon.
> Time was ticking away: He had to make a decision soon.

In both examples, the connection between the two items of information is clear, but the second one suggests a bit more urgency to
the situation. Thus, the context would determine which mark is the
most appropriate.

Note that a choice between these marks could arise only in situations involving their subtler roles—those having to do with emphasizing relationships. In the majority of cases, the roles are distinct,
with no overlap. The semicolon is the only mark that is appropriate
when you need to separate elements that wouldn't be sufficiently
distinguished if commas were used, and the colon is the only mark
that is appropriate when you need to separate a lead-in or introductory part of a sentence from what follows.

STYLE CONVENTIONS

• You may leave either one or two spaces following a colon. Just
be consistent.

• When a colon follows quoted text, place it *after* the closing
quotation mark. (See page 182.)

• If the text immediately preceding a colon is italicized, italicize
the colon as well.

• With regard to capitalization, style guides differ. Some say to always start the text that follows the colon with a lowercase letter; others say to begin it with uppercase if it's an independent clause, and lowercase if it's a sentence fragment. Whichever style you choose, be consistent. However, if you have chosen to go with lowercase, make an exception in the following situations:

1. If you feel the text that follows the colon is important enough to merit the emphasis of capitalization. For example: If the lead-in words are relatively trivial and your real point begins after the colon, you may decide that beginning this part of the sentence with lowercase would inappropriately subsume it.

2. If the colon is introducing a series of sentences of equal weight. For example:

Our procedures were as follows: First, we obtained a list of all eligible participants. Second, we contacted all those who lived within a ten-mile radius of the study site, and asked if they would be willing to take part. Third, we mailed out packets, consisting of the questionnaire and a stamped return envelope, to all subjects who agreed to participate.

The words *Second* and *Third* begin with uppercase, so *First* should be capitalized as well. If it were written lowercase, the information it introduces would not appear to have equal standing with the other information.

Period (.)

There's not much to be said about the period except that most people don't reach it soon enough.
—WILLIAM ZINSSER, *On Writing Well*

The period has two main functions:

- Ending a sentence
- Indicating abbreviations

ENDING A SENTENCE

Dear John,
I want a man who knows what love is all about. You are generous, kind, thoughtful. People who are not like you admit to being useless and inferior. You have ruined me for other men. I yearn for you. I have no feelings whatsoever when we're apart. I can be forever happy. Will you let me be yours? Gloria

Dear John,
I want a man who knows what love is. All about you are generous, kind, thoughtful people who are not like you. Admit to being useless and inferior. You have ruined me. For other men I yearn. For you I have no feelings whatsoever. When we're apart I can be forever happy. Will you let me be? Yours, Gloria
—ANONYMOUS (Note circulating on editors' forum on the Internet)

The period's basic role in ending a sentence is obvious enough, but there are a few situations that bear mention.

DON'T INCLUDE A PERIOD FOR A GRAMMATICALLY COMPLETE PARENTHESIZED SENTENCE THAT LIES WITHIN ANOTHER SENTENCE

> Hospital workers objected that the consultant's advice on business techniques didn't apply in their environment (for example, they felt that telling desperately sick patients to "have a nice day" was inappropriate) and was undermining rather than improving morale.

> The foreign ministry said that five more diplomats would be expelled (two had been ordered out of the country the week before), and that a full investigation into the activities at the embassy would be launched.

This also means that parenthesized text that lies within a sentence cannot consist of two or more grammatically complete sentences separated by a period. If you want to include a parenthesized comment that contains two discrete points, you must join these points with a colon, semicolon, dash or conjunction.

> **No:** We trudged gloomily along the trail (the weather was damp and miserable. We were also being eaten alive by mosquitoes) and looked for a suitable site to pitch the tent.
> **Yes:** We trudged gloomily along the trail (the weather was damp and miserable, and we were being eaten alive by mosquitoes) and looked for a suitable site to pitch the tent.

A stand-alone parenthesized sentence, of course, does take a period. See the section on style conventions for "Parentheses" on page 150.

USE A COMMA RATHER THAN A PERIOD TO END A SENTENCE IN DIALOGUE WHEN MORE TEXT FOLLOWS

> "I'm sure no one in the audience noticed when your toupee slid off," she said soothingly.
> "I realize you didn't blow up the house on purpose," he said plaintively. "But it's undeniably rather inconveniencing."

For other aspects of punctuation in dialogue, see the appropriate sections under "Comma," page 83, and "Quotation Marks," page 172.

DON'T INCLUDE A PERIOD IF A SENTENCE ENDS IN ANOTHER TERMINAL PUNCTUATION MARK, EVEN IF THAT MARK DOES NOT APPLY TO THE SENTENCE AS A WHOLE

They signed their divorce papers right after lunch, and then headed off to a matinée of *I Do! I Do!*

Before you begin, be sure to read the section entitled *Should I Begin?*

She has that annoying habit of ending almost every sentence with "you know what I mean?"

Readers will understand that in cases like this the question mark or exclamation point applies to just the words at the end, and that the entire sentence is not querying or exclamatory.

Note that if the words for which the other punctuation mark applies are enclosed within parentheses, you *would* put a period at the end of the sentence. See the section on style conventions under "Parentheses" on page 150.

IF A SENTENCE ENDS IN AN ABBREVIATION THAT INCLUDES A PERIOD, DO NOT ADD ANOTHER PERIOD

If you have any complaints about this product, send them in writing to Acme Manufacturing, Inc.

The list of student demands included less homework, a better selection of ice cream flavors in the cafeteria, more time allotted for surfing the Net, etc.

That is, you let the period that goes with the abbreviation do double duty as a terminal punctuation mark.

Note: You may follow an abbreviating period at the end of a sentence with a question mark or exclamation point. For example:

Is the company name followed by *Inc.* or *Ltd.*?

BE CONSISTENT WITH THE USE OF PERIODS AT THE END OF LIST ITEMS

Style guides differ as to whether a period should appear at the end of each item in a vertical list. That is, should your list be presented as:

Item 1.	OR	Item 1
Item 2.		Item 2
Item 3.		Item 3

If you are not obliged to follow a particular guide, make your own decision and treat all lists the same way. Some writers choose to include periods if each item on a list is a complete sentence, and omit them if the items consist of single words or sentence fragments. (In the interest of maintaining parallel structure, a list should not contain a mixture of both. For a discussion of parallelism, turn to page 223.)

If list items contain multiple sentences, it's preferable to include a period at the end, since it can look a bit odd to have periods for each sentence but the last. Some style guides, however, say to leave off the final period.

If you ever have a situation where you are avoiding periods as a rule but a particular list item seems to need one, consider adding them for all the other items in that list too, in the interest of uniformity.

INDICATING ABBREVIATIONS

Words may be shortened in several different ways. **Contractions**, which take apostrophes, act to make words more informal or easier to say. A contraction effectively becomes a new form of the word, and is both written and pronounced differently from the full word. (See page 191.) **Abbreviations**, which may take periods, are for purposes of efficiency rather than casualness.

Abbreviations for *multiple words* are made up of the first letter of each word, or sometimes the first couple of letters. They are pronounced either as the individual letters (NBC, CIA, LSD) or sometimes, if the letters spell out something pronounceable, as an **acronym** (ANOVA, MCAT, UNICEF).

Abbreviations for *single words* come in a variety of forms. They may consist of the first few letters of the word *(Avenue—Ave., population—pop., January—Jan.)*; its first and last letters *(Mister—Mr., Senior—Sr., foot—ft.)*; some combination of the above *(Boulevard—Blvd., Route—Rte., building—bldg.)*; or the first letter only *(Fahrenheit—F, North—N, University—U)*. Some even include letters that are not in the original word *(number—no., pound—lb., ounce—oz.)*. With a few exceptions, single-word abbreviations are pronounced as the entire word.

Some abbreviations must take periods, some optionally take them and some don't take them. Periods are more likely to be used when an abbreviation is sounded out as letters than when it is an acronym, but this distinction cannot be taken as a rule. In cases where periods are optional, the general trend today is to omit them, but this is by no means universal.

The following are rules and guidelines on when to include periods:

INITIALS OF PEOPLE'S NAMES
Always include periods.

> C.S. Lewis
> F. Scott Fitzgerald
> George C. Scott
> Franklin D. Roosevelt

TITLES, HONORIFICS
Follow the convention that is most appropriate for your audience. In North America, periods are expected.

Mrs. America	Fred Wincourt, Jr.
Mr. Magoo	Godfrey Barker, Esq.
Dr. Seuss	Screech Owl Recording Studios, Inc.
Mount St. Helen	Porcupine Quill Duvet Manufacturers, Ltd.

In Britain and some other Commonwealth countries, the period is omitted for abbreviations that include the final letter of the word: thus, *Mrs, Mr, Dr*, etc.

Note that the honorific *Ms*—or *Ms.*—is a special case. Many writers spell it with a period, and indeed some style guides say to do so. Presumably this is to make it equivalent to its male counterpart, *Mr.* However, given that the word isn't actually short for anything, leaving the period off is legitimate as well.

For academic degrees, the period is optional, or at least varies according to different style guides.

R.N.	RN	M.Sc.	MSc
M.D.	MD	Ph.D.	PhD
B.A.	BA	D.D.S.	DDS

GEOGRAPHICAL NAMES

Optional (or depends on the style guide). If you are not obliged to follow a particular guide, make your own decisions and be consistent.

U.S.A.	USA	N.Y.C	NYC
U.K.	UK	L.A.	LA

For American states and Canadian provinces, do not include periods if you are using the two-letter postal abbreviation of the name. Do include them if you are using the other shortened form.

CT	Conn.	AB	Alta.
MN	Minn.	MB	Man.
WA	Wash.	NF	Nfld.

Note that for states and provinces with two-word names, both forms of abbreviation will be the same: for example, *N.J.* or *NJ*, *S.C.* or *SC*, *B.C.* or *BC*, *N.S.* or *NS*.

TIME INDICATORS

Optional (or depends on the style guide).

A.M.	P.M.	AM	PM
B.C.	A.D.	BC	AD
B.C.E.	C.E.	BCE	CE

METRIC MEASUREMENTS

Do not include periods.

10°C
250 km
39 cm

NAMES OF COMPANIES OR ORGANIZATIONS

Follow convention. Most such abbreviations will not include periods, but some may; some style guides may say to include them and others to omit them.

NBC	H.M.O.
IBM	L.A.P.D.
NATO	N.H.L.
RCMP	A.M.A.

OTHER

For any abbreviation that doesn't fall into a clear category, it is usually appropriate to include the period. For example:

anonymous	anon.	gallon	gal.
born	b.	manager	mgr.
continued	cont.	manuscript	ms.
died	d.	miscellaneous	misc.
edition (or editor)	ed.	versus	vs.
Figure	Fig.	volume	vol.

Be particularly careful with Latin abbreviations. Writers are prone to make errors in period placement with foreign abbreviations, since they are not familiar with the original words.

e.g. (not eg.)
two abbreviated words, *exempli gratia* ("for example")

i.e. (not ie.)
two abbreviated words, *id est* ("that is")

et al. (not et. al.)
two words, but only one abbreviated: *et alia* ("and others")

cf. (not c.f.)
one abbreviated word, *confer* ("compare")

viz. (not viz)
one abbreviated word, *videlicet* ("namely") *(z* is a medieval contraction for *e-t)*

OTHER USES OF THE PERIOD

Aside from its two main functions, the period has a number of mechanical applications. The more common of these are the following:

SETTING OFF LIST NUMBERS

In numbered vertical lists, a period may be placed after each number to mark it off from the text that follows.

Here are the topics that will be covered this semester:

1. History of the world
2. The meaning of life
3. The origins of the universe
4. The applications of the semicolon

Alternatively, colons, closing parentheses or—less commonly—hyphens may be used. In lists that are merged in with the rest of the text, the mark used is generally the closing parenthesis.

SETTING OFF HEADINGS AND CAPTIONS
In subheadings and figure or table identifiers, a period may be used to separate this text from the text that follows.

The period. The period has the following functions . . .

Table 6. Short-term and long-term projections.

REPRESENTING A DECIMAL POINT
44.5   596.371

In many parts of the world, a comma is used instead.

Question Mark (?)

The question mark is a terminal punctuation mark that turns a sentence into a query. It may also be used to indicate uncertainty, tentativeness or incredulity. There are cases where it is necessary, cases where it is optional and cases where it is inappropriate.

It has the following functions:

- Indicating queries
- Optionally indicating rhetorical questions
- Optionally indicating requests
- Indicating uncertainty

INDICATING QUERIES

USE THE QUESTION MARK WHEN POSING A DIRECT QUERY

Were there any messages for me?

How does this electric cat brush work?

Just how many crates of mangoes *did* you eat last night, anyway?

USE IT TO TURN A STATEMENT INTO A QUERY

You promise not to tell anyone?

You don't really mean that?

She *really* said she would?

Note that the former way of posing a question is more likely when the speaker is seeking information, and the latter when the speaker is assuming or hoping for a particular answer.

In dialogue, both forms of questions are common.

Of course St John Rivers' name came in frequently in the progress of the tale. When I had done, that name was immediately taken up.

'This St John then, is your cousin?'

'Yes.'

'You have spoken of him often: do you like him?'

'He was a very good man, sir; I could not help liking him.'

'A good man. Does that mean a respectable, well-conducted man of fifty? Or what does it mean?'

'St John was only twenty-nine, sir.'

' "*Jeune encore*", as the French say. Is he a person of low stature, phlegmatic and plain? A person whose goodness consists rather in his guiltlessness of vice, than in his prowess of virtue?'

'He is untiringly active. Great and exalted deeds are what he lives to perform.'

'But his brain? That is probably rather soft? He means well: but you shrug your shoulders to hear him talk?'

'He talks little, sir: what he does say is ever to the point. His brain is first-rate, I should think not impressible, but vigorous.'

'. . . His manners, I think you said, are not to your taste?—priggish and parsonic?'

'I never mentioned his manners; but, unless I had a very bad taste, they must suit it; they are polished, calm, and gentleman-like.'

'His appearance—I forgot what description you gave of his appearance;—a sort of raw curate, half strangled with his white neckcloth, and stilted up on his thick-soled high-lows, eh?'

'St John dresses well. He is a handsome man: tall, fair, with blue eyes, and a Grecian profile.'

(Aside) 'Damn him!'—*(To me)* 'Did you like him, Jane?'

'Yes, Mr Rochester, I liked him: but you asked me that before.'

—CHARLOTTE BRONTË, *Jane Eyre*

USE IT FOR A STATEMENT THAT ENDS IN A WORD INFLECTED AS A QUERY

Just leave me alone, okay?

So you're quitting your job, eh?

USE IT FOR A SENTENCE THAT CONSISTS OF A DIRECT QUESTION CONTAINED WITHIN A STATEMENT

He was beginning to wonder, was she truly what she claimed to be?

The question was, why bother even trying?

You must ask yourself, Will I be better off with him or without him?

In this type of sentence, whether or not you capitalize the question portion depends on how much emphasis you wish to give it. Capitalization is allowable, but in most cases would probably give the question more prominence than it needs.

Note that such constructions can also be presented the other way around, with the question coming first. That is, the question mark may appear *within* the sentence, rather than as the terminal punctuation.

Was she truly what she claimed to be? he was beginning to wonder.

Why bother even trying? was the question.

Do not use a question mark for statements that contain indirect questions. For example, the question marks in the following sentences are *incorrect* and should be replaced with periods.

I couldn't help wondering how she had done it?

They asked us if we'd seen the film yet?

The tourists invariably asked if the glacier was still advancing?

Note, however, that sometimes such a construction can be turned into a statement that contains a direct question, in which case it does take a question mark. For example:

I couldn't help wondering, how had she done it?

They asked us, had we seen the film yet?

USE IT TO ACHIEVE A TENTATIVE INFLECTION

In dialogue, you can employ question marks to impart an uncertain, tentative tone to a character's manner of speaking. Some people have a habit of inflecting ordinary statements as questions, almost as if they're chronically expecting to be challenged on what they are saying?

Muriel said, "Once I was riding Alexander uptown on some errands for George? My company? And I'd had these two cats in the car just the day before? And I didn't think a thing about it, clean forgot to vacuum like I usually do, and all at once I turn around and Alexander's stretched across the seat, flat out."

—ANNE TYLER, *The Accidental Tourist*

INDICATING RHETORICAL QUESTIONS

A **rhetorical question**—one for which no answer is expected or for which the answer is self-evident—may end in either a question mark or an exclamation point. The context determines which will be most appropriate.

But when I reminded her of everything I'd done for her, do you think she was grateful?

Isn't her singing amazing?

Was there ever an occasion, however glorious, however mundane, that wasn't accented, augmented, and just generally raised heavenward on those upwardly mobile, happy little bubbles of the sublime Champagne?

—JÜRGEN GOTHE, *Good Gothe!*

How was I to know that asking him his age would cause him to flee the room in tears!

How can we ever thank you enough!

Breathes there the man, with soul so dead,
Who never to himself hath said,
This is my own, my native land!
Whose heart hath ne'er within him burn'd,
As home his footsteps he hath turn'd,
From wandering on a foreign strand!

—SIR WALTER SCOTT, *The Lay of the Last Minstrel*

In dialogue, it is sometimes realistic to have a speaker's rhetorical question end in a period.

117

Look, why don't we just drop the whole thing.

Well, isn't that just dandy.

Since different inflections in a speaker's voice carry different implications, sometimes the choice of punctuation for a rhetorical question will be determined by the tone you want to achieve.

So he really said that, did he?
[interested or surprised reaction]

So he really said that, did he.
[uninterested or musing reaction]

So he really said that, did he!
[indignant or excited reaction]

You can use a question mark in combination with italics to indicate shock or incredulity.

He said *what?*

At your age, you still use a *pacifier?*

INDICATING REQUESTS

For a request that is really a politely phrased order or instruction, decide what tone is intended. A question mark makes the words look more humble; a period, more peremptory. Usually, a period is more appropriate.

Would you take the garbage out when you leave?
[Translation: It would be nice if you would.]

Would you take the garbage out when you leave.
[Translation: Take out the garbage!]

Would you mind feeding the piranhas?

Would you be good enough to leave immediately.

How about if you wash and I dry?

Would you pass the salt, please.

Won't you sit down.

INDICATING UNCERTAINTY

A minor role of the question mark is to indicate uncertainty about dates.

Joan of Arc, 1412?—1431
Desiderius Erasmus, 1466?—1536

Similarly, you may choose to follow any tentative statement of fact with a question mark enclosed within parentheses. Obviously, it will not enhance the force of your writing if this device appears often.

STYLE CONVENTIONS

Style conventions for the question mark are the same as those for the exclamation point, and are presented there (page 124).

Exclamation Point (!)

The exclamation point is a terminal punctuation mark that is used in place of the period to add emphasis or emotion. It turns simple statements into forceful ones, and remarks into exclamations or outbursts. It comes up most commonly in dialogue, but has a role in nondialogue text as well.

Its functions are the following:

- Indicating importance or emotion
- Optionally indicating rhetorical questions
- Drawing attention to unlikely points

Almost all of its occurrences fall into the first category; the other two uses do not arise frequently.

INDICATING IMPORTANCE OR EMOTION

In nondialogue, the exclamation point can be used to lend emphasis or grab attention.

> The woman in the glasses politely let us squeeze past her to get to the "Special Sale" table—rookie!
>
> I found myself turning down the familiar drive—I, who had sworn never to go within ten miles of the place again!
>
> We paused to survey the result. A fine mess he'd made of it!

In dialogue, it can be used to indicate excitement, urgency, vehemence or astonishment.

'Are you guilty?' said Winston.

'Of course I'm guilty!' cried Parsons with a servile glance at the telescreen. 'You don't think the Party would arrest an innocent man, do you?' His frog-like face grew calmer, and even took on a slightly sanctimonious expression. 'Thoughtcrime is a dreadful thing, old man,' he said sententiously. 'It's insidious. It can get hold of you without your even knowing it. Do you know how it got hold of me? In my sleep! Yes, that's a fact. There I was, working away, trying to do my bit—never knew I had any bad stuff in my mind at all. And then I started talking in my sleep. Do you know what they heard me saying?'

He sank his voice, like someone who is obliged for medical reasons to utter an obscenity.

' "Down with Big Brother!" Yes, I said that! Said it over and over again, it seems. Between you and me, old man, I'm glad they got me before it went any further. Do you know what I'm going to say to them when I go up before the tribunal? "Thank you," I'm going to say, "thank you for saving me before it was too late." '

—GEORGE ORWELL, *Nineteen Eighty-Four*

'Oh, Rumpole!' It was an astonishing moment. She Who Must Be Obeyed actually had her arms around me, she was holding me tightly, rather as though I were some rare and precious object and not the old White Elephant that continually got in her way.

'Hilda. Hilda, you're not . . .?' I looked down at her agitated head. 'You weren't worried, were you?'

'Worried? Well, of course I was worried!' She broke away and resumed the Royal Manner. 'Having you at home all day would have been impossible!'

—JOHN MORTIMER, *Rumpole and the Learned Friends*

Note that exclamation points are by no means compulsory in dialogue every time a speech takes on some emphasis. You may often prefer to let your readers infer a character's emotions from wording or context.

Athough the exclamation point normally appears at the end of a sentence, it may occasionally be used as internal punctuation. The text that follows does not have to begin with a capital letter, as it is still part of the same sentence. (This text may, however, be

capitalized if it seems appropriate. See the discussion under "Capitalization" on page 269.)

> Mrs Palmer's eye was now caught by the drawings which hung
> round the room. She got up to examine them.
> 'Oh! dear, how beautiful these are! Well! how delightful! Do but
> look, mama, how sweet! I declare they are quite charming; I could
> look at them for ever.' And then sitting down again, she very soon
> forgot that there were any such things in the room.
>
> —Jane Austen, *Sense and Sensibility*

> I took the subway to group . . . and tried to concentrate on how I
> was going to tell the group what had happened to me. I felt mortified.
> Two years earlier, I had walked off into the sunset—cured! it's a miracle!
> she can walk!—and now I was back again, a hopeless cripple.
>
> —Nora Ephron, *Heartburn*

> An exclamation of horror broke from the painter's lips as he saw in
> the dim light the hideous face on the canvas grinning at him.
> There was something in its expression that filled him with disgust and
> loathing. Good heavens! it was Dorian Gray's own face that he was
> looking at!
>
> —Oscar Wilde, *The Picture of Dorian Gray*

INDICATING RHETORICAL QUESTIONS

It is sometimes appropriate to end a rhetorical question—one for
which no answer is expected—in an exclamation point instead of a
question mark.

> How do you expect me to finish all these chores by noon!
> Isn't he adorable!
> What on earth did she expect!

See also the examples of rhetorical questions under "Question
Mark" on page 117.

DRAWING ATTENTION TO A POINT

Some writers like to underline statements that are unlikely, ironic or unexpected by following them with an exclamation point enclosed in parentheses.

> After trying and failing to borrow money, first from his cousin, then from his best friend and finally from the starving artist upstairs (!), he decided there was no alternative but to sell off the private jet.
>
> After nineteen pastries (!), Albert decided he'd had enough.

While this strategy is not illegal, it demands attention a bit too loudly. It is occasionally appropriate, but as a general rule you are better off wording things so that ironies or oddities speak for themselves. (Give your readers credit for being able to pick up on subtleties.)

CAUTIONS ABOUT THE EXCLAMATION POINT

Use this punctuation mark sparingly, or it will lose its effectiveness. Relying on it to infuse excitement or importance into uninspired lines will make your writing look amateurish or—even worse—gratingly like ad copy.

It is permissible to use it in combination with other strategies for indicating emphasis, such as capital letters, boldface or italic type, but don't overdo this: Usually, a better approach is to use one strategy or the other. It is also inadvisable to use multiple exclamation points to indicate extreme astonishment or excitement *(Could you believe what she said!! The concert was incredible!!!)*. Occasionally, this may be effective in drawing the reader's attention more closely to something, but more typically it makes it look as if you're trying too hard.

Some writers fancy using a combination of a question mark and an exclamation point for extra emphasis, usually following a rhetorical question. There is in fact an obscure punctuation mark for this purpose, called an *interrobang* (‽), which merges the two marks into one. More typically, one sees them presented side by side.

> Could anyone have thought it possible?!
> Can you believe what she's done now?!

Combining a question mark and an exclamation point may occasionally be appropriate, but should be kept to a minimum.

STYLE CONVENTIONS

The question mark and exclamation point follow similar rules when it comes to style conventions and so are reviewed together here.

• When a question mark or exclamation point occurs in the middle of a sentence, do *not* follow it with a comma. This holds whether the text preceding the mark is dialogue, unvoiced thought with no surrounding quotation marks, or straight narrative.

Bart said, "Nonsense!" and ambled off.
"You don't really mean that?" she asked incredulously.
Did he really mean it? she wondered.
Now here was a pretty kettle of fish! I said to myself.
Who would blink first? was the question.
We had barely made it to the door when crash! everything collapsed.

• When a question mark or exclamation point appears at the end of a sentence, do *not* follow it with a period, even if it applies only to the last words. The context will make it clear to readers whether or not the entire sentence is querying or exclamatory. For illustrations of this, see the discussion under "Period" on page 108.

• When a question mark or exclamation point follows quoted text, place it after the closing quotation mark if it applies to the entire sentence, and before if it applies to just the quoted part. For illustrations of this, see the section on style conventions under "Quotation Marks" on page 182.

• When a question mark or exclamation point applies only to text enclosed within parentheses, it does not affect the terminal punctuation for the remainder of the sentence. See the section on style conventions under "Parentheses" on page 150.

• When a question mark or exclamation point immediately follows italicized text, italicize it as well.

Surely you didn't mean *me?*
Come here *immediately!*

Hyphen (-)

This section looks at the hyphen as a mark of punctuation, as opposed to a component of spelling. The distinction is that in its punctuation role the hyphen is not an inherent part of a word or phrase, but rather is required only when words are presented in particular combinations or ways. (For a discussion of its spelling role, turn to page 23.)

The functions of the hyphen as a punctuation mark are the following:

- Indicating word breaks at the end of a line
- Drawing together words that form a compound adjective
- Acting as a "stand-in" for a repeated word
- Indicating special intonations or pronunciations

INDICATING END-OF-LINE WORD BREAKS

During a late election Lord
Roehampton strained a vocal chord
From shouting, very loud and high,
To lots and lots of people why
The budget in his own opin-
-Ion should not be allowed to win.

HILAIRE BELLOC, *Selected Cautionary Verses*

Knowing where to break a word that's too long to fit on a line was more of an issue in the days of typewriters. (Remember them?) Nowadays, it's a rare word processor that won't automatically do the breaking for you. Still, it doesn't hurt for writers to have at least an awareness of the rules: As any newspaper reader knows, a computer's idea of word breaks can be hilarious—or worse.

(*Men-swear, wee-knight, heat-her, mans-laughter, Pen-elope, Superb-owl, prolife-rated* and *the-rapist* have all made appearances in print.) After all, some fallible human had to program the word-break software! And for the diehards still using typewriters, of course, word breaks remain an ongoing (or ong-oing) consideration.

The simplest and best advice regarding word breaks is, if you're ever in doubt, check the dictionary: Any proper one will indicate all places where breaks are acceptable. Be aware, though, that dictionaries may differ. In general, American style is to break words by their pronunciation, while British style is to break them by their etymology—that is, separating the root word from any add-ons. For example, *Webster's* breaks *knowledge* and *psychology* as *knowl-edge* and *psychol-ogy*, while *Oxford* breaks these words as *know-ledge* and *psycho-logy*. Certainly, both approaches have validity, although the former perhaps helps the reader a bit more in terms of anticipating what follows the hyphen. If you're going with one style or another, be consistent.

The rationale behind breaking words only in certain places is to prevent readers from having to struggle to make sense of the two parts. The basic rules are: Never break words of one syllable, and break multisyllabic words only between syllables. You have to be careful in the latter case, however, since not all syllable breaks are acceptable as end-of-line breaks. The rules are detailed below.

DON'T BREAK WORDS OF ONE SYLLABLE
This holds no matter how long a word is, and even if it has more than one phoneme (distinct sound unit).

No	Yes
bar-bed	barbed
thro-ugh	through
school-ed	schooled
scrun-ched	scrunched
he-arth	hearth

DON'T BREAK A WORD IF JUST ONE
LETTER WOULD BE LEFT ON A LINE
This rule applies to any three-letter word and to some longer ones as well.

No	Yes
a-do	ado
i-vy	ivy
i-dea	idea
tax-i	taxi
a-bout	about
e-nough	enough
throat-y	throaty

Similarly, with longer words that have more than two syllables, be sure not to break them in places that would cause this problem.

No	Yes
a-miable	ami-able
epitom-e	epito-me
i-dentify	iden-tify

There are also word breaks that it would be better to avoid, even if the dictionary indicates they are permissible.

RECOMMENDATION: BREAK HYPHENATED COMPOUND WORDS AT THE HYPHEN

Hyphenated compounds are those where the base words are linked by a hyphen as part of the normal spelling. In this situation, let that hyphen do double duty, functioning both as an integral part of the word itself *and* as an end-of-the-line word breaker. Having two hyphens in a word would look awkward.

No	Yes
by-prod-uct	by-product
dou-ble-edged	double-edged
tee-ter-totter or teeter-tot-ter	teeter-totter

RECOMMENDATION: BREAK CLOSED COMPOUND
WORDS BETWEEN THE WORDS

Closed compounds are those made up of two words run together. Breaking them between the base words is preferable to breaking either of the base words themselves, even if those words could be broken if they stood alone.

No	Yes
com-monplace	common-place
quar-terback	quarter-back
mead-owlark	meadow-lark

Similarly, if a word contains a prefix or a suffix, try to break between the prefix/suffix and the root word, rather than breaking either of those components themselves.

No	Yes
su-perscript	super-script
an-ticlimax *or* anticli-max	anti-climax
precon-dition	pre-condition
coun-terclockwise *or* counterclock-wise	counter-clockwise
sis-terhood	sister-hood

RECOMMENDATION: DO NOT BREAK A WORD IF TWO UNRELATED WORDS WOULD COINCIDENTALLY RESULT

Sometimes, breaking a word creates two new words, which might cause momentary puzzlement. To prevent your reader's having to backtrack to make sense of what was just seen, avoid breaks such as the following unless absolutely necessary:

No	Yes
bin-go	bingo
is-sue	issue
are-na	arena
pick-led	pickled
prose-cute	prosecute

LINKING THE PARTS OF A COMPOUND ADJECTIVE

This topic gets a bit complex, because the rules are so varied. There's a main rule, but then there are exceptions, and then there are exceptions to the exceptions. The best way to introduce this function of the hyphen is to lead up to it, so that the rationale behind all the rules is understood.

Consider the following sets of words:

deadly viral infection
large urban center
rude civil servant

The words *deadly, large* and *rude* are clearly adjectives, while *infection, center* and *servant* are clearly nouns. What about the words in the middle, though? They are also adjectives—but each one is combining with the noun that follows it to create a **compound noun**, which expresses a single concept. The reader understands that the first word modifies the next two: *Deadly* modifies the compound noun *viral infection, large* modifies *urban center*, and *rude* modifies *civil servant*.

civil rights leader
major league player
mad cow disease

Here again the first words are adjectives and the third ones are nouns, but now the middle word in each string is a noun that combines with the adjective that precedes it to create a **compound adjective**. The reader understands that the reference is to a leader in civil rights, not to a "rights leader" with good manners. Similarly, it is the league that is major, not the player, and the cow that is mad, not the disease itself.

long red braids
grumpy old man
sturdy little boy

Here, two adjectives in a row each independently modify the noun that follows. (For an explanation of why these phrases do not take commas, see page 82.) The reader understands that the reference is to braids that are long and red, a man who is grumpy and old, and a boy who is sturdy and little.

None of the above combinations of words should present any confusion or be interpreted as meaning anything other than what they do. But how about the following?

imported beef products
bad language rules
stone carving knife

Here, are the middle words meant to be combined with their pre-
decessors to create compound adjectives, or with their successors
to create compound nouns? Beef products that are imported, or
domestic products made with imported beef? Bad rules about language, or rules about bad language? A carving knife made of stone,
or a knife for carving stone?

Similarly, it may not always be clear whether an adjective that
comes after another adjective should be combined with the first one
to form a compound, or if it is independently modifying the noun
that follows.

green spotted snake
dirty blonde hair
thirty odd guests

A green snake with spots, or a snake with green spots? Hair of a
brown/blonde shade, or blonde hair that needs washing? Somewhere
between thirty and forty guests, or thirty eccentrics?

USE HYPHENS TO LINK THE WORDS OF A COMPOUND
ADJECTIVE THAT PRECEDES A NOUN IF AMBIGUITY
OR UNCERTAINTY MIGHT OTHERWISE RESULT

When two or more words are intended to collectively function as a
single adjective, link them with hyphens if they come before the
noun they modify and if there's any possibility of misinterpreting
them. Hyphens make the status of each word immediately clear and
make the sentence easier to read overall.

I wouldn't touch that line with a ten-foot pole.

A single 256-byte record allows for 256 single-byte output values.

Come take advantage of this once-in-a-lifetime opportunity to buy a set
of silver-plated lint-removal brushes at a not-to-be-believed price!

In some cases, as already demonstrated, the absence of a hyphen
could produce misinterpretation or ambiguity.

The new driver legislation will take effect next month.

This sentence is fine if what's meant is legislation that applies to all drivers. However, what if it is legislation pertaining only to people who have just received their licenses? In that case, the sentence should appear as: *The new-driver legislation will take effect next month.*

Similarly,

Ten month old babies were observed in the study.

Did the study look at ten babies, each of whom was one month old—or at an unspecified number of babies, each of whom was ten months old? In the absence of hyphens, we can't tell whether *ten* is modifying *babies* or *months*. This sentence should read either *Ten month-old babies were observed in the study* or *Ten-month-old babies were observed in the study.*

In other cases, the absence of a hyphen might not render a sentence ambiguous, but could cause momentary confusion as the reader started to process things one way and then realized that a word was misinterpreted.

The company sponsored events usually attracted a high turnout.

The office generated paperwork soon became too much for one secretary to handle.

His girlfriend related problems began to take their toll on his work.

Hyphens would make it clear that *sponsored, generated* and *related* are functioning as parts of compound adjectives, not as verbs.

Exceptions

Hyphens may be considered optional when a compound adjective consists of words that are quite commonly associated with each other, so there is little possibility of ambiguity or misinterpretation. The earlier examples of *major league player* and *mad cow disease* could quite properly be written as *major-league player* and *mad-cow disease.* However, this is more a choice than a necessity, since omitting the hyphens should not cause any problems for the reader.

In some cases, adding hyphens would be not only unnecessary but inappropriate. For example, you would not include them in phrases such as *high school student, baby boomer generation* or *carbon monoxide fumes*, where the first two words make up a very familiar compound.

Clearly, it will sometimes be a judgment call as to whether or not a particular combination calls for hyphens. The best advice is, err on the side of caution if you think a sequence of words would be harder to follow without them.

DO *NOT* LINK THE WORDS OF A COMPOUND ADJECTIVE WITH HYPHENS WHEN THEY COME AFTER THE NOUN

When a compound adjective comes *after* the noun it modifies, it does not take hyphens, since in this case no ambiguity or misreading could result from omitting them.

> Roberta is a full-time instructor who teaches graduate-level courses on up-to-date topics.
>
> Roberta teaches full time at the graduate level, on topics that are up to date.
>
> Read the easy-to-follow instructions to work your way through the ten-step process.
>
> The process has ten steps, and comes with instructions that are easy to follow.

Of course, if the compound inherently takes a hyphen, include it. In that case it is serving not to distinguish the compound from adjoining words, but as part of its proper spelling, so it naturally applies regardless of the position of the compound in the sentence.

> The back-to-back workshops were exhausting to sit through.
> The workshops were back-to-back.
>
> The cross-eyed doll seemed to be giving him a baleful look.
> The doll was cross-eyed.

Hyphenated compounds appear as their own entries in the dictionary, so it's easy to confirm if a hyphen is needed. If you don't see a compound listed, assume that it does not take a hyphen. (Note, though, that dictionaries may differ on what gets hyphenated.)

DO NOT USE A HYPHEN WHEN THE FIRST WORD OF A COMPOUND ADJECTIVE IS AN ADVERB ENDING IN *LY*

Adjectives are words that modify nouns; **adverbs** are words that modify verbs. Adverbs also modify adjectives, participles (verb forms acting as adjectives) and other adverbs. Adverbs are usually very easy to recognize: The majority are formed by taking an adjective and adding *ly* to it. (Note that some adjectives end in *ly* as well.)

The words that make up compound adjectives may individually be nouns, adjectives, verbs, participles or adverbs. For all but the last, hyphens are often necessary because, as previously discussed, word order alone may not be sufficient to clarify which words are modifying which. An adverb, however, *always* modifies the word that immediately follows it (unless it's the last word in the sentence). Since no ambiguity is possible, putting a hyphen after an adverb to link it with the next word would be redundant.

The hyphens in the following examples are *incorrect* and should be removed:

The organization was run by a highly-motivated team.

She admitted that she had poorly-developed spatial skills.

They showed him selections of beautifully-woven fabric.

Add two cups of freshly-chopped parsley.

She led the guests into an impressively-decorated sitting room.

The no-hyphen rule also applies, of course, when the adverb-adjective compound follows the noun.

The team was highly motivated.

The fabric was beautifully woven.

The parsley was freshly chopped.

Exceptions

Do include a hyphen after an *ly* adverb if the compound adjective contains at least two more components and those two are hyphenated. You wouldn't want to have part of a compound using hyphens, and part not.

The engineer emerged with some hastily-drawn-up plans.

It sounded like a poorly-thought-out strategy.

He turned in a clumsily-done-up sketch.

Very occasionally, it may not be clear whether the word that follows an adverb is linked with the adverb or with whatever lies on its *other* side. For example:

> Try as she would, she couldn't get around the maddeningly slow moving van.

Is the reference here to a moving van that is maddeningly slow or to a plain old van that's moving maddeningly slowly? If the former is intended, a hyphen to combine *maddeningly* with *slow* would make it clear which word gets linked with which.

> Try as she would, she couldn't get around the maddeningly-slow moving van.

IN MOST CASES, DO USE A HYPHEN FOR ADVERBS THAT DO NOT END IN *LY*

The rules are more complex for adverbs that do not have *ly* endings, probably because such words may not be as instantly recognizable as adverbs. Style guides do not completely agree on how to handle these situations. Rather than prescribing *the* way to do it, this section will simply describe the alternatives.

Authorities agree that in most cases, when a "non-*ly*" adverb combines with another word to form a compound adjective modifying a noun, *do* link the two with a hyphen.

> He handed in a well-written essay.
> She stared into the still-glowing embers.
> His much-loved pet gerbil was getting old.
> It was clearly an ill-advised plan.
> A fast-talking salesman cornered them and wouldn't leave.
> The cat let out a high-pitched yowl when he accidentally dropped the cantaloupe on her head.

As before, if the compound follows the noun, omit the hyphen, unless the compound takes one as part of its proper spelling. Note that the hyphen *is* part of the spelling in quite a few of these cases.

> The essay was well written.
> The embers were still glowing.
> The gerbil was much loved.

> The salesman was fast-talking.
> The plan was ill-advised.
> The yowl was high-pitched.

The disagreement lies in whether a hyphen is needed when the modifier is a **comparative** (indicating a degree of intensity) or a **superlative** (indicating one or the other extreme). Some authorities hold that hyphens would *not* appear in the following sentences:

> She's her country's best loved poet.
> He holds the dubious distinction of being the city's least trusted politician.
> The higher ranked players went on to the next level of competition.
> The most criticized questions on the exam were eventually dropped.
> The better fitting dress, unfortunately, was the wrong color.
> The less sophisticated members of the audience applauded wildly
>   between movements.

Others would say to use *best-loved poet, least-trusted politician, higher-ranked players*, etc. Make your own decision on how to handle these constructions, and be consistent.

ACTING AS A "STAND-IN" FOR A REPEATED WORD

If a word appears more than once in a sentence and each time is linked with a different modifier, it may sound ponderous to repeat the base word each time. A useful strategy is to replace all but one occurrence of this word with a hyphen, called a **suspension hyphen**. Consider the sentence:

> His critics both overestimated and underestimated his abilities.

This could appear more neatly as:

> His critics both over- and underestimated his abilities.

The hyphen informs the reader that there is something intentionally missing; that *over* is not intended as a complete word in itself but just as the first part of a compound, the remainder of which will be identified shortly. It is important to include the hyphen, for omitting it would create momentary confusion as the reader tried to make sense of *His critics both over and.* (Note that use of the suspension hyphen is unrelated to whether or not the word it is standing in for is normally hyphenated. For example, the actual word *overestimate* does *not* take a hyphen, nor need you put one in *underestimate* to match the one in *over-*.)

If the repeated word is the *second* part of a compound—either a root word that takes different prefixes, or a suffix that attaches to different root words—write the whole compound out on its final occurrence only, and use hyphens for the earlier combinations.

> You can use either a two-, three- or four-column layout.
> At one time, scientists were interested in relating endo-, ecto- and mesomorph builds to personality.
> Referrals were given for both clinic- and hospital-based services.

If the repeated word is the *first* part of a compound, write the whole compound out on its first occurrence, and use hyphens for subsequent combinations.

> The standards committee drew up guidelines to be adhered to in both ISO-7 and -8 environments.
> The department-sponsored and -initiated programs drew high praise.

Note: Even when applied correctly, the suspension hyphen has the potential of obscuring meaning or making a sentence look awkward. Think carefully before you include it, and don't overuse it.

INDICATING SPECIAL INTONATIONS OR PRONUNCIATIONS

The hyphen has a few applications in dialogue that let you achieve various effects of tone and pronunciation.

SPELLING A WORD OUT

Hyphens between each of the letters of a word indicate that it is to be pronounced letter-by-letter, rather than as a word.

> '. . . Now, then, where's the first boy?'
> 'Please, sir, he's cleaning the back parlour window,' said the temporary head of the philosophical class.

'So he is, to be sure,' rejoined Squeers. 'We go upon the practical mode of teaching, Nickleby; the regular education system. C-l-e-a-n, clean, verb active, to make bright, to scour. W-i-n, win, d-e-r, der, winder, a casement. When the boy knows this out of book, he goes and does it. It's just the same principle as the use of the globes. Where's the second boy?'

'Please, sir, he's weeding the garden,' replied a small voice.

'To be sure,' said Squeers, by no means disconcerted. 'So he is. B-o-t, bot, t-i-n, tin, bottin, n-e-y, bottinney, noun substantive, a knowledge of plants. When he has learned that bottinney means a knowledge of plants, he goes and knows 'em. That's our system, Nickleby: What do you think of it? '

'It's a very useful one, at any rate,' answered Nicholas significantly.

—CHARLES DICKENS, *Nicholas Nickleby*

A SLIGHT PAUSE FOR EMPHASIS

'She sot down,' said Joe, 'and she got up, and she made a grab at Tickler, and she Ram-paged out. That's what she did,' said Joe, slowly clearing the fire between the lower bars with the poker, and looking at it: 'she Ram-paged out, Pip.'

—CHARLES DICKENS, *Great Expectations*

A DRAWN-OUT INTONATION

"You're having a time, Sherman. What on earth are you doing?"

Without looking up: "I'm taking Marshall for a wa-a-a-a-alk."

Walk came out as a groan, because the dachshund attempted a fishtail maneuver and Sherman had to wrap his arm around the dog's midsection.

—TOM WOLFE, *The Bonfire of the Vanities*

A LILTING OR SINGSONG INTONATION

"Eddy! Boomer! Where are those [expletive] trainers?" a voice bellows. It is almost noon, and in the final panic of getting ready, laces get broken, tape and cotton are urgently needed, and it's a question we're all asking. In an eminently reasonable, hide-and-seek voice, Robinson calls out, "Oh Ed-dy, Boo-mer, you can come out now. We give up."

—KEN DRYDEN, *The Game*

ROLLED *R*'S OR HISSED *S*'S

Bilbo seeing what had happened and having nothing better to ask stuck to his question, "What have I got in my pocket?" he said louder.

"S-s-s-s-s," hissed Gollum. "It must give us three guesseses, my preciouss, three guesseses."

"Very well! Guess away!" said Bilbo.

"Handses!" said Gollum.

"Wrong," said Bilbo, who had luckily just taken his hand out again. "Guess again!"

"S-s-s-s-s," said Gollum more upset than ever. He thought of all the things he kept in his own pockets: fishbones, goblins' teeth, wet shells, a bit of bat-wing, a sharp stone to sharpen his fangs on, and other nasty things. He tried to think what other people kept in their pockets.

—J.R.R. Tolkien, *The Hobbit*

. . . [T]he Lady, who rode side-saddle and wore a long, fluttering dress of dazzling green, was lovelier still.

"Good day, t-r-r-avellers," she cried out in a voice as sweet as the sweetest bird's song, trilling her R's delightfully. "Some of you are young pilgrims to walk this rough waste."

"That's as may be, Ma'am," said Puddleglum very stiffly and on his guard.

"We're looking for the ruined city of the giants," said Jill.

"The r-r-ruined city?" said the Lady. "That is a strange place to be seeking. . ."

—C.S. Lewis, *The Silver Chair*

STUTTERING, STAMMERING OR TEETH-CHATTERING

. . . the first time Joshua had been invited there for dinner, Trimble had grasped his hand, indicated the bronzed young man scraping the dock, and said, "I want you to meet a future prime minister of Canada."

Charlie dipped his head, blushed, and said, "P-p-pleased to meet you, Mr. Sh-sh-shapiro."

—Mordecai Richler, *Joshua Then and Now*

To indicate an actual cutting off of speech, use a dash instead. For discussion of this use of the dash, turn to page 158.

Slash (/)

The slash (also known as the *diagonal* or *slant*, or more esoterically as the *solidus, virgule* or *shilling*) is a somewhat nebulous mark. There are a couple of situations where no other punctuation will do, but often it is used as a casual shorthand for more precise modes of expression. Since it runs the risk of being ambiguous, it should be applied with caution. In more formal genres of writing, such as that expected for academic journals, it may be considered too informal or imprecise to be used at all.

The functions of the slash are as follows:

- Indicating "and" or "or" relationships
- Indicating various other relationships between words or numbers
- Separating lines of poetry

INDICATING "AND" OR "OR" RELATIONSHIPS

The slash may be variously used to indicate options, dual roles and alternatives.

• As a symbol for *and*, it may be used to identify an entity that has more than one characterization or function.

> She liked to describe her position as that of vice-president of finances/
> baby-sitter.
> The trial/media circus has the city in a frenzy.
> The one room in his tiny apartment had to serve as a bedroom/workshop.

(Note that if you were vocalizing such sentences you would say, "vice-president of finances slash baby-sitter" and "trial slash media circus," since the significance of the relationship cannot be inferred from the words alone.)

Linking words with a hyphen doesn't carry the same meaning, since the function of the hyphen is to form a new compound word. With a slash, each word retains its independence. If your intention is to form a compound, the hyphen is probably the more appropriate mark.

A more formal way of expressing the type of relationship expressed by the slash is to use the Latin word *cum*, optionally italicized and linked to the other words with hyphens: *a trial-cum-media circus, a bedroom-cum-workshop.*

• The slash may serve to connect two distinct entities that are either parts of a whole or closely affiliated.

> The audio/video controls are at the back of the console.
> Her specialty is obstetrics/gynecology.
> If you enter, you will be eligible to win a washer/dryer set, a radio/cassette
>   player and other exciting prizes!

In more formal writing, use the word *and* instead, or link the related words with a hyphen (if appropriate).

• In situations that present two clear alternatives, the slash is often an acceptable symbol for *or*.

> The graduate courses are graded pass/fail.
> In the second part of the exam, the questions were true/false.
> If a player draws an ace, he/she loses a turn.
> Dear Sir/Madam:

In more formal writing, use the word *or* instead. (It should also be noted that many people balk at *he/she*—and hit the roof over *s/he*. For more on this, see the section on pronouns in "Writing With Sensitivity" on page 297.)

• Probably the most common use of the slash is in the combination *and/or*, which is an efficient way of expressing a slightly unwieldy concept. It can be useful for scenarios where the possibilities are option *a*, option *b* or both: That is, *a* and *b* do not necessarily coexist, but they are not mutually exclusive either.

> The tent offers suitable protection against cold and/or windy conditions.
> Headings may be set in bold type and/or capital letters.
> Ingredients: Sugar, glucose, fructose, palm and/or coconut oil, artificial
>   flavor and color.

Some authorities frown on this quasi-word, viewing it as a lazy substitute for more carefully crafted phrasing; others accept it. In more formal writing, it is usually better to use a few extra words in order to avoid it.

• Since a slash can indicate either "and" or "or," there are situations where it might not be clear which of these conjunctions is intended. In some cases either word would do, so the reader's interpretation doesn't really matter.

> Come to beautiful Mount Avalanche for a weekend of cross-country
>   skiing/alpine skiing.
> The new policy is aimed only at contract employees. Regular full-time/
>   part-time employees will not be affected.

In other cases, its use could result in ambiguity.

> Please do not use the library/study between noon and six.
> The figures/illustrations are not complete.

Are these two separate rooms, or one room with a dual purpose? Two different groups of artwork, or two terms for the same thing? Avoid using the slash as a hasty shorthand, when the resulting meaning could be unclear.

INDICATING OTHER RELATIONSHIPS

Apart from indicating "and" and "or" relationships, the slash may be used for the following purposes:

SEPARATING ELEMENTS THAT ARE BEING COMPARED

> The Toronto/Montreal hockey rivalry had its heyday in the sixties.

More formal alternative: *The hockey rivalry between Toronto and Montreal.*

SEPARATING ORIGINS AND DESTINATIONS
The Los Angeles/Sydney flight was fully booked.

More formal alternatives: *The Los Angeles-to-Sydney flight* or *The Los Angeles–Sydney flight.* (See "The En Dash" on page 162.)

SEPARATING THE NUMERALS MAKING UP A DATE
01/01/97
12/10/1995

INDICATING A PERIOD SPANNING TWO CALENDAR YEARS
academic year 1997/98
records from 1955/56

AS A SHORTHAND DESIGNATION FOR *PER*
$5/yard
sixty words/minute
100 km/hour

More formal alternative: *$5 per yard; sixty words per minute.*

INDICATING DIVISION OR FRACTIONS
6/3 = 2	1/2
x/y = z	2/3

SEPARATING LINES OF POETRY

Use the slash to separate lines of a poem or song that are run in with a prose sentence. (For longer excerpts, set off the lines vertically.)

"And what about his trademark, the whistle?"

"That was heard by the three people who came quickly on the scene after the Easthaven murder. One just heard a whistle, one said it sounded like a hymn and the third, who was a churchwoman, claimed she could identify it precisely, 'Now the Day Is Over.' We kept quiet about that. It could be useful when we get the usual clutch of nutters claiming they're the Whistler. But there seems no doubt that he does whistle."

Dalgliesh said: " 'Now the day is over / Night is drawing nigh / Shadows of the evening / Fall across the sky.' It's a Sunday-school hymn, hardly the kind that gets requested on *Songs of Praise*, I should have thought."

—P.D. JAMES, *Devices and Desires*

Leave a space on either side of the slash when using it for this purpose.

Parentheses ( )

The function of parentheses is to set off an element that "interrupts" a flow of thought significantly. The element must be relevant enough to merit being worked in where it is, but enough of an aside to require being set off distinctly. Text that is appropriate for parentheses is usually either an explanation, amplification or example of the topic the sentence is dealing with, or some digression that bears a relationship to the topic, but not a tight one. If a digression, it must not be a non sequitur (something with no logical connection to anything previously said): It must have some bearing on what precedes it, and this connection should be evident to the reader. Parentheses are not simply places to stash stray bits of information that don't quite fit in anywhere else.

Digressive elements may be set off with either commas, dashes or parentheses. Thus, how do you decide when it's appropriate to use each? Sometimes the decision is obvious; sometimes it's more a matter of achieving a particular tone. In general, commas serve to integrate a digressive element unobtrusively; dashes serve to draw particular attention to it; and parentheses serve to *de*-emphasize it, signaling to the reader that the text is temporarily getting off the track. These distinctions aren't hard-and-fast, though, and in some cases the effect of parentheses may be to draw more, rather than less, attention to what they enclose. It very much depends on context.

Don't overuse parentheses, as they can be distracting and may make your writing look choppy and awkward. If you find yourself sprinkling them around liberally, ask yourself whether all those asides really need to be included.

Parentheses are useful for accomplishing the following:

- Working in digressions
- Making complex text easier to follow
- Setting off minor details

WORKING IN DIGRESSIONS

You may use parentheses to enclose either digressions within a sentence or digressions of one or more stand-alone sentences.

When a parenthesized element is part of a sentence, it does not have any impact on the structure of the rest of the sentence: It may fit in grammatically, or it may not. The parts that come before and after it are treated as if it weren't there, and must mesh with each other, both grammatically and logically, just as they would if nothing intervened between them.

Within a sentence, a parenthesized element may be a single word,

> After considerable pleading, she finally got him to reveal the secret ingredient (sarsaparilla).

a sentence fragment,

> It turned out that they liked the same toppings on pizza (truffles, green peppers, sardines and a dash of coriander), which cemented their relationship.

or a grammatically complete unit;

> The race for second place (first place, of course, was a foregone conclusion) was still wide open.

or there may be more than one parenthesized segment.

> Brian gave the impression of never shutting up. This was not quite true, though, because he *did* stop talking when he slept. But when he finally flipped his cookies (as we politely said in my immediate family) or showed symptoms of schizophrenia (as one of his many psychiatrists put it) or woke up to the real meaning of his life (as he put it) or had a nervous breakdown (as his Ph.D. adviser put it) or became-exhausted-as-a-result-of-being-married-to-that-Jewish-princess-from-New York

145

(as his parents put it)—then he never stopped talking *even* to sleep. He stopped sleeping, in fact. . . .

—ERICA JONG, *Fear of Flying*

When parentheses enclose one or more independent sentences, the text following the interrupting element must pick up exactly where the text preceding it left off. The parenthesized sentences may be part of a paragraph,

As she said these words her foot slipped, and in another moment, splash! she was up to her chin in salt water. Her first idea was that she had somehow fallen into the sea, "and in that case I can go back by railway," she said to herself. (Alice had been to the seaside once in her life, and had come to the general conclusion that, wherever you go on the English coast, you find a number of bathing machines in the sea, some children digging in the sand with wooden spades, then a row of lodging houses, and behind them a railway station.) However, she soon made out that she was in the pool of tears which she had wept when she was nine feet high.

—LEWIS CARROLL, *Alice in Wonderland*

or an entire paragraph.

In the end, I always want potatoes. Mashed potatoes. Nothing like mashed potatoes when you're feeling blue. Nothing like getting into bed with a bowl of hot mashed potatoes already loaded with butter, and methodically adding a thin cold slice of butter to every forkful. The problem with mashed potatoes, though, is that they require almost as much work as crisp potatoes, and when you're feeling blue the last thing you feel like is hard work. Of course, you can always get someone to make the mashed potatoes for you, but let's face it: the reason you're blue is that there *isn't* anyone to make them for you. As a result, most people do not have nearly enough mashed potatoes in their lives, and when they do, it's almost always at the wrong time.

(You can, of course, train children to mash potatoes, but you should know that Richard Nixon spent most of his childhood making mashed potatoes for his mother and was extremely methodical about getting the lumps out. A few lumps make mashed potatoes more authentic,

if you ask me, but that's not the point. The point is that perhaps
children should not be trained to mash potatoes.)

For mashed potatoes: Put 1 large (or 2 small) potatoes in a large
pot of salted water and bring to a boil. . . .

—Nora Ephron, *Heartburn*

There is no specific limit to the length of what may be put in
parentheses, but it is inadvisable to set off *too* long a section, as the
reader may have forgotten what preceded the digression by the time
the closing mark finally appears. If you find yourself setting off anything longer than a paragraph, you should probably rethink the
structure of your work.

MAKING TEXT EASIER TO FOLLOW

Parentheses aren't always planned in advance: Sometimes their
desirability becomes apparent only after you have looked over a first
draft. If you need to cram dense amounts of information into your
writing, you might find that adding parentheses in certain places
serves to make the main points easier to follow. Consider using them
when you want to work in elements that are important, but not
primary, and you do not want these elements to distract from others
that are more vital.

This strategy is often useful in technical or academic writing,
where many complex and interrelated items of information have to
be presented as concisely as possible. For example:

The "Save As" feature lets you save an existing file to either the main drive
  or the extra drive under a new name so that you now have two copies
  of the same file.

Many readers would miss the fact that this sentence contains two
discrete pieces of information. Its main message is *The "Save As"
feature lets you save an existing file under a new name so that
you now have two copies of the same file.* The information about
where this new file can be saved, while useful, is separate and secondary. Putting it within parentheses would prevent it from distracting the reader from the main thread.

BETTER: The "Save As" feature lets you save an existing file under a new name (to either the main drive or the extra drive) so that you now have two copies of the same file.

The next example presents a similar problem:

Error messages are recorded on the local and the host message queues. The local message queue has the same name as the session. To find out the cause of the failure, use the information in both message queues.

Readers—even those who understand the jargon—might have trouble spotting that two of these three sentences are critically related. The main thread here is that there are two message queues (whatever those are!) and the user must apply the information in *both* queues in order to solve a problem. The secondary information is that one of these two message queues is identified in a particular way. Subsuming this secondary information in parentheses would make the relationship between the first and third sentences clearer.

BETTER: Error messages are recorded on the local and the host message queues. (The local message queue has the same name as the session.) To find out the cause of the failure, use the information in both message queues.

Parentheses can also be employed to make text read more smoothly and concisely.

A validity coefficient cannot exceed the square root of the reliability coefficient. For example, if the reliability of a test is .70, the test validity cannot exceed .83. If the validity coefficient exceeds the square root of the reliability coefficient, a sampling error has occurred.

Note the unwieldiness of the third sentence, which repeats the entire contents of the first. It would be nice to avoid this repetition by using a pronoun, but the second sentence prevents this, since it would intervene between the pronoun and its antecedent. (See "Referring to the Right Antecedent" on page 249.) If this sentence were enclosed in parentheses, however, the third sentence could be constructed as though it came immediately after the first. That is, the second sentence would effectively "not be there" as far as the rest of the text is concerned. Since it is just an example, subsuming it does no harm to the flow.

BETTER: A validity coefficient cannot exceed the square root of the reliability coefficient. (For example, if the reliability of a test is .70, the test validity cannot exceed .83.) If it does, a sampling error has occurred.

SETTING OFF DETAILS

Parentheses are employed to set off a variety of small details that may need to be worked into a sentence. Some common examples of this type of use are listed below.

SHORT CLARIFICATIONS

The settlement is 80 kilometers (about 50 miles) from the nearest town.

The one-way fare is $200 (U.S.).

TELEPHONE AREA CODES

For directory information for New York City, dial (212) 555-1212.

BIRTH/DEATH DATES

Marie Curie (1867–1934) was the first person to be awarded a second Nobel prize.

NUMBERS OR LETTERS USED FOR LISTING ITEMS

For lists run in with the regular text, the numbers may be set off either with parentheses on both sides or with just a closing parenthesis.

Look for the following features in a good word processing system: (1) spell-checking, (2) grammar-checking, (3) word count and (4) some minor graphics abilities.

Look for the following features in a good word processing system: 1) spell-checking, 2) grammar-checking, 3) word count and 4) some minor graphics abilities.

For list items laid out with vertical spacing, the numbers or letters may be set off with full parentheses, closing parentheses, colons, periods, hyphens or dashes.

REFERENCES

In some academic styles, citations of quoted sources (whether presented as names or numbers) are enclosed in parentheses.

> The leading proponents of this theory (Maxwell, 1986; Rosenberg & Terrence, 1995) agree that the process must be sensitive to issues of timing.
> Other researchers, however, have found conflicting results (3, 8, 12).

Some styles specify the use of square brackets or superscript numbers instead. In formal writing, you are usually expected to follow the specifications of a particular guide.

ABBREVIATIONS

If you are using an abbreviation for a name or term, it is sometimes appropriate on the first occurrence to spell out the full term followed by the abbreviation in parentheses, or (less commonly) vice versa. Once the abbreviation has been defined, it may be used without further explanation.

> The Organization of African Unity (OAU) was founded in 1963.
> Many users feel most comfortable with programs designed to be WYSIWYG (What You See Is What You Get).

Do not do this with abbreviations assumed to be common knowledge; for example, U.S.A., NBC.

STYLE CONVENTIONS

• Don't leave spaces around the enclosed text (like this). Place the opening and closing marks directly next to the text (like this).

An exception is if you are using parentheses to enclose a symbol, as might occur in some forms of technical writing. For example, (.) and (*) are easier to read than (.) and (*).

• Try to avoid putting parenthetical text within parenthetical text; the structure may become difficult to follow. If you must do so, make the inner parentheses square brackets instead.

> Subjects from the other two study sites (rural [N = 58] and urban [N = 60]) were followed for four months.

• It is permissible to use a pair of dashes within parentheses, but think before you do so. The parenthesized text is already an aside, and it can be distracting to have an aside within an aside. (See "Marking Off a Descriptive Element or Digression" on page 154.)

• Ensure that parentheses always come in pairs. Particularly with longer elements, writers occasionally forget that text is parenthetical, and neglect to close it off.

• When parentheses enclose a sentence that stands alone, put the terminal punctuation mark *inside* the parentheses.

Dealing with multiple punctuation marks in a single sentence can be tricky. (The positioning of parentheses and periods is a case in point.)
The shoe was now on the other foot. (Or was it?)
For weeks afterward, he kept a wide berth of the shop. (Evidently, he had learned his lesson!)

• When parentheses enclose just part of a sentence, observe the following conventions:

—Put the terminal punctuation mark *outside* the parentheses, even if the parenthesized element comes at the end.

The promotion was unanimously approved (although some members privately had their doubts).
Do you really think this move is necessary (because if not, we still have time to cancel it)?
After all, *someone* has to win (ridiculous as the odds are)!

(In the case of exclamation points, note that it would actually be somewhat counterproductive to put parenthesized text at the end of the sentence, since the purpose of an exclamation point is to impart excitement or urgency, and the interruption would detract from this. If you ever do construct such a sentence, analyze it carefully. It is likely that recasting it would improve it.)

—If a comma, semicolon or colon is needed between what precedes and follows the parentheses, put it *after* the closing parenthesis—not before the opening one, and not in both places.

The room contained only a sofa (much the worse for wear), a faded armchair and a carpet (if that stained and threadbare square could be called such); the other furnishings had long since been sold off.

—If the parenthesized element is a complete grammatical sentence, do not begin it with a capital letter, and do not end it with a period.

> It was well past the appointed hour (the shops had already closed, and the streetlights were coming on) when she arrived.

You may however end it in one of the other terminal punctuation marks.

> Her sour face (did it ever look otherwise?) peered suspiciously around the doorway.
> Factors that contributed to the success of the group included friendship (we actually enjoyed seeing each other!) and acceptance of criticism.

—Regardless of what punctuation appears within the parentheses, don't omit the appropriate terminal punctuation mark for the overall sentence. Remember, always treat the rest of the sentence as though the parenthesized element wasn't there.

> We actually managed to finish on time (a first!).
> Can you possibly get the report in by Tuesday (Wednesday would be the absolute latest!)?
> The reading assignments consisted of three novels and one play *(Who's Afraid of Virginia Woolf?)*.

Dashes

Dashes come in several sizes, so strictly speaking the term refers to more than one mark. There is the **en dash**, which is roughly the width of the capital letter *N* in whatever font is being used; the **em dash**, which is the width of the letter *M;* and the **2-em dash** and **3-em dash**, which are the widths of two and three side-by-side *M*'s, respectively. (Not every font will follow these specifications literally. The important point is that an en dash is distinctively longer than a hyphen, an em dash is longer than an en dash, a 2-em dash is longer than an em dash, and a 3-em dash is the longest of all.)

The em dash is by far the most commonly used of these marks and, except to sticklers such as editors and typesetters, is almost always what is meant by the unqualified term *dash*. The en dash has its uses but comes up in only a few specialized circumstances, while 2- and 3-em dashes are downright esoteric.

The Em Dash (—)

The em dash serves the following functions:

- Marking off a descriptive element or digression
- Marking an abrupt break in structure or turn in content
- Indicating interrupted or scattered speech
- Setting off the source of a quotation

MARKING OFF A DESCRIPTIVE ELEMENT OR DIGRESSION

A pair of dashes can be employed in two ways: It acts to draw particular attention to elements that you wish to emphasize, and it lets you veer off in a different direction temporarily and then get back on the original track.

In the first role, dashes may be used to set off such elements as identifying information, descriptions, examples and lists. In this role, they function much as commas do (see the discussion of parenthetical text under "Comma" on page 71). Consider using them instead of commas if you want to emphasize an element; if the element is not integral to the sentence and you want to distance it somewhat; or if the element consists of a series of subelements that already contains commas, and surrounding it by more commas might make the punctuation difficult to follow. More than one of these reasons, of course, may apply in a given situation.

Even Georgette—a girl who knew which side her bread was buttered on—had her doubts.

The board members—with the conspicuous absence of the president— met to discuss the missing funds.

Several of the neighbors—the Walkers, Goldbergs and Millhouses—
started a petition to get rid of the Boylstons' rooster.

The more subjective measures—the patients' energy levels, health
outlooks and emotional well-being—tended to correlate more highly
with the charts than did the objective measures.

In another role, dashes act much like parentheses. The difference
is that their effect is usually to emphasize a digression rather than
subsume it. In general, text enclosed by dashes is more integral to
the sentence than text enclosed by parentheses. As with parentheses, the digressive text may or may not be grammatically congru-
ent with the rest. (See "Parentheses" on page 144.)

[The hair was] grey at the root, the rest dyed a vivid metallic orange.
Dirk pursed his lips and thought very deeply. He didn't need to think
hard in order to realise who the hair belonged to—there was only one
person who regularly entered the kitchen looking as if her head had
been used for extracting metal oxides from industrial wastes—but he
did have seriously to consider the implications of the discovery that
she had been plastering her hair across the door of his fridge.

It meant that the silently waged conflict between himself and his
cleaning lady had escalated to a new and more frightening level. It
was now, Dirk reckoned, fully three months since this fridge door had
been opened, and each of them was grimly determined not to be the
one to open it first. . . .

—Douglas Adams, *The Long Dark Tea-Time of the Soul*

. . . I am now living, for economy's sake, in a little town in Brittany,
inhabited by a select circle of serious English friends, and possessed of
the inestimable advantages of a Protestant clergyman and a cheap
market.

In this retirement—a Patmos amid the howling ocean of Popery
that surrounds us—a letter from England has reached me at last. I find
my insignificant existence suddenly remembered by Mr. Franklin Blake.
My wealthy relative—would that I could add my spiritually-wealthy
relative!—writes, without even an attempt at disguising that he wants
something of me. The whim has seized him to stir up the deplorable
scandal of the Moonstone; and I am to help him by writing the account

of what I myself witnessed while visiting at Aunt Verinder's house in London. Pecuniary remuneration is offered to me—with the want of feeling peculiar to the rich. . . . My nature is weak. It cost me a hard struggle, before Christian humility conquered sinful pride, and self-denial accepted the cheque.

—WILKIE COLLINS, *The Moonstone*

Note that the distinctions between using dashes, commas or parentheses may not always be cut-and-dried, and you may sometimes want to play with the different marks to see which effect looks best.

MARKING A BREAK IN STRUCTURE OR TURN IN CONTENT

Dashes come in singles as well as doubles. Use an em dash if your text is going along in one direction, then suddenly veers off in another. That is, you can abruptly end a thought midstream, leave it hanging and start another thought, all in the same sentence. There must be some logical connectedness between what precedes and follows the dash, but there does not have to be any grammatical connectedness.

This hobbit was a very well-to-do hobbit, and his name was Baggins. The Bagginses have lived in the neighbourhood of The Hill for time out of mind, and people considered them very respectable, not only because most of them were rich, but also because they never had any adventures or did anything unexpected: you could tell what a Baggins would say on any question without the bother of asking him. This is a story of how a Baggins had an adventure, and found himself doing and saying things altogether unexpected. He may have lost the neighbours' respect, but he gained—well, you will see whether he gained anything in the end.

The mother of our particular hobbit—what is a hobbit? I suppose hobbits need some description nowadays. . . .

—J.R.R. TOLKIEN, *The Hobbit*

'I do appreciate, Mrs Sauskind,' continued Dirk, 'that the cost of the investigation has strayed somewhat from the original estimate, but I am sure that you will in your turn appreciate that a job which takes seven years to do must clearly be more difficult than one that can be pulled off in an afternoon and must therefore be charged at a higher rate. . . .'

The babble from the phone became even more frantic.

'My dear Mrs Sauskind—or may I call you Joyce? Very well then. My dear Mrs Sauskind, let me say this. Do not worry yourself about this bill, do not let it alarm or discomfit you. Do not, I beg you, let it become a source of anxiety to you. Just grit your teeth and pay it.'

—DOUGLAS ADAMS, *Dirk Gently's Holistic Detective Agency*

It is also appropriate to use an em dash when text that appears to be heading for a predictable ending suddenly takes an unexpected turn, or otherwise reaches a conclusion worthy of extra emphasis. In this case, all parts of the sentence mesh grammatically; the dash is not acting to divide grammatically independent structures, but rather to draw special attention to what follows.

> She planned the trip for months, got her hands on all the travel information she could find, booked the hotel—and then called the whole thing off.

> The room was the picture of order, the mahogany furniture gleamed, not an ornament on the shelves was out of place nor a painting on the wall askew—the only note of discord was the corpse draped over the back of the chesterfield.

> . . . In a trice, I remember'd my Poem, writ last Night upon the Tablecloth, and hastily flipp'd 'neath the Capon before the foul Debauch.
>
> I clamber'd out of Bed to seek for it, walkt gently upon the Floor so as not to wake Tunewell again, flipp'd o'er the Tablecloth—and lo! found that my Words were smudged out of the Linen! Bits of Charcoal clung here and there where my Epick's grand Opening Lines had been!

—ERICA JONG, *Fanny*

DASH OR COLON?

The colon is another punctuation mark that acts to draw attention to what follows it, and there is undeniably some overlap between it and the dash (see the discussion on page 101). However, a colon is usually most appropriate if the relationship between the opening and concluding parts of the sentence is straightforward, and a dash is appropriate if this relationship contains something unexpected. If either mark would meet your purpose, it is preferable to use the more low-keyed colon, as the dash is stronger and will lose its punch if overused. Reserve it for situations where you want its dramatic impact.

Caution: Some authors go wildly overboard with the dash, applying it wherever any sort of break in a sentence seems to be needed. Such sloppy usage may be acceptable in rough drafts and informal memos, but will not enhance serious writing.

INDICATING INTERRUPTED DIALOGUE

In dialogue, the em dash serves to indicate broken-off speech. One speaker can interrupt another:

> "Listen, I'm serious," I said. "No kidding. Why's it better in the East?"
>
> "It's too involved to go into, for God's sake," old Luce said. "They simply happen to regard sex as both a physical and a spiritual experience. If you think I'm—"
>
> "So do I! So do I regard it as a wuddayacallit—a physical and spiritual experience and all. I really do. But it depends on who the hell I'm doing it with. If I'm doing it with someone I don't even—"
>
> "Not so *loud*, for God's sake, Caulfield. If you can't manage to keep your voice down, let's drop the whole—"
>
> "All right, but listen," I said. I was getting excited and I *was* talking a little too loud. Sometimes I talk a little loud when I get excited.
> —J.D. Salinger, *The Catcher in the Rye*

A speaker can stop abruptly without being interrupted:

> ". . . I took a corkscrew from the shelf:
> I went to wake them up myself.
> And when I found the door was locked,
> I pulled and pushed and kicked and knocked.

And when I found the door was shut,
I tried to turn the handle, but—"

There was a long pause.
"Is that all?" Alice timidly asked.
"That's all," said Humpty Dumpty. "Good-bye."

—LEWIS CARROLL, *Through the Looking-Glass*

A break can come in the middle of a word:

"*Tabernac,*" growls Robinson, breaking a skate lace. "Eddy, Eddy,
I need a lace!" he shouts.
"Left or right?" a voice asks.
"Ri—," he starts, then stops angrily.

—KEN DRYDEN, *The Game*

The dash also serves to indicate speech that is scattered or falter-
ing: that is, not interrupted by a second speaker, but by the speaker
breaking off a thought and starting another, or talking in disjointed
sentence fragments.

Supper was announced. The move began; and Miss Bates might be
heard from that moment without interruption, till her being seated at
table and taking up her spoon.
'Jane, Jane, my dear Jane, where are you? Here is your tippet. Mrs.
Weston begs you to put on your tippet. She says she is afraid there
will be draughts in the passage, though everything has been done—
one door nailed up—quantities of matting—my dear Jane, indeed you
must. Mr. Churchill, oh! you are too obliging. How well you put it
on—so gratified! . . . Well, this is brilliant! I am all amazement! could
not have supposed anything—such elegance and profusion! I have
seen nothing like it since—Well, where shall we sit? Where shall we
sit? Anywhere, so that Jane is not in a draught. Where *I* sit is of no
consequence. Oh! do you recommend this side? Well, I am sure, Mr.
Churchill—only it seems too good—but just as you please. What you
direct in this house cannot be wrong. Dear Jane, how shall we ever
recollect half the dishes for grandmamma? Soup too! Bless me! I should

not be helped so soon, but it smells most excellent, and I cannot help
beginning.'

—JANE AUSTEN, *Emma*

Compare the above uses of the dash with those of the ellipsis
(page 186).

SETTING OFF THE SOURCE OF A QUOTATION

The em dash is often used between a quotation and the name of its
author or source.

An author ought to consider himself, not as a gentleman who gives a
private . . . treat, but rather as one who keeps a public ordinary, at which
all persons are welcome for their money.—Henry Fielding

I don't want to achieve immortality through my work. I want to achieve
immortality through not dying.—Woody Allen

Computers in the future may weigh no more than 1.5 tons.—*Popular
Mechanics*, 1949

640K ought to be enough for anybody.—Bill Gates, 1981

STYLE CONVENTIONS

• The em dash is not a keyboard character. If you can't produce
it on your typewriter or word processor, type two hyphens (--).
• You may either leave spaces around a dash or have the dash lie
directly against the words it adjoins. Be consistent; don't leave a
space on one side of a dash but not on the other.

He suspected — no, he knew — that something was up.
He suspected—no, he knew—that something was up.

Whichever style you choose, do not put a space before a dash
that is being used to interrupt dialogue in the middle of a word.

"But I nev—" she started.

• When a dash is being used to indicate broken-off dialogue, follow
it immediately with a closing quotation mark. Do not add a comma.

"How was I supposed to—" she sputtered indignantly.

• Do not put *any* other punctuation immediately adjacent to a dash, with the exception of a question mark or exclamation point before a closing dash. Even if the text that is broken by dashes would otherwise take a comma or semicolon, do not include it.

> She shrugged her shoulders, and he went back to arguing with the brick wall.
> She shrugged her shoulders—it was all so futile—and he went back to arguing with the brick wall.

• Text that is enclosed within dashes may contain any punctuation mark other than a period. Parentheses should be avoided if possible, as the construction of an aside within an aside would be awkward.

• Do not employ both a single dash and a pair of dashes in the same sentence, as it would then be unclear which text is enclosed by the pair. The following sentence, for example, presents a challenge:

> He had a determined goal—to bring together all the parties in the dispute—students, faculty members and administrators—and get them talking.

The En Dash (–)

The en dash has two primary functions:

- Linking elements
- Substituting for a hyphen in cases where a hyphen could be unclear

Some style guides may specify other, very specialized roles for this punctuation mark; only the main ones are reviewed here.

LINKING ELEMENTS

The main use of the en dash is to serve as a link for such things as ranges of dates, times and page numbers.

1987–1997	10:30–10:45
pp. 112–116	Elizabeth I, 1533–1603
Chapters 1–8	encyclopedia volumes Q–SC

You would also use this mark if giving the birth date of someone who is still alive.

Egbert Clodhopper, 1931–

SUBSTITUTING FOR A HYPHEN
TO LINK COMPOUNDS

The hyphen has several roles. Among other functions, it may be used to link compound words, to link a prefix or a suffix to a main word and to link words that make up a compound adjective. (See the discussions of the hyphen as a component of spelling on page 23, and as a punctuation mark on page 125.)

A tricky situation can arise when two of these situations combine: that is, if you need to link two entities that themselves contain hyphens. For example:

> The anti-conscription-pro-conscription debate was turning into a
>   shouting match.

In situations such as this, use the longer en dash to link the compounds.

> The anti-conscription–pro-conscription debate was turning into a
>   shouting match.

You face a similar problem with an open compound (a compound where each word stands alone) because it may look like only the word closest to the hyphen is linked to what precedes or follows. For example, writing *the ex-prime minister* looks—just a little— like a reference to a minister who is no longer in his prime! Again, the solution is to use an en dash in place of the hyphen.

> the ex–prime minister
> a non–computer expert
> a credit card–sized calculator
> the Quebec City–Montreal flight

STYLE CONVENTIONS

• If you can't create an en dash, use a hyphen or an em dash. If your text is going to be properly typeset, the mark will be changed before publication.

• Do not leave spaces around an en dash: Always have it lie directly against the adjoining text on both sides.

2-Em (——) and
3-Em Dashes (———)

A 2-em dash is used to indicate missing letters within a word. In fiction, the device of dropping letters to disguise names or to sanitize vulgarities or profanities was once more commonly employed than it is today.

> 'If J.E. who advertised in the ——shire Herald of last Thursday, possesses the acquirements mentioned; and if she is in a position to give satisfactory references as to character and competency; a situation can be offered her where there is but one pupil, a little girl, under ten years of age; and where the salary is thirty pounds per annum. J.E. is requested to send references, name, and address, and all particulars to the direction: "Mrs Fairfax, Thornfield, near Millcote, ——shire." '
>
> —CHARLOTTE BRONTË, *Jane Eyre*

> Matters were thus restored to a perfect calm, at which the serjeant, tho' it may seem so contrary to the principles of his profession, testified his approbation. 'Why now, that's friendly,' said he; 'D——n me, I hate to see two people bear ill-will to one another, after they have had a tussel. The only way when friends quarrel, is to see it out fairly in a friendly manner, as a man may call it, either with fist, or sword, or pistol, according as they like, and then let it be all over: for my own part, d——n me if ever I love my friend better than when I am fighting with him. To bear malice is more like a Frenchman than an Englishman.'
>
> —HENRY FIELDING, *Tom Jones*

Such uses now appear rather archaic. One does occasionally see 2-em dashes being used to tame certain words deemed unfit for family newspapers, if the reporter feels obliged to include them in a quote. Another use is in transcribed material, where it is not clear what word the original author intended.

A 3-em dash indicates an entire missing word. It too may be used to indicate a missing or unclear word in transcribed material. More commonly, it is used in bibliographies to indicate the repetition of a name, where one author (or the same set of co-authors) has successive works listed.

Williams, T.R. "The structure of the socialization process in Papago Indian society." *Social Forces*, 36 (1958): 251–256.

———. A Borneo childhood. New York: Holt, Rinehardt, & Winston, 1969.

STYLE CONVENTIONS

• With a 2-em dash, do not leave any space between it and the remaining letters of the word.

• With a 3-em dash, leave spaces before and after, just as you would with the word it is standing in for.

Brackets [ ]

People often interchange the words *brackets* and *parentheses*, but, aside from some minor overlaps, these punctuation marks have quite distinct uses.

Brackets have two primary functions:

- Identifying changes to quoted material
- Enclosing digressions within parentheses

IDENTIFYING CHANGES TO QUOTED MATERIAL

If you changed any of the text in a quoted passage and did not indicate that you had done so, you would be guilty of misquoting. You may, however, make minor changes provided you clearly attribute them to yourself. The convention for identifying which words are your own is to enclose them in square brackets. Some writers use parentheses instead, which may be problematic because parentheses serve other purposes. That is, if the original material contains any parentheses of its own, readers would have a hard time distinguishing the original author's digressions from your insertions. Brackets, in contrast, are unambiguous.

Brackets may be applied to quotes derived from oral sources, such as interviews or press conferences, as well as from printed sources. They are actually more likely to be necessary in the former case, because speakers tend to choose their words more casually than writers, leading to a more frequent need for clarification.

There is no specific length limit on the text you put in brackets, but it should usually be quite brief; it is, after all, an interruption of someone else's words. If you want to make a lengthy clarification or editorial comment, it would be better to finish the quotation and then add your comments.

If you simply want to remove parts of a quoted passage that are not relevant or necessary, use ellipses instead (see page 184).

The possible reasons for making changes to quoted material are as follows:

• If you put down a passage verbatim, something about it might not be clear to your readers. For example, it may include a pronoun—she, his, it, those—that was clear in context but not in the selected fragment you are presenting. If that's the case, it may be necessary to replace the pronoun with the word or name that the speaker meant.

> **Original quotation**: "All my friends said I was a shoo-in for it, but I never got a nomination," Ms. Plotnick said mournfully.
>
> **Revised quotation**: "All my friends said I was a shoo-in for it [the Academy Award], but I never got a nomination," Ms. Plotnick said mournfully.
>
> **Revised quotation**: "All my friends said I was a shoo-in for [the Academy Award], but I never got a nomination," Ms. Plotnick said mournfully.

Note that your own text may either replace or be added to the original wording. (Do, of course, retain the original words if there is anything about them that is important.) If your words are replacing the original, they must mesh grammatically with the remainder of the sentence.

• You may feel that a quote will have more meaning for your readers if you add some relevant information, explanation or clarification. In this situation, obviously, you would not drop any of the original wording.

> **Original quotation**: Her library, for example, includes all the works of Grass and Day-Lewis.
>
> **Revised quotation**: Her library, for example, includes all the works of [German writer Günter] Grass and [British poet laureate Cecil] Day-Lewis.

> **Original quotation**: Researchers believe that the reading of Kana and Kanji characters may tap into different brain processes.

Revised quotation: Researchers believe that the reading of Kana [the Japanese phonetic script] and Kanji [the Japanese logographic script] characters may tap into different brain processes.

Note that the bracketed material may appear either before or after the text it is qualifying, as appropriate. Also, when the text within brackets is a comment or clarification, it does not have to mesh grammatically with the rest of the sentence.

• You may want to work a fragment of a quote into a sentence of your own, but need to alter it slightly so that it fits grammatically.

Original quotation: A waiter might as well serve one on a dirty plate as a journalist offer such untidy stuff as: *The University of London Press* hopes *to have ready the following additions to* their *series of . . .*—Fowler's *Modern English Usage*

Revised quotation: Another authority, Fowler, admonishes journalists against "[offering] such untidy stuff as: *The University of London Press* hopes *to have ready the following additions to* their *series of . . ."*

• If you have dropped part of a quotation by using an ellipsis and are picking it up again in the middle of a sentence, you may prefer to present the partial sentence as if it were complete—that is, capitalize it. If you do this, some formal styles of writing require that you enclose the opening capital letter in brackets to indicate that it did not appear this way in the original.

Original quotation: It need hardly be said that shortness is a merit in words. There are often reasons why shortness is not possible; much less often there are occasions when length, not shortness, is desirable. But it is a general truth that the short words are not only handier to use, but more powerful in effect; extra syllables reduce, not increase, vigour. —Fowler's *Modern English Usage*

Revised quotation: It need hardly be said that shortness is a merit in words. . . . [S]hort words are not only handier to use, but more powerful in effect; extra syllables reduce, not increase, vigour.

• You may wish to highlight something in a quote, either because you feel it holds particular significance or because it makes some point that you want to dissociate yourself from. One way to do this is to italicize the relevant text and then follow it with the words *italics mine, italics added* or *emphasis added*, in brackets. For an illustration of this, see "Underscoring a Point in a Quote" under "Italics" on page 284.

Under some circumstances, it may suit your purposes better to follow the text with an explicit comment in brackets; obviously, however, this is more intrusive. Other times, it will be best to simply present the entire quote in an uninterrupted way and have your comments follow.

• If a quotation contains a misspelling, misused word or factual error, you may want to make it clear to your readers that it's not *your* slip. The convention is to follow the offending text with the Latin word *sic*, which means "thus" or "so" (essentially, this is saying it appeared thus in the original—I didn't mistranscribe it!). Traditionally, this word is italicized and enclosed in brackets, although one sometimes sees it appear in roman type and/or in parentheses. It is always in lowercase.

> In his statement, the education minister said: "Grammar standards in our schools today is [*sic*] slipping sadly, and I intend to do something about this."
> The time is immanent [*sic*] for a popular uprising.
> He won great acclaim in the Battle of Britain in 1941 [*sic*], and after the war went on to a distinguished political career.

You may sometimes want to put *sic* after an unusual term or spelling that was used deliberately, in order to assure readers that the nonstandard word isn't a typo.

> The band's new album, *Total Waist of Time* [*sic*], contains little that is original.

Usually, however, such exceptions will speak for themselves.

The advantage of *sic* is that it provides a relatively unobtrusive way of pointing out errors. However, it must be used with discretion; applying it too enthusiastically can make you look overly earnest or even obnoxious. Don't stoop to adding it just to get in a little jab at an author's ignorance or to draw attention to errors that are irrelevant or trivial. If the error is a misspelling, it may be best to just quietly fix it, unless the blooper is somehow relevant. If the quote is from a culture or an era with different rules of spelling or usage, it would be inappropriate to imply that incidences of these are errors.

ENCLOSING DIGRESSIONS WITHIN PARENTHESES

Digressions in text are typically enclosed in parentheses, but what do you do if you need to put a digression within a digression? Placing parentheses inside parentheses could be confusing, as readers might mistake the closing parenthesis of the nested unit as indicating the close of the whole thing. The convention is to enclose the inner digression in square brackets, since brackets and parentheses are easily distinguished. Examples of this type of construction come up most often in academic or scientific writing. For an illustration, see the style conventions under "Parentheses" on page 150.

Brackets within parentheses may look awkward, so avoid this construction unless absolutely necessary. If possible, try to either recast the sentence or see if commas could be used instead (see the discussion of parenthetical commas on page 71).

OTHER USES OF BRACKETS

Apart from their main functions, brackets have a few roles to play in certain types of specialized writing.

• In stage and film scripts, they may be used instead of parentheses to enclose stage directions.

• In scholarly writing, they are sometimes used instead of parentheses to enclose reference citations, which may be either names or numbers. For example, the appearance of [1] following a quote or description means that this information is attributable to the first author listed in the reference section. Some style guides specify to cite the author's name and date of publication instead: For example, [Leung, 1996].

• If a word in a document is missing or illegible, the publisher or editor may surmise what it should be and fill it in, enclosed in square brackets to clarify that it was not in the original. Note that this situation is far likelier to arise with older, handwritten manuscripts than with modern writing.

By Mrs Hurst and Miss Bingley they were noticed only by a curtsey; and, on their being seated, a pause, awkward as such pauses must always be, succeeded for a few moments. It was first broken by Mrs Annesley, a genteel, agreeable-looking woman, whose [endeavour] to introduce some kind of discourse proved her to be more truly well-bred than either of the others; and between her and Mrs Gardiner, with occasional help from Elizabeth, the conversation was carried on.

—JANE AUSTEN, *Pride and Prejudice*

• In mathematical equations, various styles of brackets are used to clarify which numbers are grouped with which. The placement of parentheses and brackets is reversed from what it is with text, with parentheses appearing within brackets. For example:

$$a = [(b + 1)/(x)] - [(2b)/(x + 3)]$$

Other styles of brackets are curly brackets { } and angle brackets < >, which are usually reserved for specialized uses in certain technical and mathematical fields.

STYLE CONVENTIONS

• Don't leave spaces around the text enclosed by brackets [like this]. Place the opening and closing marks directly next to the text [like this].

• Unlike parentheses, brackets may be immediately preceded by other punctuation, such as a comma. Simply treat the rest of the quotation as you would if it still contained the original words.

Original quotation: Well, they may be in their infancy right now, but there's some very exciting work being done on them.

Revised quotation: Well, [bibliographic visualization tools] may be in their infancy right now, but there's some very exciting work being done on them.

Quotation Marks (" ")

Quotation marks have several distinct functions:

- Setting off dialogue
- Setting off citations
- Setting off words that are meant in a special way
- Setting off titles

SETTING OFF DIALOGUE

This function, of course, is a very familiar one. In text that includes dialogue, quotation marks serve to set off speech from narrative, and one speaker's words from another's. Quotation marks are required at the beginning and end of each speaker's lines.

Begin a new paragraph each time the speaker changes.

> They watched the news, dutifully, and then they went out to the sun porch and sat at their grandparents' card table. They played something called Vaccination—a card game they'd invented as children, which had grown so convoluted over the years that no one else had the patience to learn it. In fact, more than one outsider had accused them of altering the rules to suit the circumstances. "Now just a minute," Sarah had said, back when she still had hopes of figuring it out. "I thought you said aces were high."
>
> "They are."
>
> "So that means—"
>
> "But not when they're drawn from the deck."
>
> "Aha! Then why was the one that Rose drew counted high?"
>
> "Well, she did draw it after a deuce, Sarah."

"Aces drawn after a deuce are high?"

"No, aces drawn after a number that's been drawn two times in a row just before that."

Sarah had folded her fan of cards and laid them face down—the last of the wives to give up.

—ANNE TYLER, *The Accidental Tourist*

This convention may occasionally be broken if the spoken lines are brief and if the effect of the writing would be enhanced by breaking the paragraph only when the scene changes.

"We're going through!" The Commander's voice was like thin ice breaking. He wore his full-dress uniform, with the heavily braided white cap pulled down rakishly over one cold grey eye. "We can't make it, sir. It's spoiling for a hurricane, if you ask me." "I'm not asking you, Lieutenant Berg," said the Commander. "Throw on the power lights! Rev her up to 8,500! We're going through!" The pounding of the cylinders increased: ta-pocketa-pocketa-pocketa-*pocketa-pocketa*. The Commander stared at the ice forming on the pilot window. He walked over and twisted a row of complicated dials. "Switch on No. 8 auxiliary!" he shouted. "Switch on No. 8 auxiliary!" repeated Lieutenant Berg. "Full strength in No. 3 turret!" shouted the Commander. "Full strength in No. 3 turret!" The crew, bending to their various tasks in the huge, hurtling eight-engined Navy hydroplane, looked at each other and grinned. "The Old Man'll get us through," they said to one another. "The Old Man ain't afraid of Hell!"

"Not so fast! You're driving too fast!" said Mrs. Mitty. "What are you driving so fast for?"

—JAMES THURBER, *The Secret Life of Walter Mitty*

As a rule, however, follow the standard form of starting a new paragraph for each speaker.

If one speaker's dialogue runs more than a paragraph, put opening quotation marks at the start of each paragraph but a closing mark only at the end of the last one, since the closing mark is the signal that the speech has ended.

Frodo sat silent and motionless. Fear seemed to stretch out a vast hand, like a dark cloud rising in the East and looming up to engulf him. 'This ring!' he stammered. 'How, how on earth did it come to me?'

'Ah!' said Gandalf. 'That is a very long story. The beginnings lie back in the Black Years, which only the lore-masters now remember. If I were to tell you all that tale, we should still be sitting here when Spring had passed into Winter.

'But last night I told you of Sauron the Great, the Dark Lord. The rumours that you heard are true: he has indeed arisen again and left his hold in Mirkwood and returned to his ancient fastness in the Dark Tower of Mordor. That name even you hobbits have heard of, like a shadow on the borders of old stories. Always after a defeat and a re-spite, the Shadow takes another shape and grows again.'

—J.R.R. TOLKIEN, *The Lord of the Rings*

Nondialogue text may appear in the same paragraph as dialogue.

'Nice furniture!' said Haresh, in the belief that this was the kind of small talk that needed to be made.

Meenakshi looked at him and forbore from comment.

But Mrs Khandelwal gazed at him with her sweetest, most charming expression. He had provided her with an opportunity to say what she had been waiting to say. 'Do you think so?' she asked Haresh. 'It has been done by Kamdar's—Kamdar's of Bombay. Half our rooms are decorated by them.'

Meenakshi looked at the heavy corner-settee—in dark, solid wood with dark blue upholstery. 'If you like this sort of thing, you can always get it in Calcutta,' she said. 'There's the Chowringhee Sales Bureau, for instance, for old-fashioned furniture. And if you want something more modern in style, there's always Mozoomdar. It's a little less'— she paused for a word—'a little less ponderous. But it depends on your taste. These pakoras are delicious,' she added by way of compensation, helping herself to another one.

Her bright laugh tinkled across the china, though there was nothing very obviously humorous in her previous remarks.

'Oh, but I think,' said Mrs Khandelwal, oozing charm, 'I do think that the quality of workmanship and the quality of wood at Kamdar's is unbeatable.'

And the quality of distance, thought Meenakshi. If you lived in Bombay, you'd be importing your furniture from Calcutta. Aloud she said: 'Well, Kamdar's is Kamdar's, of course.'

'Do have some more tea, Mrs Mehra,' said Mrs Khandelwal, pouring it out herself.

—Vikram Seth, *A Suitable Boy*

Quotation marks are generally not used to enclose words that a character is thinking silently rather than saying aloud. Be certain, of course, that you make the status of such words perfectly clear so that the reader does not confuse them with the rest of the narrative.

An occasional writer will use artistic license to omit quotation marks around all dialogue, perhaps using dashes or some other punctuation to set it off. There are respected literary precedents for this, but most writers would do better to stick with the conventions.

Note: Do not, of course, use quotation marks in scripts and screenplays, where every line is dialogue.

SETTING OFF CITATIONS

When you cite someone else's words verbatim, you must set them off in some way. This applies whether the original words had been spoken or had appeared in print.

Style guides differ on the precise conventions. In formal writing, citations that run more than a few lines are customarily set off not by quotation marks but by space: blank lines left above and below, sometimes distinctive line spacing, sometimes indented margins on one or both sides and sometimes reduced type size. If you are writing to the specifications of a particular guide, follow its instructions. Style guides also differ as to whether the text introducing such a quotation should end in a period, a comma, a colon or no punctuation at all. Sometimes, the context may dictate using one form or the other.

Quotation marks are used to set off shorter citations that lie within the regular text. They are required whether the quoted words constitute an entire statement or just a fragment.

> Humphries (1995) states that the five considerations for writing good academic prose are "fluency, clarity, accuracy, economy, and grace."

> The delegates agreed that proposals unveiled by the government are "incomplete and contain some irritants."

> The reporter would only say that the report had been leaked to him by a "congressional source."

> "Omit needless words!" cries the author on page 23, and into that imperative Will Strunk really put his heart and soul.
> —E.B. WHITE, *The Elements of Style*

When quoted material lies within text that itself is enclosed by quotation marks, the inner quotation marks must be distinguished from the outer ones. If the outer marks are double, make the inner ones single, and vice versa. For more detail, see page 181.

> "This is the end of a perfect day, Jeeves. What's that thing of yours about larks?"
> "Sir?"
> "And, I rather think, snails."
> "Oh yes, sir. 'The year's at the spring, the day's at the morn, morning's at seven, the hillside's dew-pearled—' "
> "But the larks, Jeeves? The snails? I'm pretty sure larks and snails entered into it."
> "I am coming to the larks and snails, sir. 'The lark's on the wing, the snail's on the thorn—' "
> "Now you're talking. And the tab line?"
> " 'God's in His heaven, all's right with the world.' "
> "That's it in a nutshell. I couldn't have put it better myself."
> —P.G. WODEHOUSE, *The Code of the Woosters*

ALTERING A CITATION

Unless you are clearly paraphrasing a quote, you must use the writer's (or speaker's) exact words, since if you made any changes it would look as if they were part of the source. If you want to alter a quote in some way to make it fit your needs better, you must distinguish your input from the original. The strategies to achieve this are to use square brackets to indicate changes or additions, ellipses to indicate omissions, or italics or the word [*sic*] to dissociate yourself from a misspelling, factual error or controversial opinion. For details, see the discussions under "Brackets" on page 166, "Ellipsis" on page 184 and "Italics" on page 284.

SETTING OFF SPECIAL TEXT

Quotation marks around a word or phrase serve to call special attention to it. There are several reasons for enclosing text this way.

COINED OR UNUSUAL WORDS

If you are introducing a word, term or phrase that you yourself have just coined, or that most people would consider specialized or obscure, enclosing it in quotation marks sends a reassuring signal to your readers that they aren't expected to have prior acquaintance with it. Without this signal, readers might momentarily be nonplussed; some might even glance back a paragraph or two to see if they had missed something. Quotation marks make it immediately clear that a word is appropriate, if unusual. If an explanation of the term is required, it should, of course, immediately follow. Do not use quotation marks on subsequent appearances of the word.

> It was not until the advent of von Krankmann, one of Fruitlooper's more brilliant students, a tireless theoretician and jogger and, later, founder of the "neo-Fruitloopian school" of psychoanalysis, that interest in vegetarianism was renewed.
> —GLENN C. ELLENBOGEN, *Oral Sadism and the Vegetarian Personality*

> Some early writing systems used the "boustrophedon" style of alternating the direction of the lines.

> There are now software programs available that you can use to determine the "Fog Index" of your writing.

Sometimes the absence of quotation marks can make a sentence outright difficult to follow, as the reader struggles to figure out what part of speech an unfamiliar word represents. For example:

> A transom is a horizontal crossbar in a window; over the transom is a
>   publisher's term for unsolicited manuscripts.
> **BETTER:** A transom is a horizontal crossbar in a window; "over the
> transom" is a publisher's term for unsolicited manuscripts.

Quotation marks make it clear that these words make up a phrase.

> In a questionnaire, skip instructions tell the respondent to skip certain
>   questions if they are not relevant.
> **BETTER:** In a questionnaire, "skip instructions" tell the respondent to skip
> certain questions if they are not relevant.

Quotation marks make it clear that *skip* is part of a compound noun, not a verb.

> Check any utilities issuing blocking ineligible warnings.
> **BETTER:** Check any utilities issuing "blocking ineligible" warnings.

Quotation marks make it clear—or at least clearer—that "blocking ineligible" is the type of warning that certain utilities are issuing.

With technical and academic terms, note that esotericism is a relative matter. Words that would be unusual to the layperson may be basic terminology to a specialist, so know your audience. It could verge on insulting to set off a term your readers consider standard, as it would imply that you thought they wouldn't know it.

Quotation marks may also be appropriate for terms that you want to acknowledge as special or unusual in some way, even if they are familiar enough not to have to be defined. For example, they may serve to set off literary references.

> The language of "Newspeak" is alive and well in political circles today.
> On the surface all was friendliness, but the "green-eyed monster" was
>   starting to raise its head.

WORDS USED IN A SPECIAL SENSE

If you are introducing a word or phrase that is not unusual in itself, but which you intend in some specific or nonstandard sense, enclose it in quotation marks to alert the reader to this fact.

> As applied to technical communicators, the concept of "early
> involvement" does not mean being present as observers in the initial
> stages of product development, but having direct participation.
> The outcome was considered to be "poor" if the patient was unable to
> function for one or more days in the preceding month.
> Note that the national norms are not necessarily "normal" in the sense
> of being optimal for good health.

Other candidates for quotation marks are phrases or clichés used
in a nonliteral manner:

> Physicians need a reliable mechanism that lets them "take the pulse" of
> their practices so that they can respond to issues of concern to their
> patients.
> Manuals dealing with the same product should all have the same "look
> and feel."

Some phrases benefit from being set off by quotation marks when
they are functioning as adjectives, in order to stand out better:

> Her "so what" attitude was beginning to wear on the others.
> The "family values" crowd was gaining control of the agenda.

WORDS USED IRONICALLY

Quotation marks around a term make it clear that your use of it is
ironical or satirical.

> Four soldiers were killed by "friendly fire."
> The "collateral damage" extended to two schools and a medical clinic.
> She would be seen at nothing but the "best" dinner parties.

Note that quotation marks are only needed for this purpose if
omitting them might make it look as if you personally endorsed some
absurd term or concept. If the irony of a term is self-evident, leave
it alone. For example, it would hardly enhance the following passage
to have quotation marks around *honest tradesman*:

> While Sydney Carton and the sheep of the prisons were in the
> adjoining dark room, speaking so low that not a sound was heard,

179

> Mr. Lorry looked at Jerry in considerable doubt and mistrust. That honest tradesman's manner of receiving the look did not inspire confidence; he changed the leg on which he rested, as often as if he had fifty of those limbs; he examined his finger-nails with a very questionable closeness of attention; and whenever Mr. Lorry's eye caught his, he was taken with that peculiar kind of short cough requiring the hollow of a hand before it, which is seldom, if ever, known to be an infirmity attendant on perfect openness of character.
>
> —CHARLES DICKENS, *A Tale of Two Cities*

SETTING OFF TITLES

Quotation marks are often used to set off references to short stories, poems, magazine or journal articles, book chapters and songs.

> He walked on, tunelessly whistling "Paperback Writer."
> One of the assigned readings was Guy de Maupassant's "The Necklace."
> The entire kindergarten class rose to recite "The Owl and the Pussycat."

They may also be used to set off the titles of books, newspapers, magazines, journals, plays, films, and radio and television programs, although for these more major works it is more conventional to use italics. Not all titles need be set off; for example, names of political parties, geographical locations and institutions are not, and newspapers and journals often are not. In short, there are many variations and exceptions. If you are writing to the specifications of a style guide, check its rules.

STYLE CONVENTIONS

In addition to knowing *when* to apply quotation marks, writers need to be familiar with the mechanics of applying them correctly. Quotation marks vary in both appearance and position.

SHAPE AND NUMBER

• If you are working on a regular typewriter, you are limited to typing quotation marks that look something like this: (" ")

On a word processor, you likely have the ability to create more elaborate marks, with the opening ones in the shape of miniature *6*s and the closing ones like miniature *9*s: (" ")

The latter look a bit more professional, but there's nothing wrong with the former. If you have the ability to type both marks, be careful that you are consistent—don't "mix and match."

• Quotation marks come in both doubles (" ") and singles (' '). The American standard is to use double ones for all purposes: for marking off dialogue, citations from someone else's writing, titles of works, or terms or phrases with special meaning. (The occasional style guide may instruct you to use double marks for some purposes and single marks for others, but most keep things simpler.)

If you have one quotation fall within another, make the inner marks single, to distinguish them.

> "Well?" said Miss Higgins. "Are we about to hear your 'the dog ate my homework' explanation again?"

If a double and a single mark abut, separate them with one space—a narrower-than-standard space, if you have such a function on your keyboard.

> The authors argue that alphabetic systems "may be the only systems of writing that take full advantage of the processing functions of the so-called 'language hemisphere' " (1982).

If you ever need to set off a quote within a quote within a quote, you go from double to single to double—and so on. However, most arbitrators of good writing would probably agree that at this point, it's probably time to recast the sentence!

British style is traditionally—though not invariably—the reverse: That is, start with single marks, then use double marks for quotes within quotes (and single marks for quotes within quotes within quotes). Canadians can go either way, but are likelier to start with double marks.

A caution about using single quotation marks: The closing one is indistinguishable from an apostrophe, so if used to enclose a phrase that includes an actual apostrophe, this could lead to momentary confusion. For example, putting the expression 'ladies' man' within single quotation marks could make it look as though the word *ladies* is set off in quotes. If such a situation arises, it is probably better to recast the sentence.

POSITION

When text within quotations is immediately followed by some other punctuation, the placement of that other mark relative to the closing quotation mark depends on several factors.

• When the quote marks enclose *dialogue*, the closing punctuation for the dialogue always goes inside the quotations.

She declared, "I won't go."	[period]
"I won't go," she declared.	[comma]
"I won't go!" she declared.	[exclamation point]
"Will you go?" he asked.	[question mark]
"No, I always—" she began.	[dash]

When quotations set off *nondialogue* text, the rules vary for different marks.

• For *commas and periods*, there are two styles: one American and one British. (Canadians may go either way.) In the United States, the convention is to place the comma or period *inside* the quotation marks.

A questionnaire may include options such as "Don't know," "No opinion," or "Undecided."

In Britain, it is more conventional to place the comma and period *outside*.

A questionnaire may include options such as "Don't know", "No opinion", or "Undecided".

• *Semicolons and colons* always go outside the quotation.

A questionnaire may include the option of "No opinion"; however, in some cases it may be preferable to force the respondent to make a choice.
How should I handle things if too many respondents answer "No opinion": should I revise the question?

• *Question marks and exclamation points* go outside the quotation if they apply to the entire sentence, and inside if they apply to just the quoted part.

Perhaps it would be better in this case to just "live and let live"?
[entire sentence is a question]

Small wonder audiences are calling her "the human pretzel"!
[entire sentence is exclamatory]

I really have problems with his attitude of "what's in it for me?"
[only quoted part is a question]

Several of the members cried, "Hear, hear!"
[only quoted part is exclamatory]

In the last two examples, note that although these sentences would be pronounced as though they ended in a period, they do not take one, since a sentence never takes more than one terminal punctuation mark. Readers understand that it is only the last segment, not the entire sentence, that is a query or an exclamation.

Ellipsis (. . .)

The ellipsis (from the Greek "to leave out" or "fall short") has three distinct functions:

- Indicating omissions in quoted material
- Indicating hesitation or trailing off in spoken words
- Imparting extra significance to a sentence

INDICATING OMISSIONS

You may abridge a quotation, but you must not pass off your abridged version as the original. If you take anything out, you must put an ellipsis in its place to let the reader know that something is missing.

Ellipses are needed only when you drop something from *within* a quoted passage, or if you need to clarify that a quotation is beginning or ending in midsentence. Do not use them if you are presenting selected excerpts or obvious sentence fragments.

There is no limit to how many words you may take out of a quotation, but be sure that the fragments you leave hold together grammatically. More importantly, be certain that you are not distorting or misrepresenting the meaning of the original. It is fine to drop words that are irrelevant for your purposes, but the message and the spirit of the source must be retained.

If you are altering or adding any text to a quotation, use brackets instead (see page 166).

The following shows how an original passage may be abbreviated using ellipses.

Oʀɪɢɪɴᴀʟ Qᴜᴏᴛᴀᴛɪᴏɴ:

Dear Theo,

    Toulouse-Lautrec is the saddest man in the world. He longs more than anything to be a great dentist, and he has real talent, but he's too short to reach his patients' mouths and too proud to stand on anything. Arms over his head, he gropes around their lips blindly, and yesterday, instead of putting caps on Mrs. Fitelson's teeth, he capped her chin. Meanwhile, my old friend Monet refuses to work on anything but very, very large mouths and Seurat, who is quite moody, has developed a method of cleaning one tooth at a time until he builds up what he calls "a full, fresh mouth." It has an architectural solidity to it, but is it dental work?

Vincent

—Wᴏᴏᴅʏ Aʟʟᴇɴ, If the Impressionists Had Been Dentists

Rᴇᴠɪsᴇᴅ Qᴜᴏᴛᴀᴛɪᴏɴ:

Toulouse-Lautrec. . . . longs more than anything to be a great dentist, and he has real talent, but he's too short to reach his patients' mouths and too proud to stand on anything. . . . he gropes around their lips blindly. . . . Meanwhile, . . . Monet refuses to work on anything but very, very large mouths and Seurat . . . has developed a method of cleaning one tooth at a time until he builds up what he calls "a full, fresh mouth." It has an architectural solidity to it, but is it dental work?

Ellipses can also be used to indicate the omissions in a one-sided dialogue, typically a phone conversation or a conversation where the writer wants to report what only one character is saying.

    I was going to ask to see the rubies when the phone rang, and Gatsby took up the receiver.

    "Yes. . . . Well, I can't talk now. . . . I can't talk now, old sport. . . . I said a *small* town. . . . He must know what a small town is. . . . Well, he's of no use to us if Detroit is his idea of a small town. . . ."

    He rang off.

—F. Sᴄᴏᴛᴛ Fɪᴛᴢɢᴇʀᴀʟᴅ, The Great Gatsby

INDICATING HESITATION OR
TRAILING OFF OF SPEECH

In dialogue, ellipses can be used to indicate speech that pauses or trails off (in contrast to the dash, which is used to indicate speech that is abruptly broken off because of an interruption or sudden change of mind).

The effect of ellipses can be to make speech appear indecisive or nervous,

> "Could we go there and take a look at it?"
> Sherman's mouth had gone dry. He could feel his lips contracting.
> "The car?"
> "Yes."
> "When?"
> "Soon's we leave here's good a time as any, for us."
> "You mean *now?* Well, I don't know . . ." Sherman felt as if the muscles of his lips were being constricted by a purse string.
> "There's certain things that's consistent with an incident like this. If a car don't have those things, then we keep on going down the list. At this point we're looking for a car. We don't have a description of a driver. So—that okay with you?"
> "Well . . . I don't know . . ." No! Let them look at it! There's nothing for them to find! Or is there?
>
> —Tom Wolfe, *The Bonfire of the Vanities*

laid-back or musing,

> They said when Healey arrived he had got the highest ever marks in a scholarship entrance. Once, in his first term, Cartwright had been bold enough to ask him why he was so clever, what exercises he did to keep his brain fit. Healey had laughed.
> 'It's memory, Cartwright, old dear. Memory, the mother of the Muses . . . at least that's what thingummy said.'
> 'Who?'
> 'You know, what's his name, Greek poet chap. Wrote the Theogony . . . what *was* he called? Begins with an "H".'
> 'Homer?'

'No, dear. Not Homer, the other one. No, it's gone. Anyway.
Memory, that's the key.'

—STEPHEN FRY, *The Liar*

or mysterious or dreamy.

"Little man," I said, "I want to hear you laugh again."
But he said to me:
"Tonight it will be a year . . . My star, then, can be found right
above the place where I came to the Earth, a year ago . . ."
"Little man," I said, "tell me that it is only a bad dream—this affair
of the snake, and the meeting-place, and the star . . ."
But he did not answer my plea. He said to me, instead:
"The thing that is important is the thing that is not seen . . ."
"Yes, I know . . ."

—ANTOINE DE SAINT-EXUPÉRY, *The Little Prince* (translated by
Katherine Woods)

Ellipses can also be used to indicate multiple speakers completing
a single sentence. (Dashes could serve this purpose as well, but
would convey an impression of a series of forcible interruptions
rather than of one speaker pausing to let the next one begin.)

Ten minutes. I strap on my right pad. Preoccupied with time and
equipment and not yet the game, the room is quieter, if no more
serious. Too quiet. Uneasy, thinking of Cournoyer, the team's captain,
at home, his distinguished career probably over, Lapointe says, "Hey,
let's win this one for Yvan," and instantly the room picks up. "Poor
little guy," he continues, "his back all busted up, probably just lyin' at
home . . ." and as he pauses as if to let his words sink in, Shutt and
Houle jump in before anyone else can.
". . . havin' a little wine . . ."
". . . a little Caesar salad . . ."
". . . poor little bastard," Lapointe muses sadly, and we all laugh.

—KEN DRYDEN, *The Game*

IMPARTING EXTRA SIGNIFICANCE TO WORDS

In nondialogue writing, ending a sentence in an ellipsis rather than a period adds a certain ineffable weight to it.

The effect can be to underscore a point that need not be stated explicitly,

> "I don't care what you do with your whiskers; I don't care what *anybody* does with his whiskers," said the King, still soothing his own tenderly; "I want the King of Euralia's blood." He looked round the Court. "To anyone who will bring me the head of the King, I will give the hand of my daughter in marriage."
>
> There was a profound silence. . . .
>
> "Which daughter?" said a cautious voice at last.
>
> "The eldest," said the King.
>
> There was another profound silence. . . .
>
> —A.A. MILNE, *Once on a Time*

to impart a haunting, surreal or dreamy aspect,

> The sea is high again today, with a thrilling flush of wind. In the midst of winter you can feel the inventions of spring. A sky of hot nude pearl until midday, crickets in sheltered places, and now the wind unpacking the great planes, ransacking the great planes. . . .
>
> I have escaped to this island with a few books and the child—Melissa's child. I do not know why I use the word 'escape'. The villagers say jokingly that only a sick man would choose such a remote place to rebuild. Well, then, I have come here to heal myself, if you like to put it that way. . . .
>
> —LAWRENCE DURRELL, *The Alexandria Quartet*

or to create a sense of suspense.

> It was a fine night and he walked home to Bertram's Hotel after first getting into a bus which took him in the opposite direction. It was midnight when he got in and Bertram's Hotel at midnight usually preserved a decorous appearance of everyone having gone to bed. The lift was on a higher floor so the Canon walked up the stairs. He came

to his room, inserted the key in the lock, threw the door open and entered!

Good gracious, was he seeing things? But who—how—he saw the upraised arm too late. . . .

Stars exploded in a kind of Guy Fawkes' display within his head. . . .

—AGATHA CHRISTIE, *At Bertram's Hotel*

STYLE CONVENTIONS

• Leave spaces between the points that make up an ellipsis. That is, type them as (. . .), not (...).

• An ellipsis always consists of three points, although it sometimes appears to have four. Use three points in the following situations:

—In quotations, if you are omitting text in the middle of a sentence or at the beginning of the first sentence.

—In dialogue, to indicate a pause in the middle of a sentence or when a sentence trails off unfinished.

• A four-point ellipsis is actually a three-point ellipsis plus a period. (The marks, of course, are indistinguishable.) Use four points in the following situations:

—In quotations, if you are omitting either the last part of a sentence, the beginning of a sentence other than the opening one (here, the first point is the period of the previous sentence) or an entire sentence or more. If the sentence whose last part is being omitted (or the sentence that precedes the one whose first part is being omitted) ends in a question mark or an exclamation point rather than a period, then instead of four points, use that mark plus three points.

—In a one-sided telephone conversation (here, the first point is the period ending the speaker's words).

—In dialogue, to indicate a pause that follows a complete sentence (here, the first point is the period ending that sentence).

- When using an ellipsis at the end of a sentence to impart significance or suspense, some writers put down three points, and some four.

- With three points, leave a space on either side of the ellipsis. With four points, place the first one immediately next to the text that precedes it.

- In quotations, if you drop the first part of a sentence, you may either capitalize the word that now begins that sentence or keep it lowercase (which is truer to the original). A third option is to capitalize it and enclose the first letter in square brackets to indicate your change. For an illustration of this, see "Identifying Changes to Quoted Material" under "Brackets" on page 166.

- In quotations, you may choose to either drop or retain any punctuation that immediately precedes an ellipsis, depending on whether or not it helps readability. You may, for example, find it desirable to keep a semicolon or colon that comes before the text you dropped.

Apostrophe (')

The apostrophe often is'nt used correctly: Peoples' misunderstand-ings about it's function range from omitting it when its required, to putting it in the wrong place, to adding bevy's of apostrophe's where they dont' belong. Not too many sentences contain as many apostro-phe errors as the above (seven), but misuses show up alarmingly often. The confusion over this much-abused mark probably arises out of the fact that it has three completely independent uses, each of which applies under some circumstances but not others. These functions are the following:

- Indicating omissions in contracted words
- Indicating possessives
- Indicating plurals

INDICATING OMISSIONS IN CONTRACTED WORDS

The apostrophe is used as a "stand-in" for missing letters in a con-traction, signaling that something has been taken out. Contractions may derive from two words that are combined into one, from single words or from numerical dates.

TWO-WORD CONTRACTIONS

When two words are run together and one or more letters get dropped in the process, the apostrophe takes the place of the miss-ing letters.

She **couldn't** make it.	[could not]
You're looking great.	[you are]

We've no time to lose.	[we have]
They'd rather not do it.	[they would]
They'd finished the job.	[they had]
Let's go.	[let us]
Who's on first?	[who is]
Who's got the time?	[who has]
'Tis a pity.	[it is]
It's a pity.	[it is]
It's already been done.	[it has]

These types of contractions are not appropriate for all genres of writing: In particular, they are often viewed as too informal for academic journals (which isn't to say they may never be used there, just that they must be used with discretion). On the other hand, they are fine for informal writing and virtually mandatory for dialogue, as speech would sound ridiculously stilted and unnatural without them. In fact, in dialogue you can (provided you don't overdo it) even get away with double contractions such as "You shouldn't've said that" or "I'd've known him anywhere."

Different words may sometimes form the same contraction. This doesn't usually create a problem, since the context should make your intentions clear, but occasionally you might need to spell things out to avoid ambiguity. For example, your readers might not be able to distinguish whether *I'd let* means "I would let" or "I had let."

SINGLE-WORD CONTRACTIONS
Single words are sometimes shortened to make them less formal. Letters may be dropped anywhere in a word: from the beginning, the end, the middle or both ends.

For some such contractions, an apostrophe is mandatory. Since the contraction is not a "real" word, the apostrophe is needed as a signal that something is intentionally missing. If you omitted it, it might look as though you were simply ignorant of how the word should properly appear.

So, how's life in the **'burbs**?

How are you **doin'**?

Please hurry, **'cause** we're late.

C'mon, let's go.

In other cases, the contraction may be considered a legitimate variant, so the apostrophe is optional. That is, it's not incorrect to include it, but the shortened form of the word may stand alone as well.

> **'Copter** Pilot Safe After Crash
> **Copter** Pilot Safe After Crash
>
> If I had my **'druthers,** we'd be elsewhere.
> If I had my **druthers,** we'd be elsewhere.
>
> We've been working **'round** the clock.
> We've been working **round** the clock.

In other cases (usually involving phrases), the contracted form has actually become the standard spelling, and is what appears in the dictionary entry.

> Their son turned out to be a **ne'er**-do-well.
> His girlfriend sings in a rock **'n'** roll band.
> She's always pursuing will-o'-the-wisp ideas.

And in still other cases, the shortened form has come to replace the original word, or has at least become the more common version. Here, including the apostrophe would look pedantic or old-fashioned rather than correct. After all, language continuously evolves, and today's slang may be tomorrow's standard usage. Few modern writers would think to put apostrophes in the following:

> She went home by **bus.**   [original: omnibus]
> He's sick in bed with the **flu.**   [original: influenza]
> She plays the **cello.**   [original: violincello]

It may be debatable as to whether a given contraction has become "standard" enough to lose its apostrophe, so judgment is needed in some cases. Go by your own comfort level and the tone of your writing: more formal—keep the apostrophe; less formal—drop the apostrophe.

NUMERICAL CONTRACTIONS
If the century of a date is obvious, it is often permissible to drop the first two digits. (This may not be encouraged in more formal styles of writing.)

> Remember the summer of '68?
> He was born in the '30s.

This is simply the numerical equivalent of writing *remember the summer of 'sixty-eight* or *he was born in the 'thirties*.

If there could be any question as to what the missing numbers are, do not omit them. Presumably most dates refer to the present century, so dropping the first two digits shouldn't leave any ambiguity; similarly, if your text is dealing exclusively with some other era, the context should make any abbreviated dates there sufficiently clear. (Everyone knows when Clementine's father, the 'forty-niner, was around.) Just be certain there's no possible doubt.

If a shortened date contains an apostrophe for some other purpose, do not use an apostrophe to indicate the contraction, as it would look awkward to have more than one.

> The **80's** excesses gave way to the frugality of the **90s**.
> [apostrophe indicates a possessive]

INDICATING POSSESSIVES

This section first presents the basic rules about possessives and then details the exceptions and problem areas. There are admittedly quite a few aspects to this topic; fortunately the basic rules cover the vast majority of situations.

FOR SINGULAR NOUNS, ADD AN APOSTROPHE PLUS *S*

> the hamster's nose
> that student's books
> Mr. Smith's apartment

FOR PLURAL NOUNS THAT END IN *S*, ADD JUST AN APOSTROPHE

> both hamsters' noses
> those students' books
> the Smiths' apartment

FOR PLURAL NOUNS THAT DON'T END IN *S*, ADD AN APOSTROPHE PLUS *S*

> children's books
> men's shoes

the people's choice

the alumni's lounge

Note that this rule means that words where the plural is the same as the singular will have the same possessive form in both cases: For example, *the sheep's wool* could refer to the wool of one sheep or of multiple sheep. If you are ever faced with this sort of construction, make sure that the context makes your meaning unambiguous.

FOR PERSONAL PRONOUNS, ADD JUST *S*

This one is yours.

That one is hers.

The house on the left is ours.

I'll do my share if they do theirs.

Put everything in its place.

A particularly common error is to confuse the possessive *its* (no apostrophe) with the contraction *it's*, which means "it is" or "it has." (Consider the difference in meaning between *A wise dog knows its master* and *A wise dog knows it's master!*) Those who insist that the possessive *its* take an apostrophe because a possessive "always" takes one should take note of the fact that none of the other personal pronouns take one either. For more on this, see the discussion under "Pronouns" on page 248.

FOR JOINT POSSESSION, MAKE ONLY THE LAST NOUN
POSSESSIVE; FOR SEPARATE POSSESSION,
MAKE EACH NOUN POSSESSIVE

my mother and father's house

Arthur and Lisa's daughter

Robert and Martha's partnership

the Browns and the Murphys' vacation plans [if these families travel
together]

Montreal's and Toronto's subway systems

my brother's and sister's weddings

cats' and dogs' grooming habits

the Browns' and the Murphys' vacation plans [if these families do not
travel together]

SPECIAL SITUATIONS

Even armed with the above rules, writers often feel they are on shaky ground in certain circumstances. In some cases there are genuine exceptions to the rules; in others, people mistakenly *think* that something is an exception, and so fail to follow a rule when it should apply. These problem areas are described below.

SIBILANTS

Writers are often unsure how to deal with the possessives of nouns ending in *s* or another sibilant sound *(ce, x, z)*, or in a silent *s*. The answer is, in most cases treat such words exactly as you would any other. Thus, to form the possessive of the singular, add apostrophe *s*; to form the possessive of the plural, add *es* to the singular to make it a plural, and then add an apostrophe.

Ms. Jones's property	the Joneses' property
Mr. Harris's store	the Harrises' store
the actress's contract	the actresses' contracts
the box's contents	the boxes' contents
the quiz's answers	the quizzes' answers

However, if it would sound awkward to have two *s*'s next to each other (one belonging to the word itself and another added to make the word possessive), you may consider dropping the second one. A sensible way of deciding which way to go is to say the word aloud, spontaneously. If it feels natural to pronounce the second *s*, include it; otherwise, drop it. Many authorities would consider either of the following acceptable:

Dickens's novels	Dickens' novels
Lloyd Bridges's films	Lloyd Bridges' films
Mr. Williams's dog	Mr. Williams' dog
the Riverses' car	the Rivers' car

If you're not sure which way to go, it's usually best to include the extra *s*, since technically it is correct. There is really no excuse for creating constructions such as *Charles' wife* or *the Ferris' house*.

In a few cases (very few, mind you), convention dictates that the possessive *s* must be dropped.

Achilles' heel
Euripides' plays
Graves' disease
Brahms' lullaby
Mr. Rogers' Neighborhood
for goodness' sake
for appearance' sake

Some such phrases have their own dictionary listing, so often you can turn to the dictionary to confirm if a possessive *s* is needed.

COMPOUND NOUNS

With compound nouns, whether closed, open or hyphenated, put the possessive apostrophe at the end of the compound, rather than on the principal word. The possessive appears the same way for the singular and the plural.

the passerby's umbrella	the passersby's umbrellas
her brother-in-law's business	her brothers-in-law's business
the postmaster general's duties	the postmasters general's duties

Undeniably, these constructions can get awkward for plural possessives. You may find it preferable to recast them as, for example, *the duties of the postmasters general.*

WORDS WITH *Y* SINGULARS

Writers often make errors with words whose singular ends in *y* and plural in *ies.* Yet such words simply follow the standard rules: apostrophe plus *s* for the singular possessive; apostrophe alone for the plural possessive.

the baby's crib	the babies' cribs
the lady's purse	the ladies' purses
the daisy's petals	the daisies' petals

INANIMATE POSSESSION

Some authorities hold that it is not good idiom to create possessives for inanimate things, since they are not capable of ownership. For instance, with reference to some earlier examples, rather than *the quiz's answers* and *the 80's excesses,* one should write *the answers to the quiz* and *the excesses of the 80s.* Other authorities argue that this restriction can lead to unnecessarily stilted constructions and should be disregarded.

In a number of cases, the possessive is prescribed by convention or idiomatic expression: *a week's vacation, a stone's throw away, a minute's reflection.*

INDICATING PLURALS

It's far more often the case that apostrophes are mistakenly added to plural words than they are mistakenly omitted. The only time such an apostrophe is appropriate is when a word might be hard to interpret without it.

PLURALIZING NUMERALS OR LETTERS

Most authorities agree that the plural of a numeral or a single letter should take an apostrophe if it is likely to be misread without one.

One such scenario is when the combination of a letter or numeral and the pluralizing *s* may coincidentally look like another word.

> The binary system uses **0's** and **1's**.
> [otherwise could look like "0s" and "1s"]

> The game tonight is against the Oakland **A's**.
> [otherwise could look like "As"]

> To put the program in "Insert" mode, type two **i's**.
> [otherwise could look like "is"]

Another scenario is when the pluralizing *s* could not otherwise be distinguished from the root word, because they are both of the same case (upper or lower). For example, you might need to make a reference to 10 cc's (not ccs) or 5 Btu's (not Btus). Or say you are writing a technical manual and need a heading for a section that describes how to create an entity referred to by its abbreviation of DBC. The title of this section, then, is "Creating DBCs." With lowercase letters, this works fine without an apostrophe. If, however, your style requires that headings be set in uppercase, the title becomes "CREATING DBCS"—that is, it now looks as though the

S is part of the term itself. Writing it as "CREATING DBC'S" would avoid this problem.

In cases of numbers and letters where no ambiguity is likely, some authorities say to include an apostrophe; others say not to. The trend today is toward the latter, but this is certainly not universal. Whichever approach you take, be consistent.

> The school is strong on the three **R's**.
> The school is strong on the three **Rs**.
>
> His best work was done in the **1980's**.
> His best work was done in the **1980s**.
>
> He refuses to fly in anything but **747's**.
> He refuses to fly in anything but **747s**.
>
> She belongs to two **YWCA's**.
> She belongs to two **YWCAs**.
>
> The hospital has a shortage of **RN's**.
> The hospital has a shortage of **RNs**.

PLURALIZING NON-NOUN WORDS

When a word that is not a noun is used as one and appears in plural form, an apostrophe often helps make it clearer to the reader just how that word is intended. Without the apostrophe, the reader might have to pause or backtrack to pick up on the meaning.

> Editors must know their **which's** from their **that's**.
> I'm not taking any more "**sorry's**."
> Her speech was riddled with "**you know's**" and "**um's**."
> The response from the class was a chorus of **no's**.

Using an apostrophe in these cases can be a matter of judgment. Some writers would exclude them in such familiar expressions as "no ifs, ands or buts"; others would include them. Make your decisions about such plurals on a case-by-case basis.

WHEN *NOT* TO USE A PLURALIZING APOSTROPHE

Common errors are to include apostrophes when pluralizing words that end in a vowel, words that end in *y*, and names. Consider the following:

Apostrophe's can be tricky.
No quota's have been set yet.
The tomato's are three for a dollar.

Both baby's were screaming at once.
Jamaican patty's sold here.
The galley's haven't been checked yet.

The Smith's were invited to dinner.
The Schultz's can't make it.
Be sure to send a card to the Jenkins'.

In the first set, the nouns should appear simply as *apostrophes, quotas* and *tomatoes* (note the added *e*). Just because a word ends in a vowel doesn't mean it should be treated any differently from one that ends in a consonant.

For nouns whose singular ends in *y*, the majority form the plural as *ies*: thus, *babies* and *patties*. A few, such as *galleys*, keep the *y*. In no case is an apostrophe needed.

And treat names just as you would any other noun: thus, the *Smiths, Schultzes* and *Jenkinses* (note the *es* ending for names ending in sibilants).

For more on this, see "Plural Formations" on page 42.

PART FOUR

Grammar

The very mention of the word "grammar" makes some writers quail, evoking an image of unfathomable, rigid and often arbitrary rules buttressed by a mountain of terrifying terminology. In fact, for the most part grammar consists of sensible conventions designed to support unambiguous and meaningful expression. Grammar is concerned with the form and sequence of words in a sentence, and it's often the case that if a rule isn't followed, some uncertainty or misinterpretation could result.

Achieving clear expression shouldn't be the only motivation for observing the rules. Unconventional grammar may be taken as an indication of carelessness or ignorance on the part of a writer, with the result that readers may end up viewing the content itself less seriously. Thus, even though some conventions undeniably are based more on tradition than on logic, the mere fact of their existence means that it is usually in a writer's interests to abide by them.

This chapter does not review all the parts of speech, since any competent English speaker intuitively understands most aspects of sentence structure. Instead, the focus is on a few topics that present frequent stumbling blocks to even educated and articulate users of the language. These topics are agreement between subject and verb (ensuring that these words match each other in form), parallel construction (ensuring grammatical similarity between elements that play similar roles), positioning of modifiers (ensuring that a word or group of words meant to describe a subject doesn't act on the wrong part of the sentence) and use of pronouns (ensuring the correct form of the words used to represent nouns). A final section looks at how some aspects of grammar thought by many to be unshakable rules may in fact often be safely disregarded.

Agreement Between Subject and Verb

The dog barks/The dogs bark. He is most hospitable/They are most hospitable. My class has begun/My classes have begun. Most nouns, pronouns and verbs have singular and plural forms, and English speakers are instinctively aware that when a noun or pronoun is singular, the verb that applies to it is singular; and when the noun or pronoun is plural, the verb is plural. This is known as **agreement between subject and verb**.

When sentences are straightforward, errors in agreement are rare: Few people would say *The dogs barks, He are most hospitable* or *My classes has begun.* When the structure becomes more complex, however, mistakes become more likely. The causes fall into two general categories: uncertainty as to what constitutes the subject, and so matching the verb to the wrong noun; and uncertainty as to whether a given subject is in fact singular or plural.

Difficulties in the first category may arise when sentences contain any of the following:

- Compound subjects
- Alternative subjects
- Distracting parenthetical nouns
- Distracting modifying nouns
- Distracting predicate nouns
- Inverted subject-verb order

Difficulties in the second category may arise when sentences contain any of the following:

- Collective nouns
- Terms of quantity

- Problem pronouns
- Problem phrases
- Unusual plurals and singulars

These problem scenarios are illustrated in the following sections. In the example sentences, the subjects are shown in bold type, and the verbs underlined.

Note: For discussion of another aspect of this topic, see "Agreement Between Pronoun and Antecedent" on page 253.

Problem Category 1:
The Subject, the Whole Subject and Nothing but the Subject

The **subject** of a sentence can be any sort of entity: a person, a place, an object either concrete or abstract—in short, a noun. It can also be a pronoun that refers to an entity identified elsewhere, or a verb form (a gerund or infinitive) functioning as a noun. The subject is the *focus* of the sentence: the actor or the center of interest. It either does something, has something done to it or is described in some way. Thus, it is always tied to an accompanying verb. (For a more complete description, see "Basic Sentence Structure" on page 55.)

This section describes scenarios where writers often fail to recognize precisely which words make up the subject, and hence treat what should be a plural as a singular or vice versa.

COMPOUND SUBJECTS

A sentence may contain a compound subject: two or more nouns, pronouns, gerunds or infinitives that share the same verb and are linked by *and*. With a few exceptions, the verb for a compound subject is always plural. This applies whether each part of the compound is itself singular or plural.

Your **enthusiasm** and **participation** <u>have</u> been much appreciated.
[both parts singular]

The **books** and **records** <u>go</u> in the study.
[both parts plural]

Frank's **résumé** and **reference letters** <u>are</u> ready to be photocopied, now that the **typos** and **grammatical mistake** <u>have</u> been fixed.
[one part singular, one part plural, either order]

When the element closest to the verb is singular, some writers mistakenly make the verb agree with just that part. Consider the following examples:

Her understanding and attention span has improved greatly.

The verb should be *have*.

Whether a relationship between these events actually exists and if so whether it is causal remains to be shown.

The verb should be *remain*.

Desktop publishing may not yield the same quality achieved by traditional typesetting, but its cost-effectiveness and the control that it offers to editors makes it attractive to many publishers.

The verb should be *make*.

Note that it is particularly easy to miss the fact that there is more than one subject if the elements are long, complex or abstract.

Exceptions

• If two elements refer to the same entity, treat them as if they constitute a single subject.

Rum and Coke <u>was</u> his preferred drink.
[*rum* and *Coke* combine to form one beverage]

The **president and CEO** <u>expects</u> to attend.
[*president* and *CEO* describe the same person]

Drinking and driving <u>is</u> a crime.
[*drinking* and *driving* are not crimes in isolation, only in combination]

Sometimes the status may be a matter of interpretation:

Plucking and **cleaning** a chicken <u>was</u> an unpleasant task for many of our grandmothers.
Calculating and **plotting** the points on a graph <u>is</u> the most time-consuming part of the analysis.

In each of these sentences, the closely related actions may be considered to function as a single activity. It would be grammatical to use plural verbs and change the descriptions to *tasks* and *parts,* but that would slightly alter the implied relationships.

• Another exception is when the elements are preceded by the pronoun *each* or *every,* which then becomes the subject. These pronouns are treated as singulars, even in combination.

The **invoice** and **purchase order** <u>have</u> to be approved by the manager.

But:

Each invoice and purchase order <u>has</u> to be approved.
Every invoice and purchase order <u>has</u> to be approved.
Each of the invoices and purchase orders <u>has</u> to be approved.
Every one of the invoices and purchase orders <u>has</u> to be approved.
Each and every invoice and purchase order <u>has</u> to be approved.

Note: If *each* follows a compound subject rather than precedes it, the verb is plural. (No one ever said English was logical.)

The invoice and purchase order (or the invoices and purchase orders) each have to be approved.

ALTERNATIVE SUBJECTS

When two subjects that share a verb are linked by *or, nor* or *but,* the verb agrees with whichever part is closest to it.

The carpets or the chairs <u>are</u> giving off a musty smell.
[both parts are plural, so verb is plural]

Either **Zeke** or his **sister** <u>is</u> going to attend.
[both parts are singular, so verb is singular]

Either **Zeke** or his **parents** <u>are</u> going to attend.
[*parents* is plural, so verb is plural]

Either Zeke's **parents** or his **sister** <u>is</u> going to attend.
[*sister* is singular, so verb is singular]

One or the **other** of you <u>has</u> to compromise.
Neither the **gloves** nor the **scarf** <u>needs</u> washing.
Neither the **moon** nor the **stars** <u>were</u> visible.
Not the **weather** but the **bus schedules** <u>make</u> it difficult for her to come.
Not his **looks** but his **manner** <u>turns</u> me off.

Not only the **patient** but also her **family members** <u>feel</u> that the nursing care is excellent.

Not only the **students** but also the **teacher** <u>has</u> signed the petition.

Whether the **workers** or the **supervisor** <u>was</u> responsible was a matter of debate.

Whether the **tablecloth** or the **placemats** <u>go</u> on the table is up to you.

Note that constructions that include a plural subject but use a singular verb may sound awkward. A simple solution is to switch the components around: *Either Zeke's sister or his parents are going to attend; Not only the teacher but also the students have signed the petition.* Or avoid the issue by using a verb form that doesn't change with number: *Either Zeke's parents or his sister will attend; Not only the students but also the teacher signed the petition.*

DISTRACTING PARENTHETICAL NOUNS

When a subject is followed by a phrase that refers to another entity, writers sometimes mistake this entity for the second part of a compound subject. Consider the following sentences:

Theodora and her **daughter** <u>are</u> taking classes in Bulgarian.

Theodora, as well as her daughter, <u>is</u> taking classes in Bulgarian.

The first example contains a compound subject, *Theodora and her daughter*, and hence takes a plural verb. The second one contains a singular subject, *Theodora*, followed by a parenthetical phrase that refers to Theodora's daughter but is not part of the subject. Thus, *Theodora, as well as her daughter, are taking classes in Bulgarian* would be incorrect. If a parenthetical phrase is taken out, the sentence should still read grammatically. It is obvious that you would not say *Theodora are taking classes in Bulgarian.*

Similarly,

His chronic **tardiness**, as well as his negative attitude, <u>disrupts</u> the class.

The **professor**, together with her graduate students, <u>was</u> just entering the building.

The new **workload**, on top of my other duties, <u>is</u> unreasonable.

Pat, like the others, <u>was</u> determined to finish on time.

A parcel, along with a multitude of letters, <u>was</u> delivered the next day.

The house, with all its contents, <u>was</u> heavily insured.

Anxiety about her health, in addition to her financial woes, <u>has</u> led her to seek counseling.

Mitzi, accompanied by her husband, <u>was</u> trundling up the path.

His perseverance, no less than his pleasant manner, <u>makes</u> him a credible candidate for the job.

Their country place, including the guest cottage, <u>is</u> worth about fifty thousand.

The entire room, except the two side doors, <u>is</u> to be painted.

Of course, if the subject preceding the parenthetical phrase is plural, the verb is plural. Just be sure to disregard the parenthetical text when determining the form of the verb.

Note: The parenthetical phrases in the above examples are enclosed in commas. While technically these are proper, some writers may choose to drop them for reasons of style. If you omit the commas, this does not affect the rule described above: You would still disregard the parenthetical text as far as the verb is concerned. For example:

The library as well as the chapel <u>stands</u> on a rolling green hill.

A final word on these types of construction: They may be correct, but there is no denying they sometimes sound awkward. You may in some cases want to consider joining the subjects with *and* instead.

The professor and her graduate students were just entering the building.

A parcel and a multitude of letters were delivered the next day.

DISTRACTING MODIFYING NOUNS

When a subject is followed by a phrase that further defines it, writers sometimes mistake the noun contained in this phrase for the subject itself. Consider the following three sentences:

This set <u>is</u> not complete.

These instructions <u>are</u> not complete.

This set of instructions <u>is</u> not complete.

In the last sentence, it would be an error to say *This set of instructions are not complete*. The subject is the singular *set*; the plural word *instructions* is merely part of a phrase that modifies the subject.

Similarly,

> The **inclusion** of intervening words between subject and verb often causes confusion.
> An extensive **collection** of measures is maintained in the laboratory.
> **Engaging** in dangerous contact sports is not for the faint of heart.
> The **shape** of the eyebrows is sometimes affected by facial expression.
> An **assortment** of ribbons and bows was lying in the drawer.
> One **thing** after another has conspired to make me late.

Note: Errors attributable to this type of sentence structure seem restricted to when the subject is singular and the phrase contains a plural noun. When it's the other way around, the effect of the intervening words is less distracting. Few people would say *The pupils in her class is extraordinarily well behaved* or *The inscriptions on the tombstone was almost worn away*.

Exceptions

• In some cases, the subject and its modifier could be interchanged, with little effect other than a slight change in emphasis:

> The committee has come up with a **set** of guidelines that makes the process easier to follow.
> The committee has come up with a set of **guidelines** that make the process easier to follow.

Both these constructions are grammatically acceptable; the difference in nuance is that in the first case the guidelines seem to be acting as a unit, and in the second case to be acting independently.

• The phrase *a number of* is always treated as a plural, even though *a number* looks like a singular entity.

> **A number of vouchers** have already been handed out.

DISTRACTING PREDICATE NOUNS

The subject is the center of interest in a sentence, and the **predicate** is what provides information about the subject: either describing it or identifying an action that it performs or that is performed upon it. (For a more complete description, see "Basic Sentence Structure" on page 55.)

If the predicate is a description that contains a noun, writers sometimes mistake this predicate noun for the subject itself. This will cause errors in agreement if the subject happens to be singular and the predicate noun plural, or vice versa.

Consider the following two sentences:

Her ongoing **grievances** <u>are</u> the biggest issue.
The biggest **issue** <u>is</u> her ongoing grievances.

In the first example, the subject is the plural *grievances*: Don't be decoyed by the singular *issue*. In the second example, the wording is turned around so that the reverse is true.

Similarly,

The only deductible **item** on my tax return <u>is</u> my travel expenses.
My **travel expenses** <u>are</u> the only deductible item on my tax return.
Her best **feature** <u>is</u> her eyes.
Her **eyes** <u>are</u> her best feature.
The never-ending **crises** and **tantrums** in the office <u>were</u> a nightmare.
The main **thing** needed <u>is</u> cooler heads.
The only **problem** with the house <u>was</u> its creaky floors.

Writers are likelier to focus on the wrong noun if other words intervene between the subject and the verb. Remember, it is not proximity that determines which word acts as the subject.

INVERTED SUBJECT-VERB ORDER

In English, the subject usually precedes the verb: *Lauren* <u>is</u> a hard worker; the *fox* <u>jumps</u> over the dog; his *idea* <u>was</u> pooh-poohed. However, this order is reversed in sentences that are constructed as questions, that open with phrasings such as *there were* or *it is*, or that say *what* was done before saying *who* did it. In these situations, writers are more apt to make errors in agreement, either because they focus only on whatever immediately follows the verb and neglect to look ahead, or because they get distracted by a noun that precedes the verb. However, the same rules described above apply here as well.

<u>Do</u> your **brother** and his **friend** need a place to stay tonight?
[compound subject, both parts singular; verb plural]

Walking purposefully up to the house <u>were</u> the **trainer** and his **assistants**.
[compound subject, one part singular and one plural; verb plural]

There <u>are</u> a **desk** and ten **chairs** in the classroom.
[compound subject, one part singular and one plural; verb plural]

<u>There's</u> no **desk** or **chairs** to be found anywhere.
[alternative subject with singular element closest to the verb; verb
   singular]

<u>Are</u> neither my **rights** nor my **reputation** to be considered?
[alternative subject with plural element closest to the verb; verb plural]

<u>There's</u> neither **prestige** nor **profits** to be gained.
[alternative subject with singular element closest to the verb; verb
   singular]

Into each project <u>go</u> **hours** of hard work.
[subject is *hours*, not *project* or *work*; verb plural]

Included in the total <u>are</u> the five spare **components**.
[subject is *components*, not *total*; verb plural]

Among the guests coming tonight <u>is</u> my cousin's new **fiancé**.
[subject is *fiancé*, not *guests*; verb singular]

Here <u>are</u> the **copies** of the letter.
[subject is *copies*, not *letter*; verb plural]

If you're ever uncertain about how to deal with an inverted sentence, try mentally turning it around or dropping any distracting elements:

the **components** <u>are</u> included
my cousin's **fiancé** <u>is</u> coming
the **copies** <u>are</u> here

Be particularly careful when using contractions for *there is, it is* and the like, since contractions tend to obscure the verb. One often sees faulty constructions such as *What's the main issues at stake here?* or *Where's my shoes?* or *There's still tons of debris to be cleared.* Such errors are common in speech, and indeed are sometimes inevitable because speakers may start a sentence with a singular subject in mind and then go on to form a plural. Also, using a plural in this type of sentence would sometimes sound overly formal in speech. Writers, however, must be held to a higher standard.

Problem Category 2:
Forest or Trees?

This section describes scenarios where writers often mistake a singular subject for a plural one or vice versa, and hence match the wrong verb to it.

COLLECTIVE NOUNS

A **collective noun** refers to an entity made up of more than one thing or person: *crowd*, *government*, *flock*. Whether such a word functions as a singular or a plural depends on several factors.

SOME ARE ALWAYS SINGULAR OR ALWAYS PLURAL

The **mob** <u>was</u> turning ugly.

A mob is treated as a unit, since by definition the people who make it up could not individually exhibit mob traits.

The **supplies** <u>were</u> running low.

You can have *a supply of* something, but when the reference is to provisions, this word is always plural.

Where <u>are</u> the **binoculars?**

Items that are made up of two connected parts often take a plural construction—*scissors*, *slacks*, *glasses*, *pants*, *pliers*. They are only properly used as singulars if preceded by the phrase *a pair of*.

SOME ARE SINGULAR WHEN USED IN ONE SENSE, AND PLURAL IN ANOTHER

The new **headquarters** <u>are</u> in Paris.
[the physical entity]

Headquarters is waiting for an answer.
[the corporate entity]

Statistics is the most difficult course in the program.
[the field or body of knowledge]

The **statistics** show that highway accidents are decreasing.
[the individual items of information]

SOME CAN GO EITHER WAY

That is, you treat them as either plurals or singulars depending on whether you want the focus to be on the unit or on the members it comprises.

The **staff** seems very competent.
The **staff** seem very competent.

The **couple** has a young daughter.
The **couple** have a young daughter.

My **family** wants the best for me.
My **family** want the best for me.

SOME ARE DETERMINED BY CONTEXT

Even for those collective nouns that can normally go either way, the context sometimes dictates whether one form or the other is appropriate.

The **staff** have many specialized skills.
[reference is to the individual staff members]

The **couple** get along very well together.
[reference is to the two individuals who make up the couple]

My **family** is very close-knit.
[reference is to the unit]

BE CONSISTENT WITH COLLECTIVE NOUNS

With a collective noun that can go either way, be careful that you do not start referring to it as singular and then switch to plural, or vice versa. This can entail using either the wrong verb form or the wrong pronoun. For example, the following sentences are *incorrect:*

The couple <u>lives</u> in New York but <u>go</u> to Florida for the winters.
The committee <u>is</u> adamant that <u>their</u> recommendations be adopted.
My company <u>has</u> an employment policy that <u>they've</u> adhered to for
   years.
After <u>their</u> big win, the team <u>feels</u> it can take it easy for a while.
The group of ticketholders <u>was</u> furiously demanding refunds of <u>their</u>
   money.

If you have created such a construction, think about whether the focus should really be on the whole or on the individuals it comprises—and whichever way you go, be consistent.

The couple <u>live</u> in New York but <u>go</u> to Florida for the winters.
The committee <u>is</u> adamant that <u>its</u> recommendations be adopted.

For more on this topic, see "Agreement Between Pronoun and Antecedent" under "Pronouns" on page 253.

TERMS OF QUANTITY

Although most plural subjects take plural verbs, nouns that refer to measurements of money, time or distance are treated as singulars. That is, the sum is viewed as a unit.

Two hours <u>is</u> plenty of time.
Twelve yards of material <u>seems</u> like more than enough for a doll's dress.
Lying there in plain view <u>was</u> the missing **four hundred thousand**
   dollars.
Eleven cents <u>is</u> hardly going to cover lunch.

Of course, if the emphasis is intended to be on the individual items, use a plural.

The **forty minutes** of the class <u>were</u> dragging by with agonizing
   slowness.
The **thirteen dollars** <u>were</u> dropped into the till one by one.

Optionally, you may treat other terms of quantity as singulars as well, if they are describing something that is singular in sense.

Six cups of flour <u>is</u> what the recipe calls for.
<u>Is</u> **three pinches** of salt too much?

A generation ago, no one in the world of professional skating would have believed that **four revolutions** in the air <u>was</u> possible.

PROBLEM PRONOUNS

Most pronouns don't cause difficulty when it comes to agreeing with a verb (*it is*, *they are* and so on). The ones that tend to be misused are those that refer to multitudes but are singular in construction, and those that go both ways.

Pronouns in the first category include *each*, *every*, *either*, *neither*, *everything*, *everyone*, *everybody*, *anyone* and *anybody*.

Either candidate <u>seems</u> credible.
Either of the candidates <u>seems</u> credible.
Neither of us <u>wants</u> to go.
Neither of the options <u>is</u> acceptable.
Everything in the boxes <u>goes</u> into the large filing cabinet.
Where <u>has</u> **everybody** gone?

They are even singular when used in combination.

Anything and everything <u>goes</u>.
Anybody and everybody <u>is</u> welcome.
Each and every dish <u>was</u> chipped.

As with nouns, don't be distracted by parenthetical or modifying phrases intervening between subject and verb.

Everything about her presentation, the examples, the slide show and the handouts, <u>was</u> rated highly.

Pronouns in the second category include *all*, *more*, *most*, *some*, *any* and *none*. These pronouns take a plural verb when associated with a multitude, and a singular verb when associated with a unit.

All the chores <u>have</u> been completed.
All the snow <u>was</u> melted.
<u>Is</u> there **any** salt in the shaker?
<u>Are</u> there **any** questions?

The pronoun *none* poses a particular challenge. Strictly speaking it is a contraction for *not one*, a singular, but sometimes the singular construction sounds a bit pedantic. And in certain cases it can be taken to mean *not any*, which could be associated with either a singular or a plural. Thus, the decision as to how to treat it depends partly on whether a singular or a plural notion predominates, and partly on how formal a tone you wish to achieve.

> The candidates seem interchangeable; **none** <u>stands</u> out as the best leader.
> [not one; verb is singular]

> **None** but the foolhardy <u>eat</u> at this place.
> [not any; verb is plural]

> **None** of these options <u>is</u> satisfactory.
> **None** of these options <u>are</u> satisfactory.
> [singular form is more correct, but plural form is acceptable]

PROBLEM PHRASES

When it comes to subject-verb agreement, certain phrases cause more than their share of confusion. Some particularly troublesome ones are *one of, the only one of, more than one, one or more, one in*. . . [a certain number], *a number of* and *the number of.* (Not surprisingly, these problem wordings all have something to do with notions of singularity or plurality.)

Exercise

In the following, which of the verbs in parentheses is correct?

> Horatio is one of those people who (is, are) late for everything.
> Albertine is the only one of the guests who (needs, need) a lift.
> As the witnesses filed out, more than one (was, were) overcome by emotion.
> Included with each set (is, are) one or more evaluation forms.
> It is estimated that one in four adults (has, have) difficulty reading.
> A number of students (has, have) already registered.
> The number of cases (was, were) surprising.

Answers

> Horatio is one of those people who <u>are</u> late for everything.

The key to understanding this undeniably tricky construction is to realize that there is more than one subject here. (A sentence is not limited to one.) Effectively, this sentence is saying two things: There are some people who are late for everything, and Horatio is one of them.

Albertine is the only one of the guests who <u>needs</u> a lift.

Again, there are two subjects here, but the focus is different. Effectively, this sentence is saying that there is one guest who needs a lift, and that one is Albertine. It is not saying that there are guests, plural, who need lifts.

As the witnesses filed out, more than one <u>was</u> overcome by emotion.

Logically, *more than one* implies a plural, but by convention this construction is treated as singular. (Note that you would refer to *more than one witness*, not *more than one witnesses*.)

Included with each set <u>are</u> one or more evaluation forms.

One might argue that this is a case of alternative subjects linked by *or* where the part closest to the verb is singular and hence the verb should be singular. However, by convention, the phrase *one or more* is taken to be plural.

It is estimated that one in four adults <u>has</u> difficulty reading.

Although constructions such as this obviously refer to a plurality, grammatically the subject is *one*, so the verb is singular. However, many authorities say, with some reasonableness, that the plural form should be considered acceptable as well. Which way you choose to go may depend on the level of formality of your writing.

A number of students <u>have</u> already registered.

The phrase *a number of* is always treated as plural.

The number of cases <u>was</u> surprising.

The phrase *the number of* is always treated as singular.

UNUSUAL PLURALS AND SINGULARS

As discussed under "Plural Formations" on page 42, not all nouns in English form their plurals by adding *s*. The majority of nonstandard plurals do not cause confusion, but a few are regularly misused as singulars. Conversely, some singular nouns are taken to be plurals.

Misunderstandings of either type lead to errors in subject-verb agreement; sometimes because the subject is wrong, sometimes because the verb is wrong.

Exercise

Correct the following sentences:

The kudos for this extraordinary film go to the scriptwriter.

The main criteria for admission is an excellent grade point average.

The media of television is a powerful means of influencing people.

Rickets are best prevented by adequate vitamin D and exposure to sunlight.

We won't know the outcome until our data has been fully analyzed.

The phenomena of shooting stars has fascinated people throughout history.

Graffiti was scrawled all over the walls.

Dominoes are an easy game to learn.

At the border crossing, customs usually process us quickly.

The mathematics of the problem haven't been worked out yet.

Answers

The **kudos** for this extraordinary film <u>goes</u> to the scriptwriter.
Kudos, of Greek origin, is a singular noun meaning praise or credit. There is no such thing as an individual "kudo." (Another caution about this word: More than one slightly confused writer has offered *kudus* to recipients who might not be all that grateful to be presented with large African antelopes.)

The main **criterion** for admission <u>is</u> an excellent grade point average.
A commonly misused plural. One criterion *is*; multiple criteria *are*.

The **medium** of television <u>is</u> a powerful means of influencing people.
Another commonly misused plural. One medium *is*; multiple media *are*. The plural form is properly used when referring to some combination of television, radio, newspapers, magazines, etc., or to the people who work for such entities, as in *The media were swarming around the hotel.* (Note though that *multimedia* would be treated as singular, because it refers to a field rather than to the components

that constitute a multimedia product. See the example for *mathematics,* below.)

Rickets is best prevented by adequate vitamin D and exposure to sunlight. Despite its *s* ending, rickets is simply the name of a disorder, and hence is singular. The same holds for some other diseases: for example, *shingles, measles, mumps.*

We won't know the outcome until our **data** have been fully analyzed. *Data* is the plural of the rarely (if ever) used *datum,* meaning a single piece of factual information, such as a measurement or a statistic. As a plural noun, it properly takes a plural verb. However, it is increasingly being treated as a singular noun meaning the total body of facts accumulated. Which way you handle it may depend on the expectations of your audience. In scientific and academic writing, plural usage is the only correct way; in linguistically laxer environments, such as corporations, singular usage is accepted and may even be required. (It must be acknowledged that words do evolve. For example, the uncontroversial singular *agenda,* a list of individual to-do items, originated as a plural of *agendum.*)

The **phenomenon** of shooting stars **has** fascinated people throughout history.
Like *criteria, phenomena* is plural. One phenomenon *is*; multiple phenomena *are.*

Graffiti were scrawled all over the walls.
Graffiti is properly the plural of *graffito,* a single drawing or message scribbled on public property. The singular is unlikely to be used, but the plural should be treated as a plural.

Dominoes is an easy game to learn.
The individual pieces used in the game are plural (one domino, multiple dominoes), but when used as the name of the game, this word is simply a singular noun that ends in *s*. The same holds for other games that are described as plurals: for example, *checkers* or *draughts, horseshoes* or *quoits, ninepins* or *tenpins, tiddledywinks.*

At the border crossing, **customs** usually processes us quickly.
Used in the sense of traditions or habits, *customs* would be plural

(one custom, multiple customs), but the word referring to the agency responsible for checking travellers and baggage is singular.

The **mathematics** of the problem <u>hasn't</u> been worked out yet.

Despite the *s* ending, *mathematics* is always singular in construction. The same applies to the names of a number of other academic or professional areas: for example, *physics*, *linguistics*, *metaphysics*, *genetics*.

Achieving Parallel Structure

The versatility of the English language makes it possible to express the same concept in many ways. The problem is, this freedom makes it all too easy to start composing a sentence one way and then switch tactics midstream. The result may be a passage that is guilty of what grammarians call **faulty parallelism**—a clumsy construction in which the elements bump up against each other uncomfortably instead of meshing. In itself each element may be perfectly grammatical, but it doesn't fit with the others.

Ensuring parallelism in your writing does *not* mean that every sentence should be structured the same way. What it does mean is that if you are creating a sentence, a list or a passage that contains elements related in purpose or structure, these elements must be presented in the same grammatical form. Thus, you must not go arbitrarily from the active voice to the passive, from the second person to the third, from the present tense to the past, from a series of adjectives to a noun. You must also be consistent in your use of minor words such as prepositions, articles, pronouns and conjunctions.

The effects of faulty parallelism can range from subtle to jarring. Certain errors may be noticed only on close inspection; others may render a sentence noticeably awkward or confusing. Some writers deliberately introduce faulty parallelism out of a mistaken belief that the variety makes for more interesting reading; more typically, a writer fails to recognize a problem or simply isn't paying enough attention. Always remember to focus on the whole as well as the parts, particularly with sentences that are long and complex.

As with other rules in English grammar, you may at times decide to bend this one if you feel that a variation in grammatical form would make a sentence more vibrant or capture your intended meaning more precisely. That is, do not avoid a catchy phrasing out of an over-devotion to technicalities. Be certain, however, that you have a valid reason for rejecting the more correct alternatives.

AVOIDING FAULTY PARALLELISM

Exercise

Each of the following sentences contains a problem with parallel structure. What is it, and how would you correct it?

The lecture was long, a bore and uninspiring.

Planning a surprise party calls for organizing, scheduling and cunning.

He had always preferred talking to listening, and to give rather than to take direction.

Her responsibilities were the management of the PR department and to attend trade shows.

A computerized database index needs to be reorganized when it has become fragmented, or to correct the skewing of values.

She told him to get to the hotel by six o'clock, that he should check with the concierge for messages, leave his luggage at the front desk and to wait for her in the lobby.

The consultant objected to the proposal, saying that the costs would be exorbitant and because the training facilities were insufficient.

It may be necessary to either add or subtract items from this list.

Courses are offered in spring, summer and in fall.

The revised plan called for lower salaries, operating budgets and longer hours.

Writers who work on a freelance basis don't get steady paychecks, but one has the advantage of extra tax breaks.

Participants should sign in by noon and pick up your registration materials at the front desk.

Go to the "Options" menu to change the display colors, fonts, type size, set predefined breaks in your program or open the dictionary.

Customers may either pick up the merchandise themselves, or the company will deliver it for a small fee.

He not only shoveled the walkway, but also the stairs and balcony.

The bankruptcy proceedings involved accountants, litigation experts, tax and corporate lawyers.

The stocky and self-confessed plagiarist showed no emotion as the charges against him were read out in court.

The text editing program enables you to do the following:

—change the background color of your screen

—to select different fonts

—cutting and pasting text

—creation of complex layouts

Suggested Revisions

The lecture was long, a bore and uninspiring.

The words *long* and *uninspiring* are adjectives, while *a bore* is a noun.

BETTER: The lecture was long, boring and uninspiring.

Planning a surprise party calls for organizing, scheduling and cunning.

Despite the common endings of the last three words, they are not grammatically equivalent. *Organizing* and *scheduling* are **gerunds**: words that function as nouns by adding *ing* to verbs. The third word, *cunning*, is a straightforward noun that just happens to end in *ing*. (There is no verb "to cunn.") The series should consist of all gerunds or all nouns. *Organize* can easily be made to fit either form, but the other two must be altered somewhat.

BETTER: Planning a surprise party calls for organizing, scheduling and scheming.

OR: Planning a surprise party calls for organization, cunning and scheduling skills.

He had always preferred talking to listening, and to give rather than to take direction.

Talking and *listening* are gerunds, while *to give* and *to take* are infinitives.

BETTER: He had always preferred talking to listening, and giving over taking direction.

Her responsibilities were the management of the PR department and to attend trade shows.

The first element is a noun, the second an infinitive.

BETTER: Her responsibilities were to manage the PR department and to attend trade shows.

OR: Her responsibilities were the management of the PR department and attendance at trade shows.

> A computerized database index needs to be reorganized when it has become fragmented, or to correct the skewing of values.

The focus switches from what is happening to the database index to what the person using it should do. Since the subject of this sentence is the database index, not the user, the passive voice is more appropriate. (For more on this, see "Active Versus Passive Voice" on page 286.)

BETTER: A computerized database index needs to be reorganized when it has become fragmented or when its values have become skewed.

> She told him to get to the hotel by six o'clock, that he should check with the concierge for messages, leave his luggage at the front desk and to wait for her in the lobby.

The same wording must be used for each element. Repeating *that he should* four times would be clumsy; *to* is better. If *to* is used, it must be put either before each element in the series or just at the start.

BETTER: She told him to get to the hotel by six o'clock, to check with the concierge for messages, to leave his luggage at the front desk and to wait for her in the lobby.

OR: She told him to get to the hotel by six o'clock, check with the concierge for messages, leave his luggage at the front desk and wait for her in the lobby.

> The consultant objected to the proposal, saying that the costs would be exorbitant and because the training facilities were insufficient.

There is no reason to switch from *that* to *because*. In addition to the faulty parallelism, note that this slightly changes the meaning, turning the consultant's second objection from a matter of opinion to a statement of fact.

BETTER: The consultant objected to the proposal, saying that the costs would be exorbitant and that the training facilities were insufficient.

It would also be acceptable to drop the second *that*, since it can be inferred.

It may be necessary to either add or subtract items from this list.

If different words in a sentence take different prepositions, each preposition must be included. Writers often simply let the preposition that comes last serve for all, without checking to see if it's appropriate. In this example, it's not: You can't add something *from* something.

> **BETTER:** It may be necessary to either add items to or subtract them from this list.

Courses are offered in spring, summer and in fall.

When the same preposition applies to a series of elements, it may be either repeated for each one or used just once—but you must be consistent. Don't include it for some items and drop it for others.

> **BETTER:** Courses are offered in spring, in summer and in fall.
>
> **OR:** Courses are offered in spring, summer and fall.

The more concise version would usually be preferred, but you may sometimes for reasons of style decide to go with the repetition.

> The revised plan called for lower salaries, operating budgets and longer hours.

The adjective *lower* is intended to apply to the first two elements, but fails to connect with the second one because the next element *(hours)* takes a different adjective. In fact, the sentence is ambiguous: if *lower* is taken to apply only to salaries, a reader could assume that the plan calls not for a lower operating budget, but for its creation—that is, that no such budget existed up till now.

> **BETTER:** The revised plan called for lower salaries, lower operating budgets and longer hours.
>
> **OR:** The revised plan called for lower salaries and operating budgets, and longer hours.

> Writers who work on a freelance basis don't get steady paychecks, but one has the advantage of extra tax breaks.

The sentence switches from the plural noun *writers* to the singular pronoun *one.*

> **BETTER:** Writers who work on a freelance basis don't get steady paychecks, but they have the advantage of extra tax breaks.
>
> **OR:** As a freelance writer, one doesn't get a steady paycheck, but one has the advantage of extra tax breaks.

> Participants should sign in by noon and pick up your registration materials at the front desk.

The sentence switches from the third person to the second.

BETTER: Participants should sign in by noon and pick up their registration materials at the front desk.

OR: Sign in by noon and pick up your registration materials at the front desk.

For more on this, see "Agreement Between Pronoun and Antecedent" on page 253.

> Go to the "Options" menu to change the display colors, fonts, type size, set predefined breaks in your program or open the dictionary.

The verb *change* is intended to apply to only the first three elements, but there is no clear indication of where the next verb takes over. The sentence seems to be saying that you can use this menu to change the display colors, to change fonts, to change type size and to "change set predefined breaks in your program"—the last, of course, not making any sense.

BETTER: Go to the "Options" menu to change the display colors, fonts and type size; to set predefined breaks in your program; or to open the dictionary.

> Customers may either pick up the merchandise themselves, or the company will deliver it for a small fee.

Saying *Customers may either* implies that the *customers* will be able to do one of two things—but then the focus switches to a different actor, the company. The two options that follow *either* must be parallel. Whenever you use the combination *either/or*, check to see if the syntax still stands up if you put the second option in place of the first. The sequence *Customers may either the company will deliver it for a small fee* clearly doesn't work.

BETTER: Customers may either pick up the merchandise themselves or have it delivered for a small fee.

OR: Either customers may pick up the merchandise themselves, or the company will deliver it for a small fee.

> He not only shoveled the walkway, but also the stairs and balcony.

The contrasted items that come after *not only* must be parallel. Putting *not only* before the verb sets up an expectation that another action will follow; for example, *He not only shoveled the walkway, but also salted it.* Whenever you use the combination *not only/but also*, always put *not only* immediately before the first of the pair of elements that are being contrasted. Thus, if there are two actions involved, put it immediately before the first action; if there is one action affecting two objects, put the action first, and have *not only* come immediately before the first object.

BETTER: He shoveled not only the walkway, but also the stairs and balcony.

The bankruptcy proceedings involved accountants, litigation experts, tax and corporate lawyers.

The intention, of course, is to refer to tax lawyers and corporate lawyers, but the word *tax* is left hanging by itself. Grammatically, it's as if the sentence read *The bankruptcy proceedings involved accountants, litigation experts and tax.* Although one could ordinarily say *tax and corporate lawyers,* in this case the word *and* is serving to link the final item *(corporate lawyers)* to the rest of the sentence, and so is not available to link *tax* to *lawyers.*

BETTER: The bankruptcy proceedings involved accountants, litigation experts, tax lawyers and corporate lawyers.

OR: The bankruptcy proceedings involved accountants, litigation experts, and tax and corporate lawyers.

The stocky and self-confessed plagiarist showed no emotion as the charges against him were read out in court.

The adjectives *stocky* and *self-confessed* are not equivalent. *Stocky* can stand alone: A person can simply be described as stocky, the way he or she can be described as dark haired, athletic, grouchy, left-handed, etc. But one cannot be simply "self-confessed": By definition, one has to be a self-confessed *something*—a drug dealer, an adulterer, a chocoholic. *Self-confessed* is thus tied to the noun that follows, and the string *self-confessed plagiarist* effectively becomes a unit, leaving *stocky* without anything to latch onto. Grammatically, it is as if the sentence read *The stocky and plagiarist showed no emotion,* which clearly doesn't work. Removal of the *and* solves the problem, since *stocky* then becomes a modifier of the unit *self-confessed plagiarist.*

BETTER: The stocky self-confessed plagiarist showed no emotion as the charges against him were read out in court.

The text editing program enables you to do the following:
—change the background color of your screen
—to select different fonts
—cutting and pasting text
—creation of complex layouts

Items in a list must be presented the same way. In addition, if there is lead-in text, each list item must mesh grammatically with it so that the lead-in and the list item together form a coherent sentence.

BETTER: The text editing program enables you to do the following:
—change the background color of your screen
—select different fonts
—cut and paste text
—create complex layouts

Something else to watch for with lists is that you do not phrase some items as complete grammatical sentences and others as single words or sentence fragments. Both forms are legitimate, but not in combination. If you are creating a list where certain items must be phrased as complete sentences, rework the others so that they become complete sentences too.

PARALLELISM AS A LITERARY DEVICE

Apart from the grammatical requirement of maintaining a consistent structure, parallelism in the form of deliberate repetition can be used as a literary device to achieve a pleasing cadence or to lend additional emphasis and color. Note how it is used in the following extracts:

The jig-saw pieces came together piece by piece, the real Rebecca took shape and form before me, stepping from her shadow world like a living figure from a picture frame. Rebecca slashing at her horse;

Rebecca seizing life with her two hands; Rebecca, triumphant, leaning down from the minstrel's gallery with a smile on her lips.

—DAPHNE DU MAURIER, *Rebecca*

He was a good mixer, and in three days knew everyone on board. He ran everything. He managed the sweeps, conducted the auctions, collected money for prizes at the sports, got up quoit and golf matches, organized the concert, and arranged the fancy-dress ball. He was everywhere and always. He was certainly the best-hated man in the ship.

—W. SOMERSET MAUGHAM, *Mr Know-All*

The external world could take care of itself. In the meantime it was folly to grieve, or to think. The prince had provided all the appliances of pleasure. There were buffoons, there were improvisatori, there were ballet-dancers, there were musicians, there were cards, there was Beauty, there was wine. All these and security were within. Without was the "Red Death."

—EDGAR ALLAN POE, *The Masque of the Red Death*

In poetry, the device of deliberate repetition is common.

"One kiss, my bonny sweetheart, I'm after a prize tonight,
But I shall be back with the yellow gold before the morning light;
Yet, if they press me sharply, and harry me through the day,
Then look for me by moonlight,
Watch for me by moonlight
I'll come to thee by moonlight, though hell should bar the way."

—ALFRED NOYES, *The Highwayman*

The ice was here, the ice was there,
The ice was all around:
It cracked and growled, and roared and howled,
Like noises in a swound!

—SAMUEL TAYLOR COLERIDGE, *The Rime of the Ancient Mariner*

Positioning Modifiers Correctly

A **modifier** is an element of a sentence that describes or qualifies some other element. Adjectives and adverbs are the most common modifiers (the *leafy* trees swayed *gracefully* in the *tantalizingly cool* breeze), but a phrase or dependent clause can act as one too.

You must ensure that all parts in a sentence are positioned so that any modifying element is acting upon what it is supposed to. Failure to do so may lead to some rather disconcerting results. There are three types of problems to look out for:

- Dangling modifiers
- Misplaced modifiers
- Squinting modifiers

These are described in turn below, followed by an exercise that presents examples of all three.

DANGLING MODIFIERS

If a sentence is carelessly constructed so that the entity to be modified is implied rather than explicitly stated, the modifier is left "dangling"—left at loose ends as it were—and in the absence of the intended "modify-ee" ends up latching onto whatever element happens to be in the appropriate position. The result is a nonsense sentence. The absurdities that result from dangling modifiers can range from the obvious to the subtle; the latter are more dangerous in that they're less easy to spot. English is a forgiving language, so even when syntax is garbled, readers will often process a sentence as the writer intended it.

Dangling modifiers occur when a sentence consists of a phrase that says something about a following clause—but the subject of that clause is not what it is supposed to be. (See "Basic Sentence Structure" on page 55 for definitions of these terms.) For example:

Just two years after finishing graduate school, Gladys's career took off.

Presumably it was Gladys who finished grad school, but she makes no direct appearance in the sentence. Grammatically, what is being said here is that Gladys's *career* finished grad school and then took off (what did it do—leave her for another woman?). The problem can be remedied by rephrasing either the phrase or the clause.

Just two years after Gladys finished graduate school, her career took off.
Just two years after finishing graduate school, Gladys saw her career take off.

MISPLACED MODIFIERS

Like a dangling modifier, a misplaced modifier acts on something other than what the writer intended. In this case the problem is not that the wrong entity is functioning as the subject of the sentence, but that the modifier is in the wrong position relative to what it should be affecting. (Whenever possible, the two elements should lie right next to each other.) For example:

We put out an appeal for more volunteers to help with the fall program at last week's meeting.

Presumably what took place at last week's meeting was an appeal for help with the fall program, but the positioning of the modifier makes it sound as if the fall program itself was held at the meeting. The problem can be remedied by moving the modifying phrase.

At last week's meeting, we put out an appeal for more volunteers to help with the fall program.

SQUINTING MODIFIERS

In some cases the placement of a modifier is not so much wrong as ambiguous, in that it could apply to either the element that precedes

GRAMMATICALLY CORRECT

it or the one that follows it. These are called "squinting modifiers," as they seem to be looking in both directions. For example:

The coach said on Thursday we'd have to start working harder.

Was this said on Thursday, or would the hard work begin on Thursday? This sentence should read as one of the following:

On Thursday, the coach said we'd have to start working harder.
The coach said we'd have to start working harder on Thursday.

A squinting modifier can be particularly difficult to notice, since if you read the sentence the right way it doesn't actually contain a problem. It's a good example of why it is always advisable to have someone else look over your work: This is the sort of error a "fresh eye" is likelier to spot.

More examples of problems with modifiers follow. Note how you may have to read such sentences a couple of times before you pick up on the fact that there is something wrong with them.

Exercise
Correct the following sentences:

Upon opening the pantry door, a stack of cans flew out at her.
When loaded, type "Go" to start the program.
Unlike dashes, a writer may use parentheses to enclose an entire sentence, not just part of a sentence.
Awaiting the starter's gun, Pierre's heart began to thump rapidly.
After ransacking the house, Ben's wallet finally turned up under the dog's bowl.
Thumbing through the newspaper, my eye was suddenly caught by a small article.
Leaning over the hospital bed, she looked into the vacant man's eyes but could see no spark of recognition.
At its next meeting, the Board of Education will debate whether teachers should be allowed to administer adrenaline to students who experience severe allergic reactions without written permission.
The formerly glamorous countess is now continually mocked in the tabloids for her taste in clothing, weight and overspending.

The suspect's condition was upgraded from serious to fair after he fell from a third-story balcony while trying to evade arrest.

The gallery that was featured in the evening news recently had another major exhibit.

He liked immensely sugary desserts.

The tramp being asked to leave nastily replied that he was within his rights to be there.

Suggested Revisions

The following sentences contain dangling modifiers. Note that it is not enough to simply have the intended target of the modifier mentioned in the sentence, if it's not acting as the subject.

Upon opening the pantry door, a stack of cans flew out at her.
How did the stack of cans manage to open the pantry door?
BETTER: Upon her opening the pantry door, a stack of cans flew out at her.

When loaded, type "Go" to start the program.
Now *there's* an instruction some computer users would happily follow. The more abstemious, though, might have problems.
BETTER: When the program is loaded, type "Go" to start it.

Unlike dashes, a writer may use parentheses to enclose an entire sentence, not just part of a sentence.
This seems unfair: If writers may use parentheses this way, why shouldn't dashes be permitted to do so as well?
BETTER: Unlike dashes, parentheses may be used to enclose an entire sentence, not just part of a sentence.

Awaiting the starter's gun, Pierre's heart began to thump rapidly.
Pierre's heart must have good ears.
BETTER: Awaiting the starter's gun, Pierre felt his heart begin to thump rapidly.

After ransacking the house, Ben's wallet finally turned up under the dog's bowl.
Ben has one active wallet.
BETTER: After ransacking the house, Ben finally found his wallet under the dog's bowl.

Thumbing through the newspaper, my eye was suddenly caught by a small article.

How many thumbs does this person's eye have, exactly?

BETTER: As I thumbed through the newspaper, my eye was suddenly caught by a small article.

The following sentences contain misplaced modifiers:

Leaning over the hospital bed, she looked into the vacant man's eyes but could see no spark of recognition.

The man himself is vacant?

BETTER: Leaning over the hospital bed, she looked into the man's vacant eyes but could see no spark of recognition.

At its next meeting, the Board of Education will debate whether teachers should be allowed to administer adrenaline to students who experience severe allergic reactions without written permission.

One has to admire the discipline of those students who *do* first obtain permission.

BETTER: At its next meeting, the Board of Education will debate whether teachers should require written permission to administer adrenaline to students who experience severe allergic reactions.

The formerly glamorous countess is now continually mocked in the tabloids for her taste in clothing, weight and overspending.

What's wrong with the countess's taste in weight or her taste in overspending?

BETTER: The formerly glamorous countess is now continually mocked in the tabloids for her taste in clothing, her weight and her overspending.

OR: The formerly glamorous countess is now continually mocked in the tabloids for her weight, overspending and taste in clothing.

The suspect's condition was upgraded from serious to fair after he fell from a third-story balcony while trying to evade arrest.

Perhaps doctors should try throwing their patients off balconies to see if this improves their condition.

BETTER: The suspect, who fell from a third-story balcony while trying to evade arrest, has had his condition upgraded from serious to fair.

The following sentences contain squinting modifiers:

The gallery that was featured in the evening news recently had another major exhibit.

The gallery was recently featured, or it recently had an exhibit?

BETTER: The gallery that recently was featured in the evening news had another major exhibit.

OR: The gallery that was featured in the news had another major exhibit recently.

He liked immensely sugary desserts.

He liked such desserts immensely, or he liked his desserts immensely sugary?

BETTER: He had an immense liking for sugary desserts.

OR: He liked desserts that were immensely sugary.

The tramp being asked to leave nastily replied that he was within his rights to be there.

Who was speaking nastily: the tramp or the person asking him to leave?

BETTER: The tramp being asked to leave replied nastily that he was within his rights to be there.

OR: Upon being asked nastily to leave, the tramp replied that he was within his rights to be there.

Pronouns

Pronouns—stand-ins for nouns—are frequent stumbling blocks in English. We all know that a bull is *he,* a toaster is *it* and something that belongs to the Joneses is *theirs,* but some constructions are considerably dicier. This section looks at the following issues:

- Using the correct form of a pronoun
- Ensuring that a pronoun refers to the right antecedent
- Ensuring that a pronoun agrees with its antecedent

USING THE CORRECT FORM

> *For many weeks he pressed in vain*
> *His nose against the window-pane,*
> *And envied those who walked about*
> *Reducing their unwanted stout.*
> *None of the people he could see*
> *"Is quite" (he said) "as fat as me!"*
> *Then, with a still more moving sigh,*
> *"I mean" (he said) "as fat as I!"*
>
> A.A. MILNE, *When We Were Very Young*

Pronouns, unlike nouns, change form (**case**) depending on what role they play in a sentence. You would say *Ethelbert gave a CD player to Henrietta* and *Henrietta gave a CD player to Ethelbert,* but if the names were replaced by pronouns, these sentences would be *He gave a CD player to her* and *She gave a CD player to him.*

There are three cases: subjective, objective and possessive. A pronoun that represents the actor in a sentence is called the subject and takes the **subjective case**: for example, *I will be late*. A pronoun that represents the entity that is affected by the action of the subject is called the object and takes the **objective case**: For example, *Don't you wait for me*. The **possessive case** is used to indicate ownership, and differs depending on whether or not the possessed object follows the pronoun: *That's my chair/That chair is mine*.

No one would say *Me will be late, don't you wait for I*, but in some situations the correct pronoun is not so obvious. This section looks at a number of constructions that many writers get wrong. It does not present a comprehensive review, since English speakers intuitively use the majority of pronouns appropriately.

A word on this topic before beginning. With pronouns, probably more than any other aspect of English diction, there is considerable disparity between what the rule books say and how most people actually use the language. Educated, cultured speakers who wouldn't dream of saying *I can't go no further* or *he don't sing so good* will readily use pronouns in ways that contravene traditional grammar, often because they feel that the word that is technically correct would sound unnatural or overly formal. Or they may choose to use the "correct" form in formal and academic writing, but go with common idiom elsewhere. Most modern guides to English usage recognize this reality and stop short of dictating that every pronoun rule be followed under every circumstance. This book is no exception. It is important, however, that you be familiar with the rules so that if you choose to bend them you do so consciously. Experienced writers can distinguish between those situations where disregarding a rule would sound reasonable and those where disregarding it would sound just plain ignorant. In situations where you don't feel comfortable using either a stilted-sounding correct pronoun or a more natural-sounding but incorrect one, it may be best to recast the sentence.

PERSONAL PRONOUNS

Personal pronouns refer to people and things. The subjective personal pronouns are *I*, *you*, *he*, *she*, *it*, *we* and *they*, and the objective personal pronouns are *me, you, him, her, it, us* and *them*. Note that *you* and *it* are the same in both cases; the others change.

WHEN DO YOU USE *I* AND WHEN *ME*?
Exercise

1. (I/me) finally saw the light.
2. Felicia and (I/me) polished off the roast ox.
3. Both Aunt Minnie and (I/me) were hauled off for interrogation.
4. My brother can crochet better than (I/me).
5. The guys at the office gave Alice and (I/me) matching garden gnomes.
6. Thank you for inviting Roland and (I/me), but we both have to wash our hair that night.
7. Just between you and (I/me), I think he's lying through his teeth.
8. Sidney wanted the job more than (I/me).

Answers

1. I
2. I
3. I
4. I
5. me
6. me
7. me
8. it depends on the meaning

The pronoun is *I* when it represents the subject of the sentence: the actor or the center of interest. A subject is followed by an action or a description.

Sentence 1 is straightforward: a single subject *(I)*, followed by the action performed by that subject *(saw)*.

Sentence 2 contains a compound subject: two or more subjects that share the same verb and are linked by *and*. You treat each part of a compound subject exactly as you would if it were the only one. It should be obvious that you wouldn't say *me polished off the roast ox*.

Sentence 3 again contains a compound subject, this time one that is the recipient of an action rather than its performer. Don't be distracted by either the compound or the passive construction. It should be obvious that you wouldn't say *me was hauled off for interrogation.*

Sentence 4 is trickier: Here, it is less easy to recognize the pronoun as a subject because it is not followed by any verb. This is an example of an elliptical construction (see the discussion on page 85), in that the verb is implied but not stated. Effectively, this sentence is saying *My brother can crochet better than I can crochet:* Thus, the pronoun is a subject. It is only fair, however, to add that many people would use *me* in this type of construction, and some authorities state that it is permissible or even preferable to do so. You must determine your own comfort level.

In sentences 5, 6 and 7, the pronoun is *me* because in each case it represents the object: something that is acted on or affected by the subject. An object is not followed by an associated verb, either explicit or implied. In sentence 5, the pronoun is the target of the action *gave;* in sentence 6, it is the target of the action *inviting;* in sentence 7, it is the target of the preposition *between.* In all three cases, no action or description follows the pronoun.

When there is more than one object, people often think that *I* sounds more educated or genteel than *me.* (Some grammar books are kind enough to call this type of usage "hypercorrectness." A better term for it is "wrong.") If you are ever uncertain, mentally drop any distracting elements. It should be obvious that you wouldn't say *The guys gave I* or *Thank you for inviting I.*

Finally, in sentence 8, the pronoun is *I* if what's meant is *Sidney wanted the job more than I wanted the job* (an elliptical construction, where both *Sidney* and the pronoun are subjects), and *me* if what's meant is *Sidney wanted the job more than he wanted me* (both *the job* and the pronoun are objects). Because of the likelihood that many readers would not understand this distinction, it would often be better to fill in the implied words.

PERSONAL PRONOUNS WITH ELLIPTICAL CONSTRUCTIONS

You can apply the same strategies described above to determine when to use *she* and *her, he* and *him, we* and *us,* and *they* and *them.* That is, mentally fill in any elliptical constructions or drop any distracting nouns to help determine whether the pronoun is acting as a subject or an object.

Sally's not nearly as persnickety as *she*.
[as she is]

Louie can yell louder than *he*.
[than he can yell]

We asked the duchess and *him* to bring the dip.
[we asked him]

You and *she* should get a life.
[she should get a life]

Give the iguana to Max or *her*.
[give the iguana to her]

George and *he* were asked to dance the kazatsky.
[he was asked to dance]

Those bums have always thought they're better than *we*.
[than we are]

The tantrum thrown by the clerk and *us* had its effect.
[the tantrum thrown by us]

The space shuttle landing in the backyard excited Abe more than *them*.
[more than it excited them]

She wanted to go hang gliding as much as *they*.
[as much as they wanted to go]

In everyday speech, many people would say *Louie can yell louder than him* or *they think they're better than us*. A third option, if you are concerned about sounding too formal, is to avoid elliptical constructions and fill in the unstated verb: *Louie can yell louder than he can; They think they're better than we are*.

The following examples deal with another scenario:

Exercise
1. "Who's that tramping over my bridge?" "It's only (I/me), the smallest Billy Goat Gruff."
2. The only attendees still awake at the lecture were Miranda and (I/me).
3. "Which one is the author?" "That's (she/her) over there, on the trampoline."

4. Old King Cole was a merry old soul, and a merry old soul was (he/him).
5. It seems that my main competitor in the caber-tossing contest will be (she/her).
6. I felt that the last person I could trust with the chocolate truffles was (he/him).
7. The main suspects in the great Spam heist were (they/them).
8. A fine pair of fashion plates are (we/us)!

Answers

1. I
2. I
3. she
4. he
5. she
6. he
7. they
8. we

A pronoun following any form of the verb "to be"—am, are, is, was, were, will be, etc.—takes the subjective case, because it renames or restates the subject. In sentence 1, *I* renames the subject *it;* in sentence 5, *she* renames the subject *competitor,* and so on. If the wording were switched around, it would be clear that the pronoun is acting as the subject: *I* was the only attendee still awake at the lecture; *she* will be my main competitor.

In everyday speech, most people would probably say *it's only me, the only attendees still awake were Miranda and me, my main competitor will be her.* If you don't feel comfortable either way, consider recasting the sentence. For example, *Miranda and I were the only attendees still awake at the lecture.*

Normally a personal pronoun is used *instead* of the noun it refers to, as in all the examples above, but in some constructions it may be used *in addition* to the noun. How do you tell, then, if it takes the subjective or the objective case?

Exercise

1. (We/Us) drudges would like to have the afternoon off.
2. There's nobody here but (we/us) drudges.

3. The dean told (we/us) jocks that we'd better shape up academically.

4. The dean said that (we/us) jocks had better shape up academically.

5. For (we/us) baby boomers, the economic future is looking less rosy than the past.

6. The younger generation seem to feel that (we/us) baby boomers are a bunch of spoiled whiners.

7. There didn't seem to be much attention left over for the second-place finisher, (I/me).

8. After the tuba players, the trombonists, (he and I/him and me), threw pom-poms at the conductor.

Answers

1. we

2. us

3. us

4. we

5. us

6. we

7. me

8. he and I

When a noun and the pronoun that restates it appear side by side, simply treat the pronoun as you would if the noun weren't there. Thus, *we* would like to have the afternoon off; there's nobody here but *us;* the dean told *us;* the dean said that *we* had better shape up; for *us,* the future is less rosy; *we* are a bunch of whiners; there didn't seem to be attention left for *me; he and I* threw pom-poms. Again, in the subjective case the pronoun is the actor and is followed by a verb; in the objective case it is the target of an action and is not followed by a verb.

RELATIVE PRONOUNS

Relative pronouns are pronouns that introduce dependent clauses. (See page 57 for a definition of dependent clauses.) The most common of these are *who, whom, whoever, whomever, which* and *that.*

WHEN DO YOU USE *WHO* AND WHEN *WHOM?*

Use *who* and *whoever* when the pronoun should be in the subjective case; use *whom* and *whomever* when it should be in the objective case.

Exercise

1. (Who/Whom) shall I say is calling?
2. To (who/whom) do you wish to speak?
3. She was the one (who/whom) we wanted to support.
4. I was hoping to meet this mystery man, (who/whom) she said is her masseur.
5. (Who/Whom) do you think will win?
6. (Who/Whom) do you think they'll choose?
7. We asked only those employees (who/whom) we figured would be interested.
8. We asked only those employees (who/whom) we figured the customers would believe.

Answers

1. who
2. whom
3. whom
4. who
5. who
6. whom
7. who
8. whom

In sentences 1, 4, 5 and 7, the pronoun is associated with an action or a description (calling, being a masseur, winning, being interested), and hence takes the subjective case. In sentences 2, 3, 6 and 8, the pronoun is the target of someone else's action (being spoken to, being supported, being chosen, being believed), and hence takes the objective case.

A helpful trick is to mentally recast the phrase so that it would take either *him* or *he,* which are more intuitively understood. If it would take *him,* go with *whom* (both of which end in *m*); if it would take *he,* go with *who* (neither of which ends in *m*). (This mnemonic also works with *them* and *they,* but not with *her* and *she,* since there is no *m* in either of those words.) Thus: *He* is calling; I wish to speak to *him;* we wanted to support *him;* she said *he* is her masseur; *he* will win; they'll choose *him;* we figured *they* would be interested; we figured the customers would believe *them.*

You can use the same strategy to determine whether a sentence should take *whoever* or *whomever.* Thus,

> Would *whoever* borrowed the karaoke machine please keep it.
>
> [*he* borrowed it]
>
> *Whoever* is responsible for this mess should clean it up.
>
> [*he* is responsible]
>
> Please return that hideous lampshade to *whomever* you got it from.
>
> [you got it from *him*]
>
> Feel free to go sky-surfing with *whomever* you want.
>
> [you want *him*]

In everyday speech, most people would probably say *Who do you think they'll choose?* or *Feel free to go sky-surfing with whoever you want.* Whether or not you make the subjective/objective distinction in such cases should depend on the formality of your writing.

WHEN DO YOU USE *THAT* AND WHEN *WHICH?*

The issue here is how the information that follows the pronoun relates to the subject of the sentence.

Use *that* when the dependent clause is providing identifying information about the subject. For example: *Spiders that live underground do not spin webs.* The subject of the sentence is *spiders*—but not all spiders. The dependent clause *that live underground* applies to only some species of spider, and hence is acting to further identify the subject.

Use *which* when the clause is simply providing additional information about a subject that is already fully identified. For example: *Spiders, which have eight legs, are not classified as insects.* Again, the subject is *spiders,* and in this case we mean all spiders. The dependent clause *which have eight legs* applies to every species of spider; hence, it is not serving to further identify the subject.

For a more detailed discussion of this distinction, see page 77.

WHEN DO YOU USE *THAT* AND WHEN *WHO?*

The issue here is whether or not the subject is a human being. It is usual to use *who* when referring to people *(The Man Who Fell to Earth; The Boy Who Cried Wolf)* and *that* when referring to animals or objects *(The Mouse That Roared; The Eggplant That Ate Manhattan).*

This distinction, however, is not universally followed. Some writers use *who* for animals, at least for individual animals that are viewed (or should that be *who are viewed?*) as having personalities *(The Dog Who Wouldn't Be).* Less commonly, some writers use *who* when referring to corporate entities *(We went with the management company who offered the lowest bid).* Some authorities accept *that* for people when the reference is general rather than specific *(I can't stand people that never listen; She always seems to end up with men that only want her for her brains).* It is usually considered preferable, though, to go with *who* for people and *that* for everything else.

REFLEXIVE PRONOUNS

Reflexive pronouns are pronouns that end in *self*. It is a common error to put reflexive pronouns where they have no business going.

Exercise

1. Elmer and (I/myself) were jointly responsible for the riot.
2. Imelda gave the report directly to Hubert and (me/myself).
3. The director and (I/myself) had a long discussion about the recipe for blintzes.
4. Why did this sort of thing always happen to (me/myself)?

Answers

1. I
2. me
3. I
4. me

Some people seem to think it sounds more important or genteel to say *myself* when plain *I* or *me* would do. Wrong, wrong, wrong. If the pronoun is acting as a subject, use *I;* if it is acting as an object, use *me*. The only circumstances in which the *self* form of a pronoun is appropriate are the following:

When the subject and object are the same entity.

> You take yourself too seriously.
> She looked at herself critically.
> The machine turned itself off automatically.
> The little piggy took himself off to the market.

When you need to clarify that the subject has performed some action alone or unassisted.

> I couldn't possibly go by myself.
> She did all the cooking herself.
> Did you finish that entire sugar pie yourself?
> They cleaned up all by themselves.

When the pronoun acts to emphasize another word (in this role, it is called an **intensive pronoun**).

> I myself would never sink that low.
> Morris himself has no idea how the sour cream got into the VCR.
> We ourselves expected the worst.
> My reputation itself was at risk.

POSSESSIVE PRONOUNS

Pronouns in the possessive case differ depending on whether or not the possessed object follows the pronoun: *my* or *mine, your* or *yours, her* or *hers, his, its, our* or *ours, their* or *theirs* (note that *his* and *its* don't change). This distinction does not pose any difficulty for most writers.

However, certain possessive pronouns are often confused with their homonyms: *its* and *it's, their* and *they're, your* and *you're, whose* and *who's.* In each of these cases, the word without an apostrophe is the possessive, and the one with an apostrophe is a contraction of the pronoun plus another word.

• *Its* is the possessive of *it* (has your car had its oil checked lately; every dog has its day). *It's* is a contraction for either *it is* (it's not fair; do you think it's going to snow) or *it has* (it's barely begun; it's been a long day).

• *Their* is the possessive of *they* (is that their house; I just met their daughter). *They're* is a contraction for *they are* (I heard they're not coming; they're moving to Italy).

• *Your* is the possessive of *you* (here's your coat; how's your dog). *You're* is a contraction for *you are* (you're very welcome; you're not so easy to please).

• *Whose* is the possessive of *who* (it was an idea whose time had come; whose car is blocking the driveway; anyone whose job is done may leave now; I don't care whose fault it is). *Who's* is a contraction for either *who is* (who's driving my way; I don't care who's responsible) or *who has* (anyone who's finished may leave now; would the person who's borrowed the pencil sharpener please return it). Note that *who's* applies only to people, but *whose* can apply to either people or objects.

For more on this distinction, see page 195, under "Apostrophe."

REFERRING TO THE RIGHT ANTECEDENT

"Ugh!" said the Lory, with a shiver.

"I beg your pardon!" said the Mouse, frowning, but very politely. "Did you speak?"

"Not I!" said the Lory, hastily.

"I thought you did," said the Mouse. "I proceed. 'Edwin and Morcar, the earls of Mercia and Northumbria, declared for him; and even Stigand, the patriotic archbishop of Canterbury, found it advisable—'"

"Found what?" said the Duck.

"Found it," the Mouse replied rather crossly: "of course you know what 'it' means."

"I know what 'it' means well enough, when I find a thing," said the Duck: "it's generally a frog or a worm. The question is, what did the archbishop find?"

> *The Mouse did not notice this question, but hurriedly*
> *went on, " '—found it advisable to go with Edgar Atheling*
> *to meet William and offer him the crown. . . .' "*
>
> LEWIS CARROLL, *Alice in Wonderland*

The **antecedent** of a pronoun is the word to which it refers. For example, in the preceding sentence, the word *pronoun* is the antecedent of the pronoun *it*. The antecedent may exist in the same sentence as the pronoun or in an earlier sentence, or, less commonly, it may come after. Some pronouns logically do not have antecedents; for example, *Who was at the door?* And certain pronouns are themselves antecedents for other pronouns; more on this below.

The relationship between a pronoun and its antecedent must be crystal clear. Watch for errors such as the following:

MISSING ANTECEDENTS

Sometimes a writer uses a pronoun, failing to notice that the entity the pronoun is intended to refer to hasn't in fact been explicitly named. For example:

> Research has shown that men are generally more satisfied than women with marriage, and that they seek divorce less often. It also has shown that they live longer than bachelors.

Men live longer than bachelors? The writer obviously means *married men*, but the preceding sentence doesn't actually contain that term, so *they* ends up latching onto the wrong entity. Since the intended antecedent is not explicitly stated, it is not possible to have a pronoun substitute for it.

BETTER: Research has shown that men are generally more satisfied than women with marriage, and that they seek divorce less often. It also has shown that married men live longer than bachelors.

Similarly,

> The use of free-format tables for writing software specifications may seem counter to the general trend; however, they give the developer certain advantages.

Here, *they* is intended to refer to *free-format tables*, but note that the subject of the sentence is actually *the use of*—a singular.

Although the term *free-format tables* does appear in the sentence, it is not in a position to act as the antecedent.

BETTER: The use of free-format tables for writing software specifications may seem counter to the general trend; however, such tables give the developer certain advantages.

INTERVENING ANTECEDENTS

If a noun that could act as an antecedent—from a grammatical standpoint if not a logical one—comes between the pronoun and the "real" antecedent, the pronoun will latch onto this interloper instead. Thus, you must ensure that no interfering noun comes between a pronoun and its intended antecedent.

Keep the drug stored at room temperature. A special insulating container is provided. If it is exposed to extremes of heat or cold, its properties may degenerate.

Obviously the writer didn't intend to say that the *insulating container* may degenerate, but since this noun lies closer to the pronoun *it* than does the noun *drug*, it grabs the role of antecedent. There are three possible solutions: Repeat the intended noun instead of replacing it with a pronoun; move the intervening noun to a position where it won't cause a problem; or enclose the reference to the intervening noun in parentheses, which effectively removes it from the picture. (See the discussion under "Parentheses" on page 147.)

BETTER: Keep the drug stored at room temperature. A special insulating container is provided. If the drug is exposed to extremes of heat or cold, its properties may degenerate.

OR: Keep the drug stored at room temperature. If it is exposed to extremes of heat or cold, its properties may degenerate. A special insulating container is provided.

OR: Keep the drug stored at room temperature. (A special insulating container is provided.) If it is exposed to extremes of heat or cold, its properties may degenerate.

You also do not want to have a pronoun and its antecedent lie too far away from each other, even if no interfering noun lies between them. Readers should not have to puzzle over a *they* or an *it* popping up unexpectedly, and be faced with backtracking several sentences to find its origin.

AMBIGUOUS ANTECEDENTS

Watch out for constructions where a pronoun could refer to more than one antecedent. If this is the case, you will have to rephrase the sentence.

The dog suddenly came upon the cat, and it let out a low snarl.

Which one let out the snarl—the dog or the cat?

The dog suddenly came upon the cat, and let out a low snarl.
[the dog snarled]

The dog suddenly came upon the cat, which let out a low snarl.
[the cat snarled]

Note that the ambiguity exists only because both possible antecedents take the same singular pronoun. If there were two or more dogs and just one cat, or vice versa, there wouldn't be a problem.

The dogs suddenly came upon the cat, and it let out a low snarl.
[the cat snarled]

The dog suddenly came upon the cats, and it let out a low snarl.
[the dog snarled]

Similarly,

Marvin's uncle told him he would have to leave in a minute.

Which one would have to leave: Marvin or his uncle?

Marvin's uncle told him to leave in a minute.
[Marvin would have to leave]

Marvin's uncle told him, "I have to leave in a minute."
[the uncle would have to leave]

If Marvin's *aunt* were involved instead, the male pronoun would not be ambiguous.

AGREEMENT BETWEEN PRONOUN AND ANTECEDENT

The rules of English grammar state that within a sentence certain types of words must *agree* with certain other types of words—that is, be grammatically consistent with them. For example, a singular noun takes a singular verb and a plural noun takes a plural verb: One snowflake *falls,* multiple snowflakes *fall.* For details, see "Agreement Between Subject and Verb" on page 203.

In the case of pronouns, a pronoun must agree with its antecedent (and with any other pronouns referring to the same antecedent) in three ways: *gender, number* and *person.*

AGREEMENT IN GENDER

Agreement in gender is pretty straightforward: Male entities take *he, him, his;* female entities take *she, her, hers;* gender-neutral entities take *it, its.* Errors in this type of agreement don't arise too often. If writing about an animal, be sure you don't carelessly alternate between *it* and one of the other pronouns: for example, *The cat arched her back and switched its tail.* Also, do not write a sentence such as *Either of his sisters is likely to do well for themselves: Either* requires a singular pronoun and *sisters* makes it clear that this pronoun must be female, so the sentence should read *Either of his sisters is likely to do well for herself.*

If you have chosen to alternate between *he* and *she* when referring to persons of unspecified sex, do not do so with jarring frequency. At a minimum, finish a topic or a paragraph before switching to the other gender.

AGREEMENT IN NUMBER

No competent English speaker would say *where did I put them* when looking for a single book or *where did I put it* when looking for a stack, or refer to one's best friend as *they* or a group of friends as *he* or *she.* In most cases, we intuitively use singular and plural pronouns appropriately. There are some situations, however, where errors are likelier to arise.

• In an effort to avoid gender bias—that is, using *he* to refer to both sexes—it is common to use *they* as a singular pronoun when the sex of the person being referred to is unknown or irrelevant. For example, *If a student wants to drop a class without penalty, they must do so in the first month.* The problem is, *they* is irrefutably a plural pronoun, and using it in combination with a singular antecedent *(student)* presents a problem in agreement. This style is considered acceptable in speech, but not in formal writing. For a discussion of this issue and suggested alternatives, see "Avoiding Male-Only Pronouns" under "Writing With Sensitivity" on page 296.

• Some controversy swirls around using *they* when the antecedent is one of the indefinite pronouns *each, every, either, neither, everybody, everyone, somebody, someone, nobody, no one, anybody* or *anyone.* Despite some of these pronouns actually being plural in meaning, they are all technically classified as singulars. Many people use them as plurals, however, either because they don't realize this is incorrect or, again, because of a conscious reluctance to use *he* when both males and females are involved. Consider the following sentences:

Each poem and essay in her scrapbook had their own page.
After the storm, every tree and bush looked as if they had been coated with glass.
Each participant was asked if they could bring a snack.
Everyone should stay for the presentation, unless they have an urgent deadline.
Nobody may enter until their ticket has been validated.
Someone has lost their wallet.

The first two sentences are outright wrong: The first should read *its own page,* and the second, *it had been coated with glass.* The remaining sentences, however, are not so clear-cut. Strictly speaking they should take *he* and *his,* but many writers prefer to avoid this. Substituting *he or she* and *his or her* often sounds clumsy. Increasingly, using plural pronouns with these words is gaining acceptability. Your own decision on how to handle these constructions should depend on the formality of your writing and the expectations of your audience.

For further discussion of these pronouns, see "Problem Pronouns" under "Agreement Between Subject and Verb" on page 217.

• **Collective nouns** are those that may be treated as either singulars or plurals—but you must go one way or the other. If you have decided to treat such a word as singular, you cannot then apply a plural pronoun to it, or vice versa. The following sentences are *incorrect*:

> The committee <u>was</u> unable to get <u>their</u> report out by the deadline.
> [should be *its report*]

> Her family <u>aren't</u> usually that supportive, but <u>it</u> rallied round her this time.
> [should be *they rallied*]

For more on this, see "Collective nouns" under "Agreement Between Subject and Verb" on page 214.

• Writers are sometimes unsure which pronoun to use when there is more than one antecedent. The rule is, use a plural pronoun if the antecedents are joined with *and* (a compound subject): This holds whether the antecedents are individually singular or plural. If they are joined with *or* or *nor* (alternative subjects), have the pronoun agree with whichever antecedent lies nearest to it.

> Bayview High and Riverdale High will be holding <u>their</u> annual reunions on the same night.
> [compound subject, both antecedents singular]

> The salesclerks and the store manager said that <u>they</u> had had enough.
> [compound subject, one antecedent plural, one singular]

> Either Ellis or Herb will bring <u>his</u> camera.
> [alternative subject, both antecedents singular, pronoun singular]

> Neither the tree nor the bushes should have <u>their</u> branches pruned just yet.
> [alternative subject, last antecedent is plural, pronoun plural]

> Something was different: Either the paintings or the mirror had been moved from <u>its</u> position.
> [alternative subject, last antecedent is singular, pronoun singular]

Note that constructions such as the last two often look awkward; thus, you may want to consider recasting them even though they are grammatically correct.

AGREEMENT IN PERSON

Pronouns come in the first person (singular *I*; plural *we*), second person (*you* for both singular and plural) and third person (singular *she, he, it, one*; plural *they*). You must match the appropriate pronoun to its antecedent, and be consistent—that is, do not shift unnecessarily from one person to another. Sentences such as the following are *incorrect*:

> You shouldn't have to live behind triple-locked doors, although one has to use a bit of caution.

> A citizen has rights, but you have responsibilities too.

> All kinds of people will be affected by these funding cuts: hospital patients; immigrants learning English as a second language; people who are struggling to hold onto our present standard of living.

Apart from ensuring agreement and consistency, another issue having to do with this aspect of pronouns is deciding which person is appropriate, when there is a choice. Obviously, you would usually use *I* when referring to yourself (or having your characters referring to themselves); *you* when addressing your reader (or having one of your characters address another); and *he, she* or *they* when you are recounting anything to do with anybody else. There are a few situations, however, where there is some flexibility. When this is the case, the decision to go with the first, second or third person can make a significant difference to the tone of your writing.

• In formal or academic writing, use of the first-person singular to describe your own actions is not illegal, but is often avoided. If you have co-authored a paper, you can safely use *we*, but this sounds a bit pompous if you're the sole contributor ("the royal we"). Often writers get around this by avoiding personal pronouns entirely; for example, instead of *I divided the subjects into three groups,* the sentence is recast as *The subjects were divided into three groups*. Use of the passive voice is quite acceptable if the issue of *who* did something is not relevant. If, however, you are voicing opinions or interpretations that should be attributed to yourself, it would be better to go with *I*. (For more on this, see "Active Versus Passive Voice" on page 286.)

• In writing that addresses the reader directly, such as user manuals and how-to books, it often sounds falsely intimate to use the first person plural. Many readers would be turned off by such phrasings as *Now that we have defined our terms, let's work through an example*. The focus of "user-friendliness" should be on clear communication and avoidance of bafflegab; not on a pretense that you're holding hands with your readers as they turn the pages.

• Use of the second person is, of course, common in any writing that addresses the reader directly. Apart from this, sometimes an interesting strategy is to use it where the first person would normally go. This tends to generalize what the speaker is saying, inviting the reader or listener to relate more personally to the text even if it obviously is describing the experiences of the narrator.

> A little smoke couldn't be noticed now, so we would take some fish off the lines and cook up a hot breakfast. And afterwards we would watch the lonesomeness of the river, and kind of lazy along, and by and by lazy off to sleep. Wake up by and by, and look to see what done it, and maybe see a steamboat coughing along upstream, so far off toward the other side you couldn't tell nothing about her only whether she was a stern-wheel or a side-wheel; then for about an hour there wouldn't be nothing to hear nor nothing to see—just solid lonesomeness. Next you'd see a raft sliding by, away off yonder, and maybe a galoot on it chopping, because they're most always doing it on a raft; you'd see the ax flash and come down—you don't hear nothing; you see that ax go up again, and by the time it's above the man's head then you hear the *k'chunk!*—it had took all that time to come over the water. Once there was a thick fog, and the rafts and things that went by was beating tin pans so the steamboats wouldn't run over them. A scow or a raft went by so close we could hear them talking and cussing and laughing—heard them plain; but we couldn't see no sign of them; it made you feel crawly; it was like spirits carrying on that way in the air. Jim said he believed it was spirits; but I says:
> "No; spirits wouldn't say, 'Dern the dern fog.' "
> —MARK TWAIN, *The Adventures of Huckleberry Finn*

• Writers and speakers sometimes employ *one* instead of *I* to refer to themselves, despite *one* actually being in the third person. In dialogue, you can use this strategy to impart certain nuances, such as self-consciousness or pomposity, to a character's words.

[Bish] picked up the menu again. 'I wonder whether I should have something sweet . . . one's Bengali tooth, you know. . . .'

Lata began to wish that he were up-and-going.

Bish had begun to discuss some matter in his department in which he had acquitted himself particularly well.

'. . . and of course, not that one wants to take personal credit for it, but the upshot of it all was that one secured the contract, and one has been handling the business ever since. Naturally'—and here he smiled smoothly at Lata—'there was considerable disquiet among one's competitors. They couldn't imagine how one had swung it.'

. . . . Bish, perhaps sensing that Lata had not taken to him, made an excuse and disappeared after dinner.

—VIKRAM SETH, *A Suitable Boy*

It can also be used to achieve a tone of cynicism, detachment or slight self-mockery.

BEN. Christ, I feel awful. (*Pause.*) Do you know, all the time you were away, I didn't have one telephone call. I consider that very frightening. Not even from Tom.

JOEY. Oh. (*Pause.*) I thought you found his company intolerable.

BEN. But one likes, as they say, to be asked. Also one likes people to be consistent, otherwise one will start coming adrift. At least this one will. (*Stands up.*) Also, how does one know whether Tom is still the most boring man in London unless he phones in regularly to confirm it. This is the fourth week running he's kept me in suspense. . . .

—SIMON GRAY, *Butley*

You can also use *one* instead of using the second person (or, to put it another way, one can also use *one* instead of using the second person). That is, you may work it in as an occasional alternative to *you* in writing that speaks to the reader—although be aware that it becomes tedious if overused. It also may occasionally be an effective substitute for *he* in cases where you wish to describe something without making reference to gender. For a discussion and example, see "Avoiding Male-Only Pronouns" on page 296.

Bugbears and
Bêtes Noires:
Some Grammar
Taboos That Aren't

This is the sort of English up with which I will not put.
       —WINSTON CHURCHILL, on the notion that one shouldn't end
              a sentence with a preposition

Just as the spellings and meanings of individual words evolve, so do the rules governing how they should be strung together. In some cases, a grammar convention commonly believed to be a rule is in fact not one, despite generations of students being taught to follow it unquestioningly. When it comes to language, very little is carved in stone: Attitudes change, rules become more flexible, authorities eventually bow to common usage and adjust their dictums. There may not always be a consensus on the changes, so some writers will choose to bypass conventions they view as cobwebby while others continue to uphold them. Those conventions that are seen as having the least to contribute to clarity are the likeliest to fall by the wayside.

The present section looks at three aspects of grammar that may be considered to lie in this category: splitting infinitives, starting sentences with conjunctions and ending sentences with prepositions.

SPLITTING INFINITIVES

An **infinitive** is the *to* form of a verb: to bellow, to whine, to connive, to go. *Splitting an infinitive* means to put some word (usually an adverb) between the *to* and the verb: to loudly bellow, to peevishly whine, to cleverly connive, to boldly go.

For reasons inscrutable to many today, nineteenth-century grammarians decided that some of the rules of English grammar should conform to those of Latin. In Latin, the infinitive is not split; ergo, in English the infinitive should not be split. (The fact that in Latin the infinitive is one word and therefore *can't* be split didn't seem to trouble the rule makers.) The result is a decree that presents the modern writer with a dilemma: Should one ignore it, since breaking it usually does no real harm, or follow it, since failure to do so may be taken as ignorance?

There is obviously no definitive answer to this, but given the widespread adherence to this convention, it's probably advisable to abide by it within reason. That is, if it's just as easy to word something in a way that avoids splitting an infinitive, do so—if for no better reason than some of your readers will fault you otherwise. For example, rather than saying *Their greatest pleasure was to proudly stroll along the boardwalk with their pet armadillo,* you could put the adverb after the verb: *Their greatest pleasure was to stroll proudly along the boardwalk with their pet armadillo.* Sometimes the adverb must go in front of the *to:* Instead of *I wanted to never see him again,* you could say *I wanted never to see him again.*

In fairness, an infinitive does sometimes function best as a unit, and separating its parts can weaken it by putting undue emphasis on the intervening adverb. And certainly, even if you have no problem with splitting infinitives, don't shatter them. Constructions such as the following seriously interrupt the flow, and make comprehension difficult:

> She knew it would be a good idea to before the job interview grow out the green Mohawk.
> **BETTER:** She knew it would be a good idea to grow out the green Mohawk before the job interview.

> He asked me to as soon as I was finished grooming my newts clear off the table.
> **BETTER:** He asked me to clear off the table as soon as I was finished grooming my newts.

Virtually every modern style guide agrees, however, that it is better to split an infinitive if the alternative would introduce awkwardness or misinterpretation. For example:

It's difficult for us to adequately express our gratitude.

This sentence would sound considerably stiffer as *It's difficult for us adequately to express our gratitude* or as *It's difficult for us to express adequately our gratitude.* Either version would make it look as if you were more concerned with a nitpicky devotion to the rule book than with your reader's ear. A better alternative, if you are determined to avoid the split infinitive, would be to move the interrupter to the end of the sentence: *It's difficult for us to express our gratitude adequately.* Often this type of revision works well. In some cases, however, you may feel that it puts too much distance between the verb and its modifier.

Similarly,

We managed to just miss the tree.

Phrasing this sentence as *We managed to miss just the tree* implies that something else was hit, while *We managed just to miss the tree*, while better, seems to imply that a failed attempt was made to do something else to the tree. In this case, splitting the infinitive is the most accurate way of expressing what happened.

Or how about:

Aunt Edwina liked to mischievously fling herself down from the rooftop and startle her guests with a loud "Geronimo!"

Here, *mischievously* is modifying the joint activity of flinging and shouting "Geronimo." If it were moved farther down in the sentence, it would appear to be modifying one action only, not the combination. If it were moved before the *to,* the sentence would sound stilted.

In sum, use your ear when dealing with this type of construction, and make your decisions on a case-by-case basis. If you feel uncomfortable either splitting an infinitive or putting a modifier in what feels like an unnatural place, you're best off recasting the sentence.

STARTING A SENTENCE WITH A CONJUNCTION

And just what's so wrong with starting a sentence with a conjunction, anyway? A **conjunction** is a word that defines the relationship (forms the *junction*) between discrete units of thought: *He bought a crate of bananas <u>and</u> proceeded to hurl them at passing trains; The article annoyed me <u>so</u> I used it to line the birdcage; Patsy brushed up on her iridology skills, <u>but</u> Samantha insisted on visiting the aromatherapist; Geoffrey couldn't decide <u>if</u> he should go to dentistry school <u>or</u> become a juggler.* Such words normally go within a sentence rather than at its beginning, since they act to link one element to another.

Writers are often taught that certain conjunctions should never be put at the start of a sentence, since doing so would create a sentence fragment. (For the definition of a grammatically complete sentence, see "Basic Sentence Structure" on page 55.) In some cases, a fragment would undeniably be the result:

> There were no rugs on the floor. Or curtains at the windows.
> Try to catch me. If you can.

A sentence fragment is not illegal *per se*, though: Just because it isn't a grammatically complete unit doesn't mean it can't communicate clearly and effectively. Experienced writers may deliberately use the occasional sentence fragment for emphasis or to capture a particular flavor. Provided that this is done only sparingly and that it is justified by the context, the strategy may be effective. (Note, though, that a dash can also be used for emphasis, and should be considered preferable if the effect would be the same. For a description of this use of the dash, turn to page 157.)

And in many cases—such as this sentence—opening with a conjunction does *not* turn a sentence into something grammatically incomplete; it simply serves to connect the current information more strongly to the information or ideas that come before it. The conjunctions *and*, *but* and *however* in particular may be used to good effect this way, and sometimes will be the most forceful, concise and unambiguous means of expressing the relationship between a sentence and its predecessor.

Overdoing this type of sentence construction can make writing look clumsy or unsubtle, however, so use it with discretion. If there is an alternative wording that would allow your points to come through just as clearly and elegantly, you should go with it instead. *But* do not avoid putting a conjunction up front simply out of principle.

ENDING A SENTENCE WITH A PREPOSITION

Prepositions are the words that define the relationships between other words: Please put the skeleton *in* the closet; I'll meet you *at* the drugstore *after* the concert; we went *across* the country; she liked her salad *with* hot sauce *on* it. Many prepositions have to do with time, space or position.

A persistent myth is that a preposition may never come at the end of a sentence. For example, many students are taught that sentences such as *It's a subject I haven't thought about* and *You have to remember where he's coming from* should be worded as *It's a subject about which I haven't thought* and *You have to remember from where he's coming*. Again, the origins of this custom lie in Latin, in which a preposition cannot come after its target word. In English, however, the effect of ordering words this way is often to turn a phrasing that sounds natural and spontaneous into something tortured.

As with splitting infinitives, you may, as a general rule, prefer to avoid ending sentences in prepositions simply because of your readers' expectations. And indeed, sentences that follow the stricture sometimes do sound more elegant. For example:

There are a couple of issues I'm willing to be more flexible on.
REVISED: There are a couple of issues on which I'm willing to be more flexible.

It's astonishing that there are people this news comes as a surprise to.
REVISED: It's astonishing that there are people to whom this news comes as a surprise.

There are some questions there are no easy answers for.
REVISED: There are some questions for which there are no easy answers.

This is a matter I'd urge you to make your own decision on.
REVISED: This is a matter on which I'd urge you to make your own decision.

If the rewording would sound awkward, however, definitely leave the preposition at the end. Moving it would not "correct" your sentence; it would worsen it.

PART FIVE

Style

A sentence or passage doesn't have to contain overt errors in spelling, grammar or punctuation in order to be considered faulty. The other parts of this book deal with relatively straightforward problems: What's the right way to spell a word, should a break take a colon or a semicolon, where should a certain sentence element be positioned in order for it to be unambiguous. This part moves onto less firm ground, looking at issues such as how to avoid clumsy constructions, disorganized paragraphs, insensitive phrasings—in short, that great intangible realm known as style.

Some of the considerations addressed in the following sections are mechanical, such as the conventions governing the role of italics and capital letters in titles and headings. On other issues, however, the rules disappear. There is no single "best" style: Aside from the matter of personal tastes, different writing strategies will be appropriate for different genres, goals and audiences. Still, it is undeniable that some writers communicate more clearly, convincingly and compellingly than others. The following discussions include guidelines and suggestions on how to achieve a style that works.

Capitalization

Capital letters are used for more than just starting sentences and names. Their functions fall into two main categories:

- Creative uses—achieving certain tones and emphases
- Conventional uses—starting sentences and acting to set off important entities

CREATIVE USES OF CAPITAL LETTERS

Capital letters were once much more a part of writing than they are today. A couple of centuries ago, it was common for most nouns in English to be capitalized.

> I now began to be weary, and seeing nothing to entertain my Curiosity, I returned gently down towards the Creek; and the Sea being full in my View, I saw our Men already got into the Boat, and rowing for Life to the Ship. I was going to hollow after them, although it had been to little purpose, when I observed a huge Creature walking after them in the Sea, as fast as he could: He waded not much deeper than his Knees, and took prodigious strides: But our Men had the start of him half a League, and the Sea thereabouts being full of sharp pointed Rocks, the Monster was not able to overtake the Boat.
>
> —JONATHAN SWIFT, *Gulliver's Travels*

Modern writing is not quite as liberal with capitals, but makes occasional use of them to add humor or irony.

> 'You mean you missed me?' said Berry hungrily. 'Do you mean you missed me?'

Ann's Conscience, which up till this morning had been standing aside and holding a sort of watching brief, now intruded itself upon the scene.

'I don't want you to think I am always shoving myself forward,' said Conscience frigidly, 'but I should be failing in my duty if I did not point out that you are standing at a Girl's Cross Roads. Everything depends on what reply you make to the very leading question which has just been put to you. . . . whatever you do, let me urge upon you with all the emphasis of which I am capable not to drop your eyes and say "Yes." '

'Yes,' said Ann, dropping her eyes. 'Of course I did.'

—P.G. WODEHOUSE, *Big Money*

Our chairs were adjoining, and when Mario had finished with me and was ready to take off and shake out that cloth throwover, I never, never failed to have more of Seymour's hair on me than my own. Only once did I put in a complaint about it, and that was a colossal mistake. I said something, in a distinctly ratty tone of voice, about his "damn hair" always jumping all over me. The instant I said it I was sorry, but it was out. He didn't say anything, but he immediately started to *worry* about it. It grew worse as we walked home, crossing streets in silence; he was obviously trying to divine a way of forbidding his hair to jump on his brother in the barbershop. The homestretch on 110th, the long block from Broadway to our building, on the corner of Riverside, was the worst. No one in the family could worry his or her way down that block the way Seymour could if he had Decent Material.

—J.D. SALINGER, *Seymour: An Introduction*

In dialogue, whole words or sentences may sometimes be capitalized in order to indicate shouting or vehemence.

Alice laid her hand upon his arm, and said, in a soothing tone, 'You needn't be so angry about an old rattle.'

'But it *isn't* old!' Tweedledum cried, in a greater fury than ever. 'It's *new*, I tell you—I bought it yesterday—my nice NEW RATTLE!' and his voice rose to a perfect scream.

—LEWIS CARROLL, *Through the Looking-Glass*

> Greenery I leave to the birds and the bees, they have their worries, I have mine. At home who knows the name of what grows from the pavement at the front of our house? It's a tree—and that's it. The kind is of no consequence, who cares what kind, just as long as it doesn't fall down on your head. In the autumn (or is it the spring? Do you know this stuff? I'm pretty sure it's not the winter) there drop from its branches long crescent-shaped pods containing hard little pellets. Okay. Here's a scientific fact about our tree, comes by way of my mother, Sophie Linnaeus: If you shoot those pellets through a straw, you can take somebody's eye out and make him blind for life. (SO NEVER DO IT! NOT EVEN IN JEST! AND IF ANYBODY DOES IT TO YOU, YOU TELL ME INSTANTLY!) And this, more or less, is the sort of botanical knowledge I am equipped with, until that Sunday afternoon. . . .
>
> —Philip Roth, *Portnoy's Complaint*

Writers would be well advised to use this strategy infrequently, however. Don't fall into the error of relying on typographical tricks to infuse excitement or importance into less-than-inspired lines.

CONVENTIONAL USES OF CAPITAL LETTERS

Special effects aside, capitalization serves several purposes, the conventions of which are outlined below. In cases where there is more than one "right" approach, your main concern should be consistency.

STARTING A SENTENCE

The most common role of capital letters is, of course, to begin each new sentence. There are just a few situations here that bear mention:

• If text that is enclosed in parentheses is part of a larger sentence, do not capitalize it, even if it is a grammatically complete unit. A parenthesized sentence is capitalized only if it stands alone.

Sentences begin with a capital letter (an exception is when a parenthesized sentence lies within the structure of another sentence).
(Be certain to capitalize any stand-alone parenthesized sentences.)

For more details, see the style conventions for "Parentheses" on page 150.

• Question marks and exclamation points, normally terminal punctuation marks that signal the end of a sentence, may occasionally be used to break up what is actually a single sentence, in which case what follows usually appears in lowercase.

> The town square was all peace and tranquillity when boom! the midday cannon fired.

Sometimes either lowercase or uppercase is acceptable; just be consistent.

> How much longer would we have to wait—one hour? two? five?
> How much longer would we have to wait—one hour? Two? Five?

• In dialogue that is broken by nondialogue, lowercase the first letter of what follows the break if it's a continuation of the same sentence; uppercase it if it begins a new sentence.

> "Go six blocks past the mall," he directed. "Then turn left at the lights."
> "Go six blocks past the mall," he directed, "and then turn left at the lights."

• Although names and titles are normally capitalized, a few (a *very* few) by convention are not. Should you ever start off a sentence with one of these exceptions, you're faced with an undeniable conflict: Do you open with a capital letter, thereby presenting the name the wrong way, or with a lowercase letter, thereby breaking the rule of always starting a sentence uppercase? Either way, unfortunately, you'll be in the wrong.

> e.e. cummings died in 1962.
> k.d. lang is almost as well known for her outspokenness as for her singing.
> *the fifth estate* will be broadcasting the interview again next week.

The best strategy is to recast the sentence to avoid the problem. If that isn't possible, go with either uppercase or lowercase, and hope that your readers will be understanding.

• When a sentence contains a colon, practice varies as to whether the text following the colon should begin with upper- or lowercase. For a discussion and illustrations, see the style conventions for "Colon" on page 104.

LENDING WEIGHT

Unlike proper nouns (names of people and places), nouns that identify objects or abstract entities are normally not capitalized, but they may be if there is a reason to do so. Capitalizing a word gives it more importance, and there are several circumstances where capitalization of ordinary nouns is either mandatory or usual—or at least acceptable.

WELL-KNOWN EVENTS OR ENTITIES

If an otherwise generic word has come to be associated with a unique, well-known event or entity, capitalize it when you are using it in that specific way. For example, you would write *the depression* if referring to some current or minor historical economic downturn, but *the Depression* if referring to the period of worldwide hardship in the 1930s. Similarly,

> the Crusades
> the Holocaust
> the Black Death
> the Age of Reason
> the Bomb
> the Pill
> the Golden Rule

Many such terms will be noted in the dictionary; others may not have achieved dictionary status, but their capitalization is considered to be a matter of common knowledge.

TITLES AND IDENTIFIERS

• Capitalize a title or an identifying term when it is part of a name. If the same word is being used generically, do not capitalize it.

Prince Charles	the prince
Judge Goldberg	the judge
Professor Eng	the professor
the University of Miami	the university
the Government of Ontario	the government
New York City	the city of New York
American Sign Language	sign language

In some cases, if a person or entity is considered to be of particular significance, a title may retain its capitalization even when it is not linked with the name. For example, members of Commonwealth countries refer to the British monarch as the Queen. To a Londoner, the downtown business core is the City. The Olympics are the Games to all. To his devotees, Elvis is forever the King.

• It may sometimes be appropriate to capitalize certain descriptive or identifying names and terms that are normally lowercase. The decision to capitalize may be made on the basis of convention, policy, expectations of readers or any other reason that is specific to your circumstances. Whichever way you go, be sure you are consistent: Don't alternate between capitalizing and lowercasing.

the post office *or* the Post Office
a nursing assistant *or* a Nursing Assistant
a black candidate *or* a Black candidate
western values *or* Western values
the board of directors *or* the Board of Directors

• Words that derive from names of people (real or fictional) or places sometimes retain the capitalization of their origins, sometimes not. The dictionary will tell you which way is correct.

bowdlerize a book	sport a Vandyke beard
mesmerize a subject	make a Faustian bargain
play the saxophone	study Marxist ideology
wear a pair of bloomers	wear a Norfolk jacket
eat french fries	eat Camembert cheese

• Trade names (names of commercial products) need to be capitalized for legal reasons. Be particularly careful with those that are often unthinkingly used as generic words (Dumpster, Plexiglas, Scotch tape). A good dictionary will include trade names, so always check if you're uncertain.

The furniture was built mostly of Masonite.
He wore a pair of old, faded Levi's.
Dinner that night was broth and Jell-O.
It was really only a Band-Aid solution.

• For titles of books, plays, films, songs, etc., capitalize the opening word plus all main words. For these, as well as for titles of places or institutions, do not capitalize minor words such as articles and short (less than four letters) conjunctions and prepositions.

Arms and the Man
The Princess and the Pea
Romeo and Juliet
The Sound of Music

• For bibliographic references, some style guides say to capitalize every main word of book titles (nouns, pronouns, verbs, adjectives and adverbs) and lowercase the words that serve to introduce or join main words (articles, conjunctions and prepositions). Others say to capitalize only the first word (as well as any proper nouns, of course). Present every title the same way, regardless of how it appears on its own book cover or in someone else's reference list.

References	References
A Dictionary of Modern English Usage	*A dictionary of modern English usage*
The Chicago Manual of Style	*The Chicago manual of style*
The Elements of Style	*The elements of style*

If you are capitalizing only the first word of a title, capitalize the first word of the subtitle as well, if the book has one.

Miss Thistlebottom's hobgoblins: The careful writer's guide to the taboos, bugbears and outmoded rules of English usage
The transitive vampire: The ultimate handbook of grammar for the innocent, the eager, and the doomed

ABBREVIATIONS

Most all-caps abbreviations derive from multiword terms, where the abbreviation consists of the first letter of each word. A few cautions about capitalized abbreviations:

• Note that the article *(a* or *an)* preceding an abbreviation may differ depending on whether the abbreviation is pronounced as letters or as an acronym. If the abbreviation opens with a vowel sound, precede it with *an*, even if the first letter is a consonant. If it opens with a consonant sound, precede it with *a*, even if the first letter is a vowel.

an RCMP officer	a RAM capacity
an NBC program	a NATO meeting
a UV light	an URN publication

• Occasionally, a single word is abbreviated to two capital letters (more typically, abbreviations of single words appear in lowercase). Be certain in such cases that you capitalize *both* letters.

Each user must have a valid ID number in order to access the system.
[not Id]

If that's what you want, it's OK with me.
[not Ok]

Anything good on TV tonight?
[not Tv]

• If an all-caps abbreviation is pluralized, be sure that the pluralizing *s* appears in lowercase. If you put it in uppercase, it could look like part of the abbreviation itself.

Guests are asked to return their RSVPs as soon as possible.
[not RSVPS]

The RNs' shifts were posted by the front desk.
[not RNS']

For more on all-caps abbreviations, see the discussions under "Period" on page 109 and "Apostrophe" on page 198.

HEADINGS

• Nonfiction writing, if it is of any significant length, generally calls for headings of different levels: high-level headings to introduce main sections, lower-level headings to introduce subdivisions of a main section, still lower-level headings to introduce subdivisions of a subdivision and so on. It is very important that headings of the same level always appear the same way and that those of different levels be visually distinct. The typography of a heading serves as a visual cue to readers, informing them whether what follows is a subset of what came before, different information on the same level or a new topic altogether.

One way to achieve this distinctiveness is through capitalization. For example, the highest level headings could be in all-caps text (LEVEL ONE HEADING), the next level could have all main words capitalized (Level Two Heading) and the level below that could have only the first word capitalized (Level three heading).

You can also distinguish levels of headings through use of different type sizes, bold or italic versus regular type, centering versus flush left and more.

• If you are capitalizing all main words in a heading, you must decide how you will treat hyphenated compounds. Some writers choose to capitalize the second word of such compounds; others choose not to.

The Private Lives of Stand-Up Comedians
The Private Lives of Stand-up Comedians

English Poetry of the Mid-Eighteenth Century
English Poetry of the Mid-eighteenth Century

Confessions of a Hard-Core Mah-Jongg Player
Confessions of a Hard-core Mah-jongg Player

LISTS

If items in a vertical list consist of entire sentences, begin each one with a capital letter, just as you would with any other sentence.

If the items are single words or sentence fragments, the choice is yours (or your style guide's).

Item 1	OR	item 1
Item 2		item 2
Item 3		item 3

Note that you should not ever create a list where some items are full sentences and others not. See "Achieving Parallel Structure" on page 223.

ALL CAPS AND SMALL CAPS

If your writing is of an informative nature, such as a brochure or an instruction manual, it may occasionally be appropriate to present particularly important information in ALL-CAPS TEXT. Reserve this, however, for very short strings; preferably no more than a few words. Writers sometimes capitalize entire blocks of important information out of a belief that the reader's eye will be drawn to the larger letters, but in fact the effect may be the exact opposite—readers may impatiently skip over the all-caps section because it's tiring to wade through. How easy do you find it to skim the following passage?

AVOID UNNECESSARY USE OF ALL-CAPS TEXT, AS IT TENDS TO BE DIFFICULT TO READ. BECAUSE THE LETTERS ARE ALL EXACTLY THE SAME HEIGHT AND LACK THE DISTINCTIVE ASCENDERS AND DESCENDERS THAT CHARACTERIZE LOWERCASE LETTERS, IT OFFERS FEWER VISUAL CUES THAN LOWERCASE, AND THE READER MUST EXPEND MORE EFFORT IN PROCESSING IT.

Alternative strategies such as using bold type, outline boxes or a different color (if feasible) are usually preferable.

SMALL CAPITALS are, as their name makes obvious, characters in the shape of uppercase letters but the size of lowercase letters (those without ascenders or descenders). They come in handy when you want to present text in uppercase letters for reasons of convention rather than emphasis, as they let you avoid the jarring effect produced by all caps. Instead of jumping off the page at you, a small-caps word or phrase blends in inconspicuously with the surrounding text.

> I dig in the weediest part near the compost heap, lifting the earth and letting it crumble, sieving the worms out with my fingers. The soil is rich, the worms scramble, red ones and pink ones. . . . They're sold like apples in season, VERS 5¢ on the roadside signs, sometimes VERS 10¢, inflation. French class, *vers libre*, I translated it the first time as Free Worms and she thought I was being smart.*
> —MARGARET ATWOOD, *Surfacing*

* Meaning of phrase: Free verse.

By convention, small caps are employed for certain abbreviations: A.M. and P.M.; A.D. and B.C. (or C.E. and B.C.E., for Common Era and Before the Common Era). For design reasons, they are sometimes used to make up the opening word or words of an article or chapter. They also have a few specialized applications that may be peculiar to a particular publication or genre: For example, they may be used for the name of each speaker in a magazine interview, for synonyms in a dictionary, or (in combination with initial full caps) for the title and author's name on a book cover. In business and technical writing, small caps are often used instead of full caps for abbreviations and acronyms.

Italics

Italic type serves to make text stand out distinctively. It may be employed for stylistic reasons, lending emphasis, irony or urgency to what it encompasses, or for reasons of convention.

Its main uses are the following:

- Highlighting words that have special significance
- Emphasizing a speaker's words
- Setting off non-English words
- Setting off terms, titles and other special text
- Underscoring a point in a quote

HIGHLIGHTING SIGNIFICANT WORDS

Italicizing a word or passage draws attention to it, informing the reader that it holds particular meaningfulness.

> She twisted the dial, right, left, right again, heard the click as the lock yielded, opened the safe—*and it was empty*.
>
> After years of toil and obscurity, he could finally claim, with justifiable pride, that he was one of *them*.
>
> When my friend said she was setting me up on a blind date with a Herbert Snorkel-Winkworth, I didn't realize she meant one of *the* Snorkel-Winkworths.
>
> Given that it was *my* house he was being so generous with, I did not share his enthusiasm about putting up the entire circus troupe and their elephants for the week.

Italics are particularly important when they clarify the meaning of what is being said. Consider the nine different interpretations of the following sentence:

He knew she'd never ask him for a loan.
[Other people thought she would.]

He *knew* she'd never ask him for a loan.
[He had good reason to know she wouldn't.]

He knew *she'd* never ask him for a loan.
[Someone else would be asking him for one.]

He knew she'd *never* ask him for a loan.
[She wouldn't do so in a million years.]

He knew she'd never *ask* him for a loan.
[She might hint strongly, though.]

He knew she'd never ask *him* for a loan.
[She might ask someone else.]

He knew she'd never ask him *for* a loan.
[She'd be more likely to offer him one.]

He knew she'd never ask him for *a* loan.
[She wouldn't stop at just one.]

He knew she'd never ask him for a *loan.*
[She'd prefer an outright gift.]

As effective as italic type can be, do not rely on it excessively as a means of injecting excitement or importance. Good writers achieve emphasis through wording and punctuation, not through typographical tricks. Mostly, you should reserve italics for cases where the intended meaning would not be clear without them, or where you feel that a desired emphasis could not be made apparent through wording alone.

EMPHASIZING A SPEAKER'S WORDS

In dialogue, italics are often used to indicate words that a speaker is stressing, saying loudly or saying with particular significance. (This device should be reserved for fiction. It is usually not appropriate to include italics when quoting a real person's speech in a report or article.)

Come the crucial seventh, the Filmmakers' First Wives Club grew restive, no longer content to belittle their former husbands from afar, and moved in on the baselines and benches, undermining confidence with their heckling. When Myer Gross, for instance, came to bat with two men on base and his teammates shouted, "Go, man. Go," one familiar grating voice floated out over the others. "Hit, Myer. Make your son proud of you, *just this once.*"

—MORDECAI RICHLER, *St. Urbain's Horseman*

. . . "Perhaps this will refresh your memory." The District Attorney suddenly thrust a heavy automatic at the quiet figure on the witness stand. "Have you ever seen this before?" Walter Mitty took the gun and examined it expertly. "This is my Webley-Vickers 50.80," he said calmly. . . . "You are a crack shot with any sort of firearms, I believe?" said the District Attorney, insinuatingly. "Objection!" shouted Mitty's attorney. "We have shown that the defendant could not have fired the shot. We have shown that he wore his right arm in a sling on the night of the fourteenth of July." Walter Mitty raised his hand briefly and the bickering attorneys were stilled. "With any known make of gun," he said evenly, "I could have killed Gregory Fitzhurst at three hundred feet *with my left hand.*"

—JAMES THURBER, *The Secret Life of Walter Mitty*

Note that just part of a word can be italicized, which is a realistic representation of how people actually speak.

[Stradlater] asked me if I'd written his goddam composition for him. I told him it was over on his goddam bed. He walked over and read it while he was unbuttoning his shirt. He stood there, reading it, and sort of stroking his bare chest and stomach, with this very stupid expression on his face. He was mad about himself.

All of a sudden, he said, "For Chris*sake*, Holden. This is about a goddam *base*ball glove."

"So what?" I said. Cold as hell.

"Wuddaya mean *so what*? I told ya it had to be about a goddam *room* or a house or something."

"You said it had to be descriptive. What the hell's the difference if it's about a baseball glove?"

—J.D. SALINGER, *The Catcher in the Rye*

In fiction writing, some authors use italics to represent words that are being thought by a character, rather than spoken aloud. This is permissible, but not really necessary: Leaving off quotation marks should be sufficient to indicate your intentions (although you must be careful to distinguish these words in some way from the narrative). Because of the other purposes served by italics, using them to indicate unspoken words may appear to give those words an unintended vehemence or significance.

Another use of italics in fiction is for the text of a note or letter that a character is reading or composing: Writing within writing, as it were.

SETTING OFF NON-ENGLISH WORDS

Words from other languages are set off in italics as a signal that they should not be processed the same way as the rest of the text.

Here are a few French terms for fans at the Forum:

Bataille, Escarmouche, Bagarre générale—The three stages of mindless hockey violence. A *bataille* is generally waged by two players with no outside interference. When a third party joins the fracas, it escalates into an *escarmouche*. This is often the signal for every player on the ice to drop his gloves and go at it; the ensuing obscene spectacle is your basic Pier Six *bagarre générale*.

—MICHAEL FARBER AND MIKE BOONE, in *The Anglo Guide to Survival in Québec*

'Oh, look!' broke in Gherkins. 'Here's a picture of a man being chopped up in little bits. What does it say about it?'

'I thought you could read Latin.'

'Well, but it's all full of sort of pothooks. What do they mean?'

'They're just contractions,' said Lord Peter patiently. ' "*Solent quoque hujus insulae cultores*"—it is the custom of the dwellers in this island, when they see their parents stricken in years and of no further use, to take them down into the market-place and sell them to the cannibals, who kill them and eat them for food. This they also do with younger persons when they fall into any desperate sickness.'

. . . . The viscount was enthralled.

'I *do* like this book,' he said; 'could I buy it out of my pocket-money, please?'

'Another problem for uncles,' thought Lord Peter, rapidly ransacking his recollections of the *Cosmographia* to determine whether any of its illustrations were indelicate; for he knew the duchess to be straitlaced. On consideration, he could only remember one that was dubious, and there was a sporting chance that the duchess might fail to light upon it.

—DOROTHY SAYERS, *The Learned Adventure of the Dragon's Head*

I was in love with Kiyo Yamada. He would take me back to Osaka with him and we would live in a house with rice paper *shoji* screens and *tatami* mats. He would wear a *yukata*, and I would wear a glorious silk kimono printed with flying cranes and fresh-cut cherry blossoms.

—ANN IRELAND, *A Certain Mr. Takahashi*

Note in the above excerpt that "kimono" is not italicized along with the other Japanese words, since this is a word that has been fully incorporated into English.

Unambiguously foreign words should always be italicized, but how do you treat words that are designated as foreign, yet exist as entries in English dictionaries? The problem is, there isn't a neat distinction between foreign-derived words that have come to be considered standard English vocabulary, and those that haven't. Thus, some authors would italicize words such as *doppelgänger*, *ad hoc*, *ad nauseum*, *a priori*, *per se*, *summa cum laude*, *raison d'être*, *grande dame*, *sangfroid*, *chutzpah* and *gonif*, and abbreviations such as *e.g.*, *i.e.*, *et al.*, *ibid.*, *viz.* and *etc.* Other authors would not. Dictionaries and style guides will differ on the treatment of these types of words, so if you are not obligated to follow a particular style, make your own decisions. You may do this on a word-by-word basis, rather than resolving, say, to italicize anything in Latin. Note that modern style is inclined to use roman (regular) type for all but the most unusual or exotic words, on the reasoning that italics are necessary only if a word is likely to be unfamiliar.

Note: Never italicize foreign proper nouns—names of people or places.

SETTING OFF SPECIAL TEXT

Italic type is used to set off a variety of special words. The full range is too numerous to cover; this section reviews only the more common applications. Specialized areas such as scientific, mathematical and legal writing will all have their own particular designations.

TERMINOLOGY

In formal writing, a new term is often set off on its first appearance in some typographically distinct way. The usual strategies are to either enclose it in quotation marks (see page 177) or to put it in italic or boldface type. Other, less common options are underlining or using color.

> *Capital goods* are industrial products that are long-lived and expensive, such as heavy machinery and vehicles; *expense items* are industrial products that are cheaper and quickly consumed, such as office supplies and paper products.

After its first occurrence, the term should appear in regular type.

TITLES

It is usual to italicize the names of ships and space vehicles, and the titles of books, newspapers, magazines, films, plays, operas, and record albums or CDs. For titles of short stories, poems, book chapters, magazine or journal articles and songs, it is more common to use quotation marks instead. Note, though, that these are conventions, not absolutes. It is acceptable to use either italics or quotation marks for any of the above, or you may sometimes choose to present a title, such as the name of a newspaper or journal, without setting it off in any special way other than initial capital letters.

Style guides differ as to how titles should be presented in bibliographies. For example, one guide may specify that you must italicize titles of books and journals, but not the titles of articles within journals; a second, to italicize everything; a third, to not italicize at all.

If you are expected to use a particular guide, follow its specifications; if you are making your own rules, be sure you treat all titles consistently.

HEADINGS
If your writing contains various levels of headings, you need to clearly distinguish among them. Strategies to achieve this include centering higher-level headings and placing lower-level ones flush left; using different type sizes; using different fonts (the shape of the letters); using all caps, small caps or initial caps; and using some combination of regular, boldface and italic type. Typically, boldface type would be used for higher-level headings and italics for lower-level ones; however, there are no specific rules governing this.

STAGE DIRECTIONS
In scripts, both the names of the speakers and any directions to the actors must be easily differentiable from the rest of the text. The usual convention is to set them in italics, and to enclose the directions in parentheses or brackets.

Algernon.
. . . [T]his isn't your cigarette case. This cigarette case is a present from someone of the name of Cecily, and you said you didn't know anyone of that name.
Jack.
Well, if you want to know, Cecily happens to be my aunt.
Algernon.
Your aunt!
Jack.
Yes. Charming old lady she is, too. Lives at Tunbridge Wells. Just give it back to me, Algy.
Algernon.
(*Retreating to back of sofa.*) But why does she call herself little Cecily if she is your aunt and lives at Tunbridge Wells? (*Reading.*) 'From little Cecily with her fondest love.'
Jack.
(*Moving to sofa and kneeling upon it.*) My dear fellow, what on earth is there in that? Some aunts are tall, some aunts are not tall. That is a

matter that surely an aunt may be allowed to decide for herself. You seem to think that every aunt should be exactly like your aunt! This is absurd. For Heaven's sake give me back my cigarette case. (*Follows Algernon round the room.*)

—OSCAR WILDE, *The Importance of Being Earnest*

WORDS AND LETTERS REFERRED TO AS SUCH
Either italics or quotation marks may be used to set off words or letters that are being presented *as* words or letters.

Her *i*'s were dotted and her *t*'s were crossed.

The Tangierines—approximately 800 residents—say that their island was first settled in 1686 by a certain John Crockett, a Cornishman. There are no records of this, but the evidence of the Tangier Island speech is overwhelming. To English ears, they sound West Country. Most striking of all "sink" is pronounced *zink*. *Mary* and *merry* have a similar pronunciation, though this is common to much of the tidewater district. "Paul" and "ball" sound like *pull* and *bull*. For "creek" they will say *crik*. And they have a special local vocabulary: *spider* for "frying-pan", *bateau* for "skiff" and *curtains* for "blinds".

—ROBERT MCCRUM, WILLIAM CRAN AND ROBERT MACNEIL,
The Story of English

UNDERSCORING A POINT IN A QUOTE

If you are presenting quoted material, you may wish to highlight a particular word, phrase or passage, either because you feel it holds some critical significance or because it makes some controversial point from which you want to dissociate yourself. The way to do this is to italicize the relevant text and then, in order to clearly attribute the italics to yourself and not to the original author, follow it with the words *italics mine*, *italics added* or *emphasis added*, in square brackets.

"Of this woman's life on the plantation I subsequently learned the following circumstances. She was the wife of head man Frank . . . second in command to the overseer. His wife [Betty]—a tidy, trim woman with a pretty figure . . . was taken from him by the overseer . . . and she had a son by him whose straight features and diluted color . . . bear witness to his Yankee descent. I do not know how long Mr. King's occupation of Frank's wife continued, *or how the latter endured the wrong done to him* [italics mine]. This outrage *upon this man's rights* [italics mine] was perfectly notorious among all the slaves; and his hopeful offspring, Renty, allud[ed] to his superior birth on one occasion."

—SUSAN BROWNMILLER, *Against Our Will: Men, Women and Rape*

If italics exist in the original and you feel they may be misattributed to you, you may choose to add *italics in original*, in brackets. For more on brackets, turn to page 166.

STYLE CONVENTIONS

• If you cannot produce italic type, use underlining instead.
• In most cases, if an italicized word or phrase is followed immediately by punctuation, italicize that punctuation mark as well.

He did *what?*
For a woman of ninety, she was quite *au courant:* There was really nothing one could say to shock her.

Do not italicize parentheses, brackets or dashes that enclose italicized text, unless the entire passage that comprises these punctuation marks is italicized.

• If a whole passage is italicized for reasons other than emphasis, and you want to emphasize a word within that passage, put that word in roman (regular) type.

Active Versus Passive Voice

Grammatically speaking, **voice** refers to whether the subject of a sentence is on the performing or the receiving end of the action. In sentences written in the active voice, the subject is the doer: *Bob caught the Frisbee in his teeth* (subject is *Bob*). In sentences written in the passive voice, the subject is acted upon: *The Frisbee was caught in Bob's teeth* (subject is *the Frisbee*). In a passive construction, the person or object that is actually performing the action may be referred to in the sentence, but is not the focus of it.

The topic of voice is addressed here rather than in the chapter on grammar because misuses of voice do not constitute actual errors, but do affect tone, emphasis and readability—all of which are issues of style, not of right and wrong.

ADVANTAGES OF THE ACTIVE VOICE

Some grammar teachers issue a straight dictum to always use the active voice, never the passive. This overly simplistic advice would be better phrased as *use the active voice as a general rule, and use the passive voice only if there's a specific reason to do so.* The active voice has definite advantages over the passive: It's more direct and concise, and it can make your writing appear more vigorous and confident. The passive voice may sound clumsy, plodding or overly cautious in contrast. For example, compare the following sets of sentences:

> **PASSIVE:** When the F1 key is pressed, help information is shown.
> **MORE DIRECT:** When you press the F1 key, help information appears.
> **EVEN MORE DIRECT:** Press the F1 key to see help information.

PASSIVE: The letter received by Estella stated that legal action would be taken by the company, because her outstanding balance of fourteen cents had still not been paid.

MORE DIRECT: The company sent Estella a letter stating that it was going to take legal action, because she had still not paid her outstanding balance of fourteen cents.

If the doer of the action isn't mentioned in the sentence and isn't obvious, the result is not only clumsiness but ambiguity.

> The gifts given to Harold were much appreciated, although it was wished they smelled a little less pungent.

Who gave Harold the gifts? Who appreciated them? Who wished that they smelled less pungent? Any of the following might be possible:

> Harold was very appreciative of the gifts the herbalist gave him, although he wished they smelled a little less pungent.
>
> Harold's wife was very appreciative of the gifts the zookeeper gave him, although Harold wished they smelled a little less pungent.
>
> Harold was very appreciative of the gifts the mad chemist upstairs gave him, although the entire rest of the neighborhood wished they smelled a little less pungent.

It is good practice to scan your writing for sentences that are unnecessarily or inappropriately worded in the passive voice, and convert them to the active.

ADVANTAGES OF THE PASSIVE VOICE

To say that the passive voice is never appropriate is to misunderstand it: Why should it exist at all if its only purpose is to be held up as an example of what not to do? It is preferable to the active voice in the following circumstances:

- When the focus is on what's being done *to* something rather than *by* something.

For example, it would be better to say *The wedding cake had to be carried in by eight strong waiters* rather than *Eight strong waiters had to carry in the wedding cake,* because the cake, not the waiters, is the focus of the sentence.

Often, the decision as to which voice is more appropriate can be made only by considering the larger context. Thus, you would say *Very young babies prefer black-and-white images* if you are writing about how babies of various ages respond to colors; however, if your focus is on the colors themselves, it would be better to word this information as *Black-and-white images are preferred by very young babies.* That is, neither form is inherently better: The purpose and context of your writing should determine which voice is used.

- When the doer can be inferred or is not of interest.

It would be better to say *The cake wasn't served until two in the morning* rather than *The waiters didn't serve the cake until two in the morning,* if (a) it can be inferred that the waiters did the serving and (b) it doesn't matter anyway, and using the active voice would put an inappropriate emphasis on the wrong part of the sentence. If there were some relevance to who served the cake, that would be different: For example, *The bride herself served the cake, and the groom handed out the forks.*

- To avoid using the first-person-singular pronoun.

In academic writing, it is conventional to avoid saying *I* when referring to one's own work (although *we* is generally acceptable). The usual strategy is to word things in the passive voice: Thus, instead of *I randomly assigned the subjects to each group*, saying *Subjects were randomly assigned to each group.* Here again, the focus of the writing is on what is being done, not on who is doing it.

- To avoid using all-male pronouns.

Many writers prefer not to refer to a generic individual of unspecified sex exclusively as *he.* The problem is, there is no pronoun in English that can be used to indicate a single person of either sex, so more inventive strategies are needed. One approach is to word sentences in the passive voice to avoid the need for pronouns altogether. For example, instead of saying *The average driver trades in his car every four years*, you could say *The average car is traded in every four years.* (For a discussion of other strategies, see "Avoiding Male-Only Pronouns" on page 296.)

- To deliberately deflect responsibility or conceal information.

In speech, the passive voice is often adopted by individuals wishing to minimize or evade personal responsibility for something. A reckless driver might admit, "Well, perhaps the car was being driven a bit fast," or a guilty roommate confess, "Those cookies your mother sent you all got eaten." Sometimes, writers with uneasy consciences will choose their words in a similar fashion. The best that can be said about this strategy is, you *might* pull it off convincingly. Other than that, in some cases it may be effectively applied to dialogue to impart an evasive tone to a character's words.

The passive voice is also used by individuals who want to tell the truth and nothing but the truth, but not necessarily the whole truth. This strategy is commonly employed by writers treading on politically delicate ground, as it allows information to be presented in a way that cannot be accused of being inaccurate, but is incomplete or intentionally ambiguous. Saying *It has been alleged that Mr. Brandon knew about the takeover months in advance* is not the same as saying *Ms. Reisman has alleged that Mr. Brandon knew about the takeover months in advance.* That is, ambiguity in writing is not always the result of carelessness or inattention; sometimes it is quite deliberate. Readers often see through the evasiveness easily, so be aware that this strategy may backfire.

- To vary sentence structure.

A final legitimate use of the passive voice is for variety in your writing style: using it simply to avoid monotony. Wording every sentence the same way makes for tedious reading, so if you find that you are phrasing every sentence in the active voice, you might consider switching the occasional one to the passive. Of course, do so only in cases where the passive would not raise problems of awkwardness or ambiguity.

Writing With Sensitivity

Help the reader focus on the content of your paper by avoiding language that may cause irritation, flights of thought, or even momentary interruptions. Such sources of distraction include linguistic devices and constructions that might imply sexual, ethnic, or other kinds of biases.

—Publication Manual of the American Psychological Association

A discussion on how to use language in a way that won't annoy any of your readers—or at least not too many of them—necessarily involves treading on delicate ground, since emotions run rather higher here than on matters such as use of the serial comma. Would you describe someone in a wheelchair as disabled or challenged? Someone of a race other than Caucasian as nonwhite or a person of color? A member of a municipal government as an alderman or alderperson? Words that to one reader are simple descriptions may be perceived by another as excluding, dismissive, stereotyping, patronizing or insensitive; on the other hand, what some see as reasonable, thought-out alternatives may be viewed by others as euphemistic, grating or ridiculous.

If your intention is to provoke, that is one thing. More commonly, writers are honestly oblivious to biases or irritants in the words they have chosen, or simply feel that there is oversensitivity these days to nuances of language and that people should accept their style without reading too much into it. However, the APA admonition cited above makes a good point: Readers who are alienated by your terms or phrasings will be less receptive to the content of what you are saying—and that, after all, defeats the purpose. You want to choose your words so that they act to convey your message or ideas, not unintentionally distract from them. Entire volumes have been published on how to steer clear of sexism, racism and other 'isms in your writing. This chapter touches briefly on the topic and gives some examples.

AVOIDING LOADED WORDS

Many words carry messages under the surface that come through either subtly or not-so-subtly. You must be attuned to their full significance when you use them, to ensure that you aren't saying something more than you intended. The last couple of decades have seen a growing awareness about bias in language as it affects women and members of particular racial, cultural and social groups, but bias can have an impact on anyone.

Exercise
Each of the following sentences contains some word, phrasing or message that could give readers pause. Note that none is blatantly offensive: No racial epithets or gratuitous put-downs are included. (All are drawn or adapted from actual published material, and in no case did it seem that the writer intended to give offense.) Yet all can be rewritten in a way that fully retains the information while getting rid of something that could be viewed as insulting or patronizing.

Battered women are often reluctant to admit that they are being abused.

Most people in the world cannot speak English; therefore, software developers should design their products to be easily translatable.

The following are suggestions on how physicians can to try to change the minds of patients who refuse to participate in research studies.

Local Grandmother Wins Pulitzer Prize!

Every kid in Canada grows up dreaming of playing one day in the NHL.

Mr. Smith, who is gay and a former convict, says that the support he has received from the group has turned his life around.

In 1953, Edmund Hillary of New Zealand, accompanied by a Nepalese guide, became the first man to reach the summit of Mount Everest.

The neighborhood is rough, causing elderly residents to be scared to go out alone.

A survey from the 1930s on attitudes about immigration found that Americans viewed northern Europeans and Canadians most favorably, and blacks and Jews least favorably.

Ms. Edwards is a very large woman and moves around with difficulty, but she sparkles with intelligence and wit.

Her study looks at some of the special challenges faced by deaf people who are married to normal partners.

The islanders are a friendly and cheerful people, with a natural gift for music and dance that their Western visitors may well envy.

The rowdiest of the patrons were hauled off in the paddy wagon, and the rest soon dispersed.

Revisions

Battered women are often reluctant to **admit** that they are being abused.

Admit is a pejorative word that carries an implication of guilt; that is, that the victim has done something wrong (which may in fact be the perception of the woman herself).

BETTER: Battered women are often reluctant to reveal that they are being abused.

Most people in the world **cannot speak English;** therefore, **software developers** should design their products to be easily translatable.

While English is undeniably an asset, an inability to speak it is not exactly indicative of a personal failing and shouldn't be presented as a negative. (If it comes to that, how many other languages does the typical anglophone speak?) On a subtler level, another ethnocentric assumption made here seems to be that all software developers work in English.

BETTER: Most people in the world speak languages other than English; therefore, English-language software developers should design their products to be easily translatable.

The following are suggestions on how physicians can to try to change the minds of patients who **refuse** to participate in research studies.

Refuse—the nerve! Hard to imagine that any reasonable patient would put his or her interests ahead of the doctor's curriculum vitae. It may be true that doctor and patient often hold different social statuses, but an opposing opinion on the part of the latter shouldn't be equated with a recalcitrant child refusing to go to bed.

BETTER: The following are suggestions on how physicians can try to change the minds of patients who decline to participate in research studies.

Local **Grandmother** Wins Pulitzer Prize!

Avoid defining women by their maternal or marital roles, or by their physical appearance, unless there is direct relevance. Doing so when the focus should be on professional or personal achievement trivializes what has been achieved. To determine if you have worked any inappropriate references into a description of a woman, think for a moment if you are saying anything about her that you wouldn't bother saying about a man.

BETTER: Local Journalist Wins Pulitzer Prize!

Every **kid** in Canada grows up dreaming of playing one day in the NHL.

While the exaggeration of such a statement might be acceptable with regard to Canadian *boys*, it seems less than likely that a majority of small girls aspire to be professional hockey players. Using the word *kid* when clearly only boys are meant carries an implication that boys' interests are really the ones that matter when one refers to children.

BETTER: Every boy in Canada grows up dreaming of playing one day in the NHL.

Mr. Smith, **who is gay and a former convict,** says that the support he has received from the group has turned his life around.

To imply that homosexuality is either linked with criminal behavior or is on a par with it is simple homophobia. Sexual orientation is independent of other traits, good or bad—and indeed should only be mentioned at all if there is some relevance to it.

BETTER: Mr. Smith, a former convict, says that the support he has received from the group has turned his life around.

In 1953, Edmund Hillary of New Zealand, **accompanied by a Nepalese guide,** became the first man to reach the summit of Mount Everest.

When two or more individuals play roles of equal significance, there is no justification for treating their identities and achievements unevenly. Imagine if the above were turned around so that only the Nepalese participant was named, with Sir Edmund dismissively referred to as "a white climber."

BETTER: In 1953, Edmund Hillary of New Zealand and Tenzing Norkay of Nepal became the first men to reach the summit of Mount Everest.

The neighborhood is rough, causing **elderly residents to be scared** to go out alone.

Watch out for "ageism"—stereotyping people on the basis of how many years they've been around. There's no denying that old age can bring its problems, but do not label all individuals born before a certain date as helpless or fragile, as though individuality no longer exists. And childish words such as *scared* are not typically used to describe adult reactions.

BETTER: The neighborhood is rough, causing many elderly residents to be concerned about going out alone.

A survey from the 1930s on attitudes about immigration found that **Americans** viewed **northern Europeans** and **Canadians** most favorably, and blacks and Jews least favorably.

On the surface this statement is simply reporting the biased opinions of others, but there's a bit more to it. Americans, Europeans and Canadians are simply citizens of various countries; not ethnic groups. Presumably it was Americans who were white and Christian who expressed these views, but referring to them just as "Americans" implies that Americans by definition aren't anything else. Were black Americans surveyed? The same for northern Europe and Canada: should one assume the respondents would have welcomed British or Canadian Jews?

BETTER: A survey from the 1930s on attitudes of white Christian Americans about immigration found that they viewed people of northern European descent most favorably, and blacks and Jews least favorably.

Ms. Edwards is a very large woman and moves around with difficulty, **but** she sparkles with intelligence and wit.

Attitudes toward overweight people have been described as "the last safe prejudice": It may be politically incorrect to deride individuals for their religion or skin color, but obesity makes somebody fair game. Wording such as the above suggests that there is something unexpected or contradictory about a person who is overweight also being bright, as if fat is normally correlated with dimwittedness.

Would any writer describe a person as being "slender and active, *but* intelligent and witty"?

BETTER: Ms. Edwards, a very large woman who moves around with difficulty, sparkles with intelligence and wit.

Her study looks at some of the special challenges faced by deaf people who are married to **normal** partners.

Using the word *normal* as the simple opposite of disabled carries an implication that people with disabilities are abnormal in ways beyond their specific afflictions or conditions; also, that anyone not so afflicted meets some ideal. It is reasonable to speak of normal or abnormal hearing, vision, body movement, etc., but these words should not be applied to describe the overall person.

BETTER: Her study looks at some of the special challenges faced by deaf people who are married to hearing partners.

The islanders are **a friendly and cheerful people**, with a **natural gift for music and dance** that their Western visitors may well envy.

Racism does not always entail demonizing "the other": Condescension can be just as insidious. While it is true that just about every nation and culture tends to stereotype everyone else (parsimonious Dutch, hotblooded Italians, dour Swiss, conservative Canadians, etc.), and even though there unquestionably are traits that are more predominant in some cultures than in others, making sweeping generalizations about a group indicates a failure to recognize its members as individuals. Praise for "natural" gifts also carries a patronizing implication that a skill does not really deserve credit; that is, it is not seen as an outcome of personal application.

BETTER: Visitors to the island are made to feel welcome, and are urged to take in some of the many music and dance performances that are a strong part of the local culture.

The rowdiest of the patrons were hauled off in the **paddy wagon**, and the rest soon dispersed.

People who would never dream of saying *that's awfully white of you* or *don't try to jew me down* may in complete innocence use words whose derivations come from put-downs of other cultures: in this case, the Irish. Other such words include *gyp* (to swindle or cheat, from *gypsy*), *Indian giver* (to give only to take back) and *welsh* or *welch* (break a promise or refuse to pay a debt). It is usually not difficult to find substitutes that don't involve ethnic slurs. (It should be noted that humankind has a long if not honorable history of associating other people's ethnicities with unpleasant matters. The English used to call syphilis the French pox, and the French called it the English pox.)

> **BETTER:** The rowdiest of the patrons were hauled off in the police van, and the rest soon dispersed.

The above examples illustrate just a few ways in which language can slant or distort the impressions that readers receive; the possibilities, of course, are endless. Always take the time to look your words over very critically if you are dealing with any sort of sensitive or controversial subject.

AVOIDING MALE-ONLY PRONOUNS

The English language tends to take masculinity as the norm: The basic word for something often connotes maleness, while femaleness must be specially elucidated. (Consider the very name for our species: Man.) For writers trying to avoid this type of bias, the most challenging parts of speech to work around are personal pronouns. Grammatically, it is correct to use *he* and *him* to refer to an individual of unspecified sex, yet an increasing number of people of both sexes see this as inappropriate and excluding. How many men would feel they were being personally included in writing that used only female pronouns?

Attitudes have certainly changed on this, in both popular opinion and style guides. William Strunk, Jr., and E.B. White, authors of the classic *The Elements of Style* (first published in 1935 and still revered today for its commonsense advice on clear expression), had this to say on the matter:

> *The use of "he" as a pronoun for nouns embracing both genders is a simple, practical convention rooted in the beginnings of the English language. "He" has lost all suggestion of maleness in these circumstances. . . . It has no pejorative connotation; it is never incorrect.*

Many modern readers would not agree. An example of the turn in thinking can be found in the 1976 update of Dr. Benjamin Spock's best-selling *Baby and Child Care*, where he states in a foreword:

> *The main reason for this [revision] is to eliminate the sexist biases of the sort that help to create and perpetuate discrimination against girls and women. Earlier editions referred to the child of indeterminate sex as "he". Though this in one sense is only a literary tradition, it, like many other traditions, implies that the masculine sex has some kind of priority.*

Feeling that *he* is inappropriate when applied to both sexes is one thing; finding a graceful alternative is another. Strunk and White raised some valid objections when they went on to say:

> *Substituting* he or she *in its place. . . . often doesn't work, if only because repetition makes it sound boring or silly. . . . The furor recently raised about "he" would be more impressive if there were a handy substitute for the word. Unfortunately, there isn't—or at least, no one has come up with one yet. If you think "she" is a handy substitute for "he," try it and see what happens. Alternatively, put all controversial nouns in the plural and avoid the choice of sex altogether, and you may find your prose sounding general and diffuse as a result.*

Clearly, the "recently raised" furor hasn't gone away, but neither has anyone come up yet with a handy substitute. (For some reason, "shim" hasn't caught on.) The challenge, therefore, is to find less handy substitutes. These sometimes take a bit of ingenuity but, if successful, allow you to work around the problem without your readers even noticing. The pros and cons of various strategies are discussed below.

USING HE/SHE, S/HE, OR THEY

The solutions that are the easiest to apply are also the least likely to please: putting down *he/she* or *s/he*, or using *they* as a singular pronoun. The first two are jarring; the third ungrammatical. All three seem like cop-outs (as if you couldn't take the trouble to come up with a more imaginative strategy) and draw attention a bit too loudly to the fact that you're enlightened enough not to use all-male pronouns.

Certainly, there are some contexts where these forms are appropriate. In speech, everyone uses *they* when sex is unknown or irrelevant *(someone left this fan letter for you, but they didn't sign it)*. It sounds natural and easy and carries no ambiguity. Still, stricter standards must apply in writing, and you can't ignore the fact that grammatically, *they* refers to more than one individual. Some people argue strongly for extending its acceptability as a singular pronoun into writing as well, but until this officially happens, you run the risk of having your more fastidious readers thinking you just don't know any better. A sentence such as the following looks outright sloppy, if not ambiguous:

> Response to the new version of the program has been favorable; one customer, for example, said that they doubled their productivity within the first week.

Also keep in mind that the indefinite pronouns *each*, *every*, *anybody*, etc., are singular, so cannot be grammatically combined with *they* (although see the discussion of this on page 254). The following sentences are *incorrect*:

> Each student must hand in their own lab report.
> Every guest was given a name tag when they arrived.

He/she and *his/her* are often viewed as acceptable in less formal writing, but be aware that they become tedious if overused. The nonword *s/he*, however, has little to recommend it other than its efficiency. (How would you *pronounce* it?)

USING HE OR SHE

The expression *he or she* (along with *him or her* and *his or hers*) is an excellent solution when used sparingly, working its way into sentences in a manner that looks easy and uncontrived. The key word, however, is *sparingly*. It becomes clumsy and annoying with repetition and looks positively dreadful if used more than once within a single sentence. Any reader would find the following distracting:

> The clinician can play an important role on the research team. He or she is invaluable in gathering physical data from his or her patients, and equally useful is his or her role in gathering subjective data based on his or her impressions and feelings.

There isn't a "magic number" of how often is too often for these expressions; certainly, a few appearances in a large document is unintrusive. If the need arises frequently, however, it is best to vary *he or she* with other strategies.

Note: Some writers like to vary this expression as *she or he*, and there is no logical reason why the female pronoun shouldn't come first. Realistically though, since this phrasing isn't standard, it is likely to cause momentary distraction or annoyance on the part of some of your readers. If you recognize and accept that, then by all means go with the variation! Perhaps if enough people do, it will eventually become standard as well.

ALTERNATING HE AND SHE

In some genres of writing it works well to change about half the occurrences of *he* to *she*. This strategy can be applied to made-up scenarios or case histories, where the reference is to a single individual and a female example would fit in just as naturally as a male one.

It works less well if the reference is to a group or population. For example, in the following, it would be difficult for readers to assume that men are included:

> The survey indicated that the average newspaper reader prefers her news in a concise form.
>
> Every worker we spoke to says that she fears for her future and that of her family.

USING THE PLURAL

Going with the plural form instead of the singular is a simple and effective strategy if the context is in fact referring to more than one person. For example:

> **INSTEAD OF:** We asked each participant to speak openly about his feelings.

WORD IT AS: We asked all participants to speak openly about their feelings.

This strategy is very popular and often works smoothly and unobtrusively, but should be avoided if the plural sounds contrived or unlikely. There are many cases where a plural rather than a singular noun simply would not convey the same sense, particularly if you wish to emphasize the individuality of the actions under discussion. Bear in mind the caution about your words coming through as "general and diffuse." And, as discussed previously, don't try to get around the issue by using *they* as a singular pronoun.

USING THE INDEFINITE PRONOUN *ONE*

In some circumstances, one can substitute *one* for *he*. (This pronoun is also sometimes used as a substitute for the first or second person, as discussed on page 258.) Use of this pronoun usually carries an implication that the writer and reader belong to the same group or share some relevant characteristic or interest; in a sense, it conveys the idea of "you or I." For example, as a writer, one could work it into a book addressing other writers. (Is one making oneself clear?)

Thus, for instance, in an article aimed at physicians,

INSTEAD OF: Clinical judgment involves the physician making use of his experience, as well as his knowledge of the particular patient.

WORD IT AS: Clinical judgment involves making use of one's experience, as well as one's knowledge of the particular patient.

This approach is usually inappropriate if the intended readers would not be able to relate to the group or activity under discussion. Also, overuse of "one" can make your writing sound a bit stuffy.

USING THE SECOND PERSON

In certain types of writing, you can use *you* in order to avoid the third person—as here. This form is appropriate for genres that address the reader directly, such as instruction manuals. For example:

INSTEAD OF: The reader should familiarize himself with these terms before proceeding.

WORD IT AS: Familiarize yourself with these terms before proceeding.

Obviously you cannot use this strategy if your text is not speaking directly to the reader.

USING THE PASSIVE VOICE

Consider using the passive voice in order to avoid pronouns altogether. You want to be cautious with this strategy—the passive voice carries the risk of making sentences clumsy or ambiguous—but it can sometimes work well.

> **INSTEAD OF:** The advantage to making the surgeon responsible for acquiring the research data is that he often requires it in any case for clinical purposes.
>
> **WORD IT AS:** The advantage to making the surgeon responsible for acquiring the research data is that this information is often required in any case for clinical purposes.

For more on this, see "Active Versus Passive Voice" on page 286.

AVOIDING PRONOUNS

It is often possible to find a way of wording a sentence that eliminates the need for a pronoun, while staying in the active voice. This is often the neatest and least jarring solution. Consider the following examples:

> **INSTEAD OF:** A psychiatrist may ethically obtain research data from his patients, but his main objective must remain that of attending to their needs.
>
> **WORD IT AS:** A psychiatrist may ethically obtain research data from patients, but must not lose sight of the main objective of attending to their needs.

> **INSTEAD OF:** The bashful writer is reluctant to come right out and state his position firmly.
>
> **WORD IT AS:** The bashful writer is reluctant to come right out and take a firm position.

Sometimes it may be difficult to capture exactly the meaning you want without using a pronoun. Naturally, your meaning must take precedence over style.

Also, do not confuse gracefully recasting a sentence with simply repeating the noun:

> The writer of technical manuals is cautioned against inserting humorous comments. The writer may feel that such comments liven up a dull topic and make it more readable, but the writer should bear in mind that humor is not universal, and what the writer finds funny, another person may find annoying or offensive.

Readers of such prose would probably wish *its* writer had gone with "he" instead.

In sum, there is no single strategy that will work for all situations, and it is usually best not to use a single strategy throughout. With some effort and imagination, however, you can write around the gender problem in a way that should leave none of your readers alienated.

Writing With Finesse

BEN. . . . But tell me, how come that you've known [about Anne and Tom] for some time?
JOEY. Well, actually I got it from Reg.
BEN. From Reg? Yes? (Pause.) You know I think we're building up a case here for a conspiracy theory of personal relationships. Go on.
JOEY (sits). Tom's meeting Reg had nothing to do with me. It was something professional, I don't know what, but they got on very well and Tom told Reg and Reg told me, and then Tom phoned Reg and told Reg not to tell me or if he had told me to ask me not to tell you until he or Anne had told you.
BEN. Yes, I recognize Tom's delicate touch there in your sentence structure.

—SIMON GRAY, *Butley*

Using the language well involves a lot more than just applying the rules of grammar and punctuation. Following those rules is necessary but not sufficient, and a passage that contains no overt errors of language may still be considered badly phrased or difficult to follow for more elusive reasons. (Reasons having to do with form, that is. Content is another matter.)

Compared to the issues discussed elsewhere in this book, the matter of style is a large gray area—intangible, subjective, context-dependent. It is beyond the scope of this handbook to delve deeply into the topic; the following sections simply touch on a few aspects of style that are generally acknowledged to be consistent or not consistent with good writing. These aspects should be viewed not as hard-and-fast do's and don'ts, but as factors that are worth bearing in mind.

The following issues are looked at:

- Reading level
- Sentence length
- How much to put into one sentence ("chunking" information)
- Organizing information
- Redundancy
- Overuse of a word
- Jargon
- Accents and speech patterns
- Avoiding a "heavy-handed" style
- Assessing how well your text reads

ENSURING THAT READING LEVEL IS APPROPRIATE

"Reading level" refers to the number of years of formal education required by a reader in order to fully comprehend a piece of writing. No matter how well written a document is, it will fail in its fundamental task of communication if it is so challenging that its intended audience cannot understand it. On the other hand, if it is written at too junior a level, readers may become bored or feel patronized, and may either put it aside or take its content less seriously.

In some genres of writing, the concept of reading level is critical, the most obvious being school texts and children's books. (Children of the same age naturally exhibit a wide range of vocabulary and reading skills, but the averages are known.) In the case of adults, reading level is usually less of an issue but still must be kept in mind. For example, a writer would obviously present the same information differently in a professional journal and in a popular magazine, or in material aimed at a Ph.D. crowd versus a group of high school dropouts.

Objective determinations of reading level look at two factors: the number of words in a sentence and the number of syllables in a word. Strategies exist that can help you translate these numbers into a useful measure. The **Fog Index**, used in educational publishing, is easy to apply manually. Pick a random hundred-word chunk in your document (you may want to do this with your eyes closed, to ensure randomness), and calculate the average sentence length (that is, 100 divided by the number of sentences). Then count the number of words in the sample that have three or more syllables. Add these two numbers together, and multiply the sum by 0.4. The resulting value gives you the minimum number of years of education required by a reader in order to easily follow your writing. Repeat the calculation with several more samples, and average the results.

For example, consider the first hundred words in the preceding paragraph (beginning with *Objective determinations* and ending with *three or more syllables*). This chunk contains five sentences, for an average of 20 words per sentence, and 14 words of three syllables or more. Thus, its Fog Index is: $(20 + 14) \times 0.4 = 13.6$.

This value works out to a high school education, or high school plus one or two years of college or university, depending on the educational system. The number is high enough that readers with more education shouldn't feel that the text is talking down to them, but those with less education might find the wording challenging to follow. (Obviously, a single calculation is not likely to be representative of an entire book, so this process would have to be repeated a number of times to produce a meaningful number.)

In practice, the chunks you use for your calculations will probably be slightly under or slightly over one hundred words, since you don't want to end a sample in the middle of a sentence. To calculate the index for a chunk of any length, count (1) the number of words in the chunk, (2) the number of sentences and (3) the number of polysyllabic words. Divide (1) by (2) to get the average number of words per sentence. Divide (3) by (1) and multiply by 100 to get the percentage of polysyllabic words. Then add these last two values and multiply their sum by 0.4, as before.

The Fog Index has been around a long time, but is being supplanted these days by computerized tools that are faster and more sophisticated. The accuracy of online tools is greater, since they can scan an entire document rather than relying on random sampling. Many grammar-checkers today include this type of feature, so you may want to look for it if you are shopping around for a word processor program.

Keep in mind that this type of measure is rather simplistic, since length is just one aspect of reading difficulty. Many sophisticated words contain just one or two syllables, while many commonly used words are longer; similarly, a short sentence can pack in considerable complexity, and a lengthy one can be very easy to follow. The reading-level tools can be useful, but ultimately you must rely on common sense and intuition to ensure that you are writing in a way that your intended audience will understand.

ENSURING THAT SENTENCE LENGTH IS APPROPRIATE

What's the "right" length for a sentence? How long is too long?

There were equally excellent opportunities for vacationists in the home island, delightful sylvan spots for rejuvenation, offering a plethora of attractions as well as a bracing tonic for the system in and around Dublin and its picturesque environs, even, Poulaphouca, to which there was a steam tram, but also farther away from the madding crowd, in Wicklow, rightly termed the garden of Ireland, an ideal neighbourhood for elderly wheelmen, so long as it didn't come down, and in the wilds of Donegal, where if report spoke true, the *coup d'oeil* was exceedingly grand, though the lastnamed locality was not easily getable so that the influx of visitors was not as yet all that it might be considering the signal benefits to be derived from it, while Howth with its historic associations and otherwise, Silken Thomas, Grace O'Malley, George IV, rhododendrons several hundred feet above sealevel was a favourite haunt with all sorts and conditions of men, especially in the spring when young men's fancy, though it had its own toll of deaths by falling off the cliffs by design or accidentally, usually, by the way, on their left leg, it being only about three quarters of an hour's run from the pillar. [202 words]

—James Joyce, *Ulysses*

Now and then during the next six months he returned to town, but he did not again even see or pass the restaurant. . . . Perhaps he did not need to. More often than that he knew perhaps thinking would have suddenly flowed into a picture, shaping, shaped: the long, barren, somehow equivocal counter with the still, coldfaced, violenthaired woman at one end as though guarding it, and at the other men with inwardleaning heads, smoking steadily, lighting and throwing away their constant cigarettes, and the waitress, the woman not much larger than a child going back and forth to the kitchen with her arms over-laden with dishes, having to pass on each journey within touching distance of the men who leaned with their slanted hats and spoke to her through the cigarette smoke, murmured to her somewhere near mirth or exultation, and her face musing, demure, downcast, as if she had not heard. [123 words]

—WILLIAM FAULKNER, *Light in August*

How short is too short?

The Italians were even more dangerous. They were frightened and firing on anything they saw. Last night on the retreat we had heard that there had been many Germans in Italian uniforms mixing with the retreat in the north. I did not believe it. That was one of those things you always heard in the war. It was one of the things the enemy always did to you. You did not know any one who went over in German uniform to confuse them. Maybe they did but it sounded difficult. I did not believe the Germans did it. I did not believe they had to. There was no need to confuse our retreat. The size of the army and the fewness of the roads did that. Nobody gave any orders, let alone Ger-mans. Still, they would shoot us for Germans. They shot Aymo. . . .

—ERNEST HEMINGWAY, *A Farewell to Arms*

A blur outside the car . . . Sherman grabbed the door pull and with a tremendous adrenal burst banged it shut. Out of the corner of his eye, the big one—almost to the door on Maria's side. Sherman hit the lock mechanism. *Rap!* He was yanking on the door handle—CELTICS inches from Maria's head with only the glass in between. Maria shoved the Mercedes into first gear and squealed forward. The youth leaped to one side. The car was heading straight for the trash cans. Maria hit the brakes. Sherman was thrown against the dash. A vanity case landed on top of the gearshift. Sherman pulled it off. Now it was on his lap. Maria threw the car into reverse. It shot backward. He glanced to his right. The skinny one . . . The skinny boy was standing there staring at him . . . pure fear on his delicate face . . .

—TOM WOLFE, *The Bonfire of the Vanities*

The fact is, there is no defined minimum/maximum range, and it would be improper for any style book to dictate one. Sometimes long rambling sentences work well (provided they're punctuated into digestible chunks); the effect may be to produce a dreamy or stream-of-consciousness mood. A series of short, staccato sentences may work to set a mood of tension or drama.

In general, though—and particularly in the case of novice authors—neither extreme is advisable. The above excerpts have employed unusual sentence lengths for literary effect, but what works in the hands of a skilled novelist may fall very flat in the hands of one less experienced. And in nonfiction writing—that is, any sort of writing where the goal is to convey information, not to set a mood—very long sentences are likely to come through as disorganized and verbose, and very short ones as choppy and stilted. In some genres of writing, such as quick-reference brochures or books for young children, even moderately long sentences would be inappropriate, while in genres such as scholarly journals, too-short sentences might appear simplistic and unprofessional.

Usually, the most pleasing effect is produced by variation: most sentences of moderate length (say, between fifteen and thirty words), the occasional one notably longer or shorter. What you want to avoid is a monotonous uniformity, with every sentence looking as if it came out of the same mold.

CHUNKING INFORMATION APPROPRIATELY

Apart from the desirability of "sounding good," the issue of sentence length has a great deal to do with communicating clearly. In nonfiction writing, the decision as to how much information should go into one sentence comes down more to content than to style concerns. If two discrete items of information are closely related, putting them into a single sentence makes their connection clearer to the reader; separating them might make this connection harder to grasp. Conversely, merging distinct topics into one sentence may send a confusing signal the other way. (Of course, it's often a matter of interpretation as to what constitutes "closely related" and "distinct.")

The following examples illustrate this reasoning. Note that there is nothing really wrong with the "before's"; they're not presenting the material in any way that is actively misleading. The motive behind altering them can be described as follows: During the act of taking in information, readers form instantaneous, almost subconscious impressions and expectations, and if anything comes along that seems less than completely congruous with these expectations, they may find it necessary to pause momentarily and make some mental readjustments. If a writer can anticipate these expectations and ensure that they are met, readers will always be on top of the intended meaning.

EXAMPLE 1

It would be expensive and time-consuming to survey the entire population. What you want to do is to select a smaller, representative group (a sample). You use the data derived from this group to make generalizations about the whole.

Sentence 3 names the *purpose* of the advice given in sentence 2. This connection would come through more strongly if the two were combined.

BETTER: It would be expensive and time-consuming to survey the entire population. What you want to do is to select a smaller, representative group (a sample), and use the data derived from this group to make generalizations about the whole.

EXAMPLE 2

There are several steps you should follow when preparing a publication proposal. Basically, a proposal should contain a few paragraphs describing your goals for the book. A table of contents is helpful. Attach some completed chapters as a sample of your writing. The proposal should include a brief description of yourself, stating your experience and why you are qualified to write this particular book. The publisher may send copies of the proposal to experts in the field for peer review. Thus, it often takes a few months before you can expect to hear whether your proposal has been accepted.

This paragraph contains two subtopics: what a proposal should contain and what happens after you submit it. The bulk of the information is on the first subtopic. However, since each point begins a new sentence, it's a bit difficult to recognize where this subtopic ends and the next one begins. Combining similar information into one sentence would make the subtopics easier to distinguish.

BETTER: There are several steps you should follow when preparing a publication proposal. Basically, a proposal should contain a few paragraphs describing your goals for the book; a table of contents; some completed chapters as a sample of your writing; and a brief description of yourself, stating your experience and why you are qualified to write this particular book. The publisher may send copies of the proposal to experts in the field for peer review. Thus, it often takes a few months before you can expect to hear whether your proposal has been accepted.

Note how this merging also makes the passage more concise, since each component does not now have to be separately introduced.

EXAMPLE 3

The following section describes a method that physicians and other health practitioners can use to measure patients' physical, emotional and social functioning, which has been tested in dozens of practices, both in North America and elsewhere, to evaluate its reliability and validity, and has valuable applications in both hospital- and office-based clinical settings, as well as in research studies.

This passage packs a series of related but nonetheless discrete points into a single run-on sentence and, while not impossible to follow, is a bit of a strain. It contains three distinct items of information, and should be broken up accordingly.

BETTER: The following section describes a method that physicians and other health practitioners can use to measure patients' physical, emotional and social functioning. This method has been tested in dozens of practices, both in North America and elsewhere, to evaluate its reliability and validity. It has valuable applications in both hospital- and office-based clinical settings, as well as in research studies.

EXAMPLE 4

Our study compared the usefulness of hard copy versus soft copy help information, looking at how subjects employed one or the other of these types of help while performing tasks that included browsing, locating and reading data, and locating and using data to perform calculations.

Again, this run-on sentence can be broken into more easily digestible units.

BETTER: Our study compared the usefulness of hard copy versus soft copy help information. Subjects were asked to to employ one or the other of these types of help while performing various tasks. These tasks included browsing, locating and reading data, and locating and using data to perform calculations.

ORGANIZING INFORMATION APPROPRIATELY

Organization is critical. Sentences may be crafted perfectly on an individual level, but if they are ordered in a way that is confusing or inconsistent, they will not convey their messages clearly.

The following examples present passages that are muddled and out of sequence. The fact that they aren't impossible to follow is due mostly to the fact that they're short. On a larger scale, poor organization can cause a piece of writing to be unintelligible.

EXAMPLE 1

When you prepare a research article for publication, set it aside and read it again after a day or two. Does it say what you intended? Try to get a peer review. A fresher or sharper eye may spot areas of weakness, omissions and other problems in the manuscript that were hidden to you. Does the title accurately describe what the article is about? The discussion should stick to the topic and not ramble. Ensure that you have followed the authors' guidelines provided by the journal. Finally, be sure to run a spell-check before you print out the copy that will go to the publisher.

This information comes through as somewhat scattered, for several reasons. First, the opening two sentences tell the writer what he or she should do personally (look over the article and see if it's saying what it should); the next two deal with getting someone *else* to give some feedback; then the passage goes back to things that the writer should do. The first category should be completed before the second is begun.

Second, sentence 4 is closely related to sentence 3, in that it expounds on *why* it is important to get a peer review. This relationship will be made more obvious if the two sentences are run together.

Third, two of the aspects that the writer is advised to check for are presented as questions, and two are presented as statements. Apart from the faulty parallelism (information on equivalent matters should be presented in an equivalent way, to make the relationship more obvious), this structure almost makes it look as though the text following each question is providing an answer to that question.

BETTER: When you prepare a research article for publication, set it aside and read it again after a day or two. Does it say what you intended? Does its title accurately describe what it is about? Does the discussion stick to the topic and not ramble? Have you followed the authors' guidelines provided by the journal? Try to get a peer review—a fresher or sharper eye may spot areas of weakness, omissions and other problems in the manuscript that were hidden to you. Finally, be sure to run a spell-check before you print out the copy that will go to the publisher.

Note that the final sentence has been left where it was, even though it's in the category of things to do oneself. This is because it is stated to be the last step in the process.

EXAMPLE 2

The important thing to remember about an oral presentation is that you have only about ten minutes to tell the world about your work; hence, preparation is crucial. Design your slides so that you don't find yourself apologizing for tiny details that aren't showing up clearly. There are no absolutes about how much information should go on a single slide, but use judgment. Don't include anything that you are not planning to talk about.

Begin your talk by explaining the objectives of your study, and then move on to the methods and findings. Leave enough time for a mention of what future directions you hope to take. In your slides, avoid dark colors, which often do not project well. Don't put too much text in a slide, as it's often better to give details orally. If possible, familiarize yourself beforehand with the slide equipment; for example, ensure that there is a pointer available and that you know how to handle the projector and the room lighting. Keep each slide in mind as you talk so that there is no mismatch between your oral and visual messages. And finally, try to end on a strong note: don't trail off on some feeble line like, "Well, that's all I've got to say."

This text is scattered both timewise and contentwise, alternating between how to prepare for a presentation and what to do during it. An improved organization would be as follows:

First paragraph: Introductory sentence; what a slide should look like; what a slide should contain; what to do just before you start.

Second paragraph: What to do during the presentation (in chronological order); concluding sentence.

BETTER: The important thing to remember about an oral presentation is that you have only about ten minutes to tell the world about your work; hence, preparation is crucial. Design your slides so that you don't find yourself apologizing for tiny details that aren't showing up clearly, and avoid dark colors, which often do not project well. There are no absolutes about how much information should go on a single slide, but use judgment. Don't put in too much text, as it's often better to give details orally, and don't include anything that you are not planning to talk about. If possible, familiarize yourself beforehand with the slide equipment; for example, ensure that there is a pointer available and that you know how to handle the projector and the room lighting.

Begin your talk by explaining the objectives of your study, and then move on to the methods and findings. Keep each slide in mind as you talk, so that there is no mismatch between your oral and visual messages. Leave enough time for a mention of what future directions you hope to take. And finally, try to end on a strong note: Don't trail off on some feeble line like "Well, that's all I've got to say."

AVOIDING REDUNDANCY

A common flaw in formal writing is to make some point, then immediately restate the same information a different way. Sometimes writers do this out of forgetfulness, but more often they do it intentionally, under the mistaken belief that repetition will make their points come through more clearly or emphatically. (Some have even specifically been taught to do this in high school writing classes.) The effect is actually the opposite: Since it is reasonable for readers to expect that every sentence will have something new to say, they may find it disconcerting or confusing to reencounter the same information, and end up referring back to earlier sentences to see if there's some subtle distinction they missed. (Of course, another reason why some writers employ redundancy is to pad out skimpy content, hoping no one will notice that not much is actually being said.

It's an old term-paper trick that didn't fool your profs then, and won't fool your readers now.)

The following passages present some illustrations of needless repetition:

EXAMPLE 1

In our survey of pediatricians, nearly all our respondents indicated that their clinical activities should include both diagnosis and subsequent follow-up of child abuse cases. Over 97 percent of those returning the survey said that they believed that they should be detecting and treating this problem.

The second sentence adds little here. The terms *detecting* and *treating* are really just restatements of *diagnosing* and *following up* (or if there is a distinction, it's a pretty fine one), and *respondents* are obviously the same people as *those returning the survey*. The only actual addition is a specification of what was meant by *nearly all*, and this information is easily incorporated into the first sentence.

BETTER: In our survey of pediatricians, nearly all our respondents (over 97 percent) indicated that their clinical activities should include both diagnosis and subsequent follow-up of child abuse cases.

EXAMPLE 2

The validity of a test that measures coping traits is restricted to the population for which the test was designed. A measure that is valid when administered to one type of population may not be valid for another, and there are no standardized tests in this field that are appropriate in all situations. It is not possible to develop or refine a test for measuring coping traits that can meet all requirements and perform well in all circumstances. Therefore, researchers must be careful to select a test that is appropriate for their specific situation.

The second-to-last sentence here merely restates what is already clear, so the passage does not lose any information if this sentence is deleted.

BETTER: The validity of a test that measures coping traits is restricted to the population for which the test was designed. A measure that is valid when administered to one type of population may not be valid for another, and there are no standardized tests in this field that are appropriate in all situations. Therefore, researchers must be careful to select a test that is appropriate for their specific situation.

Note: The advice on avoiding redundancies should *not* be taken to mean that you should never restate anything. In many forms of writing, summaries or recaps at the end of a chapter are suitable. In long works, or in books that are not expected to be read cover to cover, it may be appropriate to repeat important information wherever it is relevant. Just be certain that you have a sound rationale for putting down anything that has been explained elsewhere.

AVOIDING OVERUSE OF A WORD

A form of redundancy that can be particularly annoying to your readers is to have the same word appear an inordinate number of times. Sometimes writers are so intent on emphasizing an important term or concept that they use it to death, to the point where it is more distracting than informative.

Strategies to get around this include using pronouns, synonyms and elliptical constructions, or dropping unnecessary references altogether. If you are having a hard time coming up with synonyms, remember that a thesaurus can be an invaluable tool.

EXAMPLE 1

The family-oriented approach to medical care involves recognizing that an ailment of one family member will have an impact on all family members. A family is continually subject to both the inner pressures coming from its own members and to outer pressures that affect family members. A serious illness of one of its members increases both the internal and external demands placed on the family. Internally, the illness of a family member forces an adaptation by other family members of their roles and expectations. Externally, in this age of specialized medicine, a family member's illness typically demands interaction with multiple health care settings and personnel. Thus, a key focus of family assessment in health-related research and practice must be on family stress and coping.

This passage, just six sentences long, contains the word *family* eleven times and *member* (or *members*) eight times. These counts can easily be reduced to four and three, respectively.

BETTER: The family-oriented approach to medical care involves recognizing that an ailment of one family member will have an impact on all. A family is continually subject to both inner and outer pressures, and a serious illness of one of its members increases both these types of pressure. Internally, the illness forces an adaptation by other members of their roles and expectations; externally, in this age of specialized medicine, it typically demands interaction with multiple health care settings and personnel. Thus, a key focus of family assessment in health-related research and practice must be on stress and coping.

EXAMPLE 2

The Software Development Manager program provides software development organizations with a mechanism for efficiently managing the components of a software application throughout all development stages of the application. Software Development Manager enables a group of software developers to create and manage multiple versions of a software application. This software manager program also maintains the integrity of the application by not allowing one developer to overwrite another developer's changes to the source.

Here, in three sentences, the word *software* appears seven times, *develop* (or some derivation of it) seven times, *manage* (or some derivation of it) five times and *application* four times. Below, these counts are reduced to three each.

BETTER: The Software Development Manager program provides a mechanism for efficiently managing the components of a software application throughout all stages of its development. This program enables a group of software developers to create and manage multiple versions of an application, and maintains the integrity of the application by not allowing one group member to overwrite the source changes of another.

Note: The advice about not overusing a word should *not* be taken to mean that it's a good idea to use different terminology to describe the same concept. In many fields, particularly those in science and technology, terms have very precise meanings, and calling the same thing by different names will only lead to confusion and misinterpretation. Although it is preferable to avoid using the same word over and over, *never* do so at the expense of clarity.

USING JARGON APPROPRIATELY

The term **jargon** can be understood in two ways. At its best, it refers to the vocabulary of a specialized field of knowledge: law, medicine, sports, car mechanics, computer programming, musicology, publishing and so on. Every field has terms that may be obscure or unintelligible to outsiders, but serve the purpose of labeling things unambiguously and capturing complex ideas in a concise manner. If such terms didn't exist, it would be necessary to use wordy definitions and explanations.

When you write on complex topics, you may be faced with a decision as to whether you should use jargonistic words or substitute terms that would be more generally understood. The answer comes down to the following: Know your audience. Some terms may not be appropriate for the average layperson—for example, you'd want to avoid obscure medical jargon in a pamphlet aimed at patients (or at least follow the terms with explanations, if they're unavoidable). However, to use the simpler words in an article on the same subject aimed at physicians would verge on insulting.

If you feel that you personally are a reasonable representative of your intended readership, do not include any unexplained terms that you yourself do not understand (or must look up in order to understand). Conversely, if you are being hired to write something for an audience that is trained in ways you are not, and have been provided with information that includes professional jargon, do not automatically delete or replace terms just because you are not familiar with them.

Jargon is without merit when it is used not because no more precise terms exist, but in order to inflate the importance of what's being said (or often, to disguise the fact that nothing very important is being said in the first place). This isn't to say that you should "dumb down" your style: Very often a longer or more exotic word *does* capture a meaning more precisely or effectively. What you ought to avoid is putting down pretentious words when perfectly good simpler equivalents are available. There is no need to say *utilize* when you mean *use*, to call a *building* a *facility* or to *commence dialoguing* when you mean *start a conversation*.

Another absurd use of jargon is when it is applied to soften unwelcome messages. Obfuscating words may temporarily confuse your readers, but ultimately they don't fool them. Certain fields seem more prone to bafflegab than others: Education, big business, government and the social sciences come to mind. Laid-off employees have been *downsized*; pupils showing unsatisfactory performance are *emerging*. In fairness, however, offenders exist in every field.

CAPTURING ACCENTS AND SPEECH PATTERNS APPROPRIATELY

In fiction writing, capturing colloquial accents can add color—although note that overdoing it might make things a bit challenging for the reader, if the dialect is a strong one.

> I departed to renew my search; its result was disappointment, and Joseph's quest ended in the same.
>
> "Yon lad gets war un' war!" observed he on re-entering. "He's left th' yate at t' full swing, and miss's pony has trodden dahn two rigs o' corn, and plottered through, raight o'er into t' meadow! Hahnsomdiver, t' maister 'ull play t' devil to-morn, and he'll do weel. He's patience itsseln wi' sich careless, offald craters—patience itsseln he is! Bud he'll not be soa allus—yah's see, all on ye! Yah mun'n't drive him out of his heead for nowt!"
>
> —EMILY BRONTË, *Wuthering Heights*

However, if you are creating characters whose first language is not English, don't go overboard in spelling their words as you think they would sound. The effect may come through as ridiculing of the group the character represents, as well as making the dialogue difficult to read. This isn't to say you shouldn't convey foreign accents at all; just use moderation. A dropped letter here and a misused word there will usually be effective enough.

If you are quoting a real-life individual who happens to have an accent, either foreign or colloquial, it is better not to try to reproduce the accent phonetically at all, unless it has some direct relevance to the story. Direct quotes must include the exact words used, but you do not have to carry this to the extent of reproducing intonations.

With regard to style of speech, it is important to make your fictional characters talk realistically. *You* should have a firm handle on the rules of grammar, but you obviously don't want to put perfect diction into the mouths of characters who are meant to be uneducated or rustic.

> Every night now I used to slip ashore toward ten o'clock at some little village, and buy ten or fifteen cents' worth of meal or bacon or other stuff to eat; and sometimes I lifted a chicken that warn't roosting comfortable, and took him along. Pap always said, take a chicken when you get a chance, because if you don't want him yourself you can easy find somebody that does, and a good deed ain't ever forgot. I never see pap when he didn't want the chicken himself, but that is what he used to say, anyway.
>
> —MARK TWAIN, *The Adventures of Huckleberry Finn*

Do not, however, carry rustic dialect to the point of parody.

AVOIDING A HEAVY-HANDED STYLE

In fiction writing, the better writers understand the art of holding back. As a rule, it isn't needful to name every last shade of color in a sunset or to describe a character's features in photographic detail. The beauty of writing is that it leaves something to the reader's imagination. Obviously you want to present enough detail to convey a picture, but it's not always best to do so with lumbering thoroughness or dedicated realism. For example, qualifying each line of dialogue with descriptive adverbs, such as *"That dress makes you look like a walrus," he said insultingly* or *"Do you think I should dye my hair purple?" she asked teasingly*, can come through as heavy-handed. As much as possible, try to make the dialogue itself and the context convey the speaker's mood or motivations; spelling things out on every occasion carries an implication that you don't expect your readers to pick up on much themselves. This isn't to suggest, of course, that you should fall back on a flat "he said/she said" for each line of dialogue. But before you qualify, modify or elaborate on anything, think about whether your addition is truly having an enhancing effect.

If you are experimenting with different approaches, note that an indirect description is sometimes catchier and more effective than a straight-out one. In the following account of a miffed girlfriend dumping her swain for an evening to go out with somebody else, mark how the portrayal of one character is serving equally to convey a picture of another.

> Tall, tanned, solicitous Derek Burton . . . wore a Westminster Old Boy's tie, carried a furled umbrella, and did not instantly sink to the sofa, kicking off his shoes, but remained standing until she had sat down, and lit her cigarette with a slender lighter he kept in a chamois pouch, and raised his glass to say, cheers. He didn't have to be asked how she looked, grudgingly pronouncing her all right, and taking it as an invitation to send his hand flying up her skirts, but immediately volunteered that she looked absolutely fantastic. Outside, he opened his umbrella, and held it over her. Derek drove an Austin-Healey with a leather steering wheel and what seemed, at first glance, like six head-lights and a dozen badges riding the grille. There were no apple cores in the ashtray. Or stale bagels in the glove compartment. Instead, there were scented face tissues mounted in a suede container. There was also a coin dispenser, cleverly concealed, filled with sixpences for park-ing meters. As well as a small, elegant flashlight and a leather-bound log book. Once at the restaurant, Derek tucked the car into the smallest imaginable space, managing it brilliantly, without cursing the car ahead of him, or behind, in Yiddish. Then she waited as he fixed a complicated burglar-proof lock to the steering column. Jake would absolutely hate him, she thought, which made her smile most entic-ingly and say, "How well you drive."
>
> —Mordecai Richler, *St. Urbain's Horseman*

In the following account of a chess game, note how no moves are actually described. The sense of concentration and excitement is conveyed in a completely intangible way.

During my first tournament, my mother sat with me in the front row as I waited for my turn. I frequently bounced my legs to unstick them from the cold metal seat of the folding chair. When my name was called, I leapt up. My mother unwrapped something in her lap. It was her *chang,* a small tablet of red jade which held the sun's fire. "Is luck," she whispered, and tucked it into my dress pocket. I turned to my opponent, a fifteen-year-old boy from Oakland. He looked at me, wrinkling his nose.

As I began to play, the boy disappeared, the color ran out of the room, and I saw only my white pieces and his black ones waiting on the other side. A light wind began blowing past my ears. It whispered secrets only I could hear.

"Blow from the South," it murmured. "The wind leaves no trail." I saw a clear path, the traps to avoid. The crowd rustled. "Shhh! Shhh!" said the corners of the room. The wind blew stronger. "Throw sand from the East to distract him." The knight came forward ready for the sacrifice. The wind hissed, louder and louder. "Blow, blow, blow. He cannot see. He is blind now. Make him lean away from the wind so he is easier to knock down."

"Check," I said, as the wind roared with laughter. The wind died down to little puffs, my own breath.

—AMY TAN, *The Joy Luck Club*

No two writers will have the exact same style, and it cannot be overemphasized that there are no rights and wrongs, no absolutes in this realm. Study what strategies are used by your own favorite authors, and consider whether your own style might be improved by borrowing or adapting any of these.

SUGGESTIONS ON SELF-ASSESSMENT

The following are some techniques for improving your writing style, and for assessing how well your efforts are succeeding. Not all these strategies will work for everyone, but many writers find them helpful.

READ YOUR TEXT ALOUD TO YOURSELF

This strategy may be particularly helpful if your writing is intended for oral presentation, but can be useful for other genres as well.

Hearing your own words, as opposed to looking at them, may provide you with a very different impression of them and expose weaknesses such as pretentious-sounding terms, wooden dialogue or rambling sentence structures.

ALWAYS LOOK OVER A PRINTOUT

If you're writing on a word processor (which is becoming the norm these days), don't do all your revisions online and then print off a final copy without looking it over. It's hard to explain why, but words often present themselves differently when viewed on a page rather than a screen. The effects can range from suddenly noticing a typo you'd been staring at all along without seeing it, to sensing that your tone is coming through as too brusque, too hesitant, too formal, too casual—in sum, you may at this point pick up more clearly on certain intangible aspects of your writing that can make a critical difference to its readability or credibility. Just why such nuances should emerge more clearly on a hard copy is not clear, nor is this effect universal, but many writers experience it.

FOCUS ON THE WHOLE AS WELL AS THE PARTS

Any time you add or revise an element, reread what surrounds it to ensure that everything still fits. Often, a change in one place will necessitate a change in another. Naturally you must focus on each line as you create it, but as soon as you have the first draft in place, back up a few lines and read through the earlier text again. You will frequently find that the latest addition doesn't fit in quite as it should—perhaps it restates a point already made, or doesn't make a smooth enough transition from what came before. As you form each new sentence, keep going back and rereading it from the start to ensure that all its elements mesh together. As you form each new paragraph, keep rereading it from its first line to see how its sentences fit together: Perhaps the topic shifts enough that the paragraph should be broken up, or perhaps a particular word is repeated too many times within a short space.

PUT YOUR WORK ASIDE FOR A WHILE
AND THEN COME BACK TO IT

You may feel you have polished your arguments into their final form, only to find that when you look at them a little later, problems jump out at you: illogical connections, clumsy sentence structures, a strained-sounding tone, subtle grammatical errors. A lapse of time enables you to come back to your work with a more objective eye. A day or more away is ideal, but even a few hours can make a difference.

HAVE SOMEONE ELSE LOOK YOUR WORK OVER

Any writer—no matter how skilled—can benefit from getting a second opinion, because by definition one is always too close to one's own work. Given that your writing is ultimately intended for other people's consumption, it only makes sense to find out how other people perceive it. The individual whose opinion you seek need not be a better writer than you: The goal is not to have this person correct or revise what you have done. Rather, it is to provide you with feedback on how your points and your tone are coming across. If your critic doesn't get your jokes, or finds a character you meant to be funny and sympathetic merely irritating, or can't follow some instruction because you left out a step you thought would be perfectly obvious to anybody—take all this seriously (and do your best to remain on speaking terms afterward). A professional editor is ideal, but if this is not practical or affordable, try to select someone whose opinion you respect and who represents your intended readership as nearly as possible.

And finally, draft, draft, draft. Write and rewrite. And then rewrite again. This strategy is not an option or a suggestion, but a basic part of the writing process. No professional writer expects to get away without revision; the only question is, how much will be necessary. The act of writing, after all, does not involve simply transcribing ideas inside your head into words on paper: It involves developing and articulating those ideas in the first place. As you write, you can expect to shift your priorities; to change your mind about what information goes with what; to choose a different tack in order to drive some point home. Resist the temptation to hang onto passages that you labored long and lovingly over, if they no longer fit.

INDEX